D1000888

MAD PRINCES OF
RENAISSANCE GERMANY

STUDIES IN EARLY MODERN GERMAN HISTORY
H. C. Erik Midelfort, *Editor*

MAD PRINCES
OF RENAISSANCE
GERMANY

H. C. ERIK MIDELFORT

UNIVERSITY PRESS OF VIRGINIA

Charlottesville & London

THE UNIVERSITY PRESS OF VIRGINIA
Copyright © 1994 by the Rector and Visitors
of the University of Virginia

FIRST PUBLISHED 1994

Title page:
Medal, 1519, of Margrave Christoph I of Baden.
(Courtesy of the Badisches Landesmuseum, Karlsruhe)

Library of Congress Cataloging-in-Publication Data
Midelfort, H. C. Erik.
    Mad princes of renaissance Germany / H. C. Erik Midelfort.
        p.   cm. — (Studies in early modern German history)
    Includes bibliographical references and index.
    ISBN 0-8139-1486-8
    1. Psychiatry—Germany—History—16th century.   2. Princes—
Mental health—Germany.   3. Princes—Germany—History—
16th century.   4. Germany—History—Maximilan I, 1493–1519.
5. Germany—History—1517–1648.   I. Title.   II. Series.
RC450.G3M53   1994
616.89 '00943'09031—dc20   93-39116
                                                                CIP

PRINTED IN THE UNITED STATES OF AMERICA

FOR MY SISTERS

Signe · Elise · Kristin

Contents

ILLUSTRATIONS

PREFACE

This book began its life as a chapter in a larger study of madness in sixteenth-century Germany, on which I have been working for many years. When I began to write about the mad princes, however, what I had intended to be a chapter rapidly developed tyrannical tendencies and a ruthless, but I hope not insane, ambition to live independently. Like many a willful, self-indulgent prince, it also began to put on weight and to assume the contours of a book. In the end I have felt compelled both to humor and restrain these desires by clapping them between the covers of a modest volume.

As a consequence, this study alludes to topics that might seem to demand separate, more extensive treatment. This is the case with the history of Paracelsian and Renaissance Galenic medicine, with the history of exorcism and demonic possession, and with the understanding and treatment of madness among the middle and lower classes. Readers are right to suspect that there is much more to be said on such topics, but I hope that this book will stand alone.

I started work on this project with the help of a fellowship from the John Simon Guggenheim Foundation and finished most of the research with the assistance of a fellowship from the National Endowment for the Humanities. I am delighted to be able to thank then and to show them that I did get something done during all my time in Germany. It is a pleasure also to remember my happy hours in the various German archives on which much of this study rests. Without the skilled and helpful engagement of professional archivists, historians would be at a loss, and like most historians I am most grateful for their help. The generosity of Dr.

Heike Preuß of the State Archive in Düsseldorf deserves special mention because she went so far as to lend me her own working notes based on reports from the 1590s on the condition of Duke Johann Wilhelm and the ducal court at Düsseldorf. I am also most grateful to Dr. Klaus Neitmann of the state archives in Berlin-Dahlem for expert guidance in the Prussian materials. Similarly, I want to thank the authorities of the Bayerische Staatsbibliothek in Munich, and especially Adelheid Oberwegner, for granting me the use of a library study and for providing the best scholarly environment I have ever experienced.

The secretarial staff of my department are so competent that we run the risk of taking them for granted. Without the expert computer guidance and typing help of Lottie McCauley, Kathleen Miller, and Ella Wood my work would have taken much longer. I also need to thank the tireless staff of the University of Virginia Library, especially James Campbell of the bibliography department, Faustino Arao (Sonny) Daria, Jr., of Geographic Information Systems, David Seaman of the Electronic Text Center, and the remarkable staffs of the interlibrary loan office and the reference room, who helped me with the multiple obscurities of my topic.

Over the years I have also incurred debts of gratitude to friends and scholars who put me onto the trail of one or another of my mad princes or who suggested promising lines of inquiry. I may have forgotten some who helped me, but I know that I must thank Wolfgang Behringer, Peter and Renate Blickle, Thomas A. Brady, Jr., Gerhard Fichtner, Kurt Goldammer, Klaus Graf, Dana Koutná, Werner Friedrich Kümmel, Sönke Lorenz, Volker Press, Bernd Roeck, Hans-Christoph Rublack, Heinz Schilling, Georg Schmidt, Niklas Schrenck von Notzing, and Friedrich Wieland. Thomas Becker gave my manuscript an expert reading, as did Wolfgang Behringer, Thomas A. Brady, Jr., Randolph Starn, and my dear colleagues at the University of Virginia, Edward L. Ayers, Allan Megill, Duane J. Osheim, and Anne J. Schutte. Two anonymous readers for the University Press of Virginia were also most helpful. Richard Holway of the Press has been wonderfully helpful, and Pamela Holway, as copy editor, has done an excellent job. They have saved me from many an indiscretion. On various matters, of course, I am willfully incorrigible or invincibly ignorant, and so my book remains stubbornly mine, excesses, errors, and all.

Dramatis Personae:
The Mad Princes and Princesses of
Renaissance Germany

*Margrave Christoph I of Baden (1453–1527)
*Margrave Friedrich the Elder of Brandenburg (1460–1536)
*Duke Albrecht Friedrich of Prussia (1553–1618)
*Barbara of Brandenburg (1536–1591)
*Anna Maria of Brandenburg (1526–1589)
*Friedrich of Braunschweig-Lüneburg-Calenberg (d. 1495)
*Wilhelm II of Braunschweig-Lüneburg (1425–1503)
*Elisabeth of Brandenburg, Duchess of Braunschweig-Lüneburg,
    Countess of Henneberg (1510–1558)
*Anna Maria of Braunschweig (? –1568)
*Duke Wilhelm II the Younger of Braunschweig-Lüneburg (1535–
    1592)
Friedrich Ulrich of Braunschweig-Wolfenbüttel (1591–1634)
*Elisabeth of Denmark (1485–1555)
Empress Maria of Habsburg (1528–1603) (daughter of Emperor
    Charles V, wife of Emperor Maximilian II)
Archduke Ferdinand of Tirol (Habsburg) (1529–1595)
*Maria of Habsburg (1531–1581) (daughter of Emperor Ferdinand
    I, wife of Duke Wilhelm V of Jülich-Cleves-Berg)
*Emperor Rudolf II of Habsburg (1552–1612)
*Don Julius Caesar of Austria (1585?–1609)
Emperor Matthias of Habsburg (1557–1619) (brother of Rudolf II)
*Landgrave Wilhelm I of Hesse (1466–1515)
*Landgrave Wilhelm II of Hesse (1469–1509)
Landgrave Moritz the Learned of Hesse-Kassel (1572–1632)
    (whose son Otto committed suicide in a delirium)
*Duke Wilhelm V of Jülich-Cleves-Berg (1516–1592)
*Duke Johann Wilhelm of Jülich-Cleves-Berg (1562–1609)

*Phillip of Mecklenburg (1514–1557)
Anna Maria of Pfalz-Neuburg (? – ?), wife of Duke Friedrich
    Wilhelm of Saxony-Weimar-Altenburg (1573–1602)
Duke Ernst Ludwig of Pomerania-Wolgast (1545–1592)
*Friedrich of Saxony (1504–1539)
Princess Anna of Saxony (1544–1577) (daughter of Maurice of
    Saxony, wife of William of Orange)
Emilia (1570–1629) (daughter of Anna of Saxony)
Duke Johann Friedrich of Saxony-Weimar (1600–1628)
Count Sighard of Schwarzburg (? –1560)
*Count Heinrich of Württemberg (1448–1519)
Count Phillip of Ysenburg (1467–1526)

*Genealogical information regarding these persons can be found
either in table 1 (pp. 24–25) or in the appendix table.

MAD PRINCES OF
RENAISSANCE GERMANY

INTRODUCTION:
THE HISTORY OF MADNESS

In 1582 the quiet nights of Celle, a north German town of about three thousand souls known chiefly for its lively grain trade and for its brilliant new Renaissance palace chapel, were shattered by the sounds of gunfire. Out in the streets near the ducal palace, his princely grace Duke Wilhelm the Younger of Braunschweig-Lüneburg was shooting off pistols at imaginary enemies and shouting into the dark. He took unannounced trips and drank to excess. His rages frightened the ducal councilors, who felt stymied and helpless because they were used to depending on the duke or his closest relatives for direction. But Wilhelm's closest family and most intimate advisers were themselves locked in a struggle for power, and Duke Wilhelm, despite his obvious mental trouble, still commanded respect and even awe. What could be done?

About a decade later in the bustling Rhenish town of Düsseldorf, the young duke Johann Wilhelm of Jülich-Cleves disturbed all of his advisers by taking his strong Catholic sense of guilt to such extremes that he began to worry he might deserve to be imprisoned or executed in punishment for the imagined infidelity of his Erasmian-Catholic father. In other moods he stabbed and wounded his own attendants. As his depression deepened, he neglected meals and normal bedtimes, and his father had to write to him, urging that he please leave off from excessive fasts and vigils. The young prince should, for God's sake, take off his boots and spurs and get undressed before going to bed. He needed to bathe and cut his hair. Once again, physicians, councilors, and relatives felt stuck, desperate to solve the building dynastic crisis that would break over them if the prince could not be induced to straighten out and father a legitimate heir.

Altogether, the stories of nearly thirty mad German princes can be reconstructed in varying degrees of detail, and, as we shall see, many of them bubble with the barely suppressed frustrations and agonies of advisers, wives, and sons, who respected their prince and his office so highly that they could not simply depose and lock up their political father. It had not always been so. In the late Middle Ages and early sixteenth century several important German princes were, indeed, abruptly swept aside in coups d'état of startling brutality. By the mid-sixteenth century, however, such princes were much more likely to be subjected to an increasingly frenzied search for remedies. The history of the mad princes of Renaissance Germany thus opens up an unsuspected window onto the history of princely rule.

Not so very long ago it was fashionable to study the rulers of Europe simply because they were the most important people. After all, they drew up policy and decided the fates of nations. They supported artists and scholars, promoted cultural pursuits, fought in battles, and commissioned the heroic histories in which their exploits were commemorated. They styled themselves the "most Christian" or the "Defender of the Faith" and adopted postures of ostentatious public piety. About a generation ago, however, such studies of European rulers fell out of academic favor. Readers and scholars alike demanded histories of ordinary people, of popular culture, of the subaltern classes. Social historians also demanded an account of the broad sweep of socially important developments, of the "longue durée," and of anonymous but determining forces such as geography, climate, epidemics, demography, and the conjuncture of wages and prices. Such histories promised to give us a more profound account of the past than the chronicles of mere events. In the last ten or fifteen years, though, we have seen a somewhat chastened return of kings and battles and the revival of what has been called "narrative."[1] A renewed interest in early modern state formation, moreover, can hardly escape focusing attention on the head of state. It seems, for example, that even the petty monarchs of Germany's territories began to make increasing claims to absolutist majesty. We cannot understand the politics of early modern Europe without the prince.

We have also seen the growth of "microhistory" as a way of getting at important realities of the past by exploring the life and often the legal troubles of ordinary persons.[2] What I am presenting

here is a connected series of microhistories of the rich and powerful in an effort to use state records to shed light on the history
of courtly medicine, state crises, and madness in early modern
Europe.

Madness is itself a contentious term, for it is notoriously im-
precise. Psychiatrists today do not treat "madness" but mental illness, or psychosis, or emotional disorder. Jurists speak of an insanity defense and of diminished capacity, while religious writers
may prefer words like alienation or angst. The only scholars who
choose madness as their topic seem to be historians and social or
cultural constructivists who wish to emphasize an elusive but
wide-ranging set of mental and emotional disorders, of mental
transgressions, and of aberrant mental behavior, without prejudg-
ing the issue of whether a given condition or behavior was dis-
eased, immoral, or beyond the bounds of personal responsibility.[3]
These are also the reasons I refer to "mad" princes and to their
condition as madness. The word has a useful, untechnical vague-
ness. These princes may well have been ill, beyond the claims of
moral and legal responsibility, or hopelessly alienated, but I hope
that it becomes clear that, other important issues notwithstand-
ing, they were first of all princes and princesses whose thinking
had become so disordered that something had to be done about it.
Actually, one of our concerns will be to evaluate the precise terminology used by the friends, relatives, councilors, physicians,
preachers, opponents, and enemies of the mad monarch. It is
important to note whether contemporaries used legally or medically technical terms such as *furor, mania,* or *melancholia,* or
whether they used vernacular terms such as *unrichtig* (not right),
unsinnig (senseless), or *schwermütig* (heavyhearted, depressed).
The medical and legal technical terms usually had precise mean-
ings, deriving often from classical sources and commentaries on
them. Plato, Aristotle, and Cicero had all commented on the term
mania, which was connected with *mantikos,* "prophetic, oracu-
lar," thus establishing a link between madness and divination.
Furor was the technical Roman legal term for an insanity so severe
that the sufferer could not be held responsible for his deeds. *Melancholia* never entirely lost its literal sense of black bile and with
it a profoundly somatic set of connotations that were explored
with care in the Renaissance. As a disorder, melancholy resulted
in a wide range of mental abnormality from whimsy and pensive

sadness through raving fury and deranged insanity, with an occasional hint, especially among poets and painters, of genius, creativity, and greatness. In contrast, I have not been able to squeeze much systematic sense out of most of the vernacular terms, especially since some of the German words were deliberately vague euphemisms, such as *Schwachheit* (weakness), used to convey a general mental or physical debility without insulting the proud sensibilities of a duke or his duchess. We will have to learn to interrogate and relish the variety of words used in specific situations. I have tried to resist the impulse to translate sixteenth-century terms into modern diagnostic categories, while developing a sensitivity to the exact language and conceptual framework used for the mad. In that sense this book makes a contribution to the social history of ideas.

For more than thirty years, of course, the historians of early modern madness have known that their subject was much more than the history of psychiatry. Scholars have succeeded in drawing out connections between the academic and medical treatment of mental disorders and such ambient social institutions as hospitals, prisons, and poorhouses. They have also found resonances between psychiatry and certain upper-class ideologies and philosophical systems: the artistic cult of melancholy or the occult study of alchemy and astrology, for instance.[4] In recent years the connections of madness with religion and with the history of demonic possession have also become clearer.[5] But the most stunning and influential work on the history of the "social construction" and simultaneous repression of madness remains Michel Foucault's *Madness and Civilization: A History of Insanity in the Age of Reason*, first published in French in 1961 and four years later in a severely truncated English translation.[6]

MADNESS AND CIVILIZATION

With a series of dramatic images, Foucault created a symbolic history of the "experience of madness" (a deliberately ambiguous phrase),[7] and called attention to what he saw as a remarkable early modern shift from the relatively open attitude of the later Middle Ages (in which the mad occupied a "liminal" position) to a growing humanist and absolutist attitude that emphasized exclusion and confinement. Thus one could see, with Foucault's help, the transition from Sebastian Brant's and Hieronymus Bosch's world of the Ship of Fools (the 1490s) through Erasmus of Rotterdam's *Praise of Folly* to Tommaso Garzoni's imagined *Hospital of Incurable Fools* (1586) and on finally to the Great Confinement in France, that fateful absolutist social policy, begun in 1656, which swept together the poor, the crippled, the vagrant, and the blind, along with prostitutes, petty criminals, beggars, and the mad. The internment of these unfortunates in vast cities of exile called *hôpitaux généraux* shifted the governing accent from charity toward culpability and thus set the stage for the subsequent development and deployment of the concept of deviancy in the eighteenth and nineteenth centuries.[8] In Foucault's hands the history of reason and the Enlightenment became inseparable from the history of power and repression. In the *hôpitaux* enlightened Reason could confine, define, and discipline an Unreason that might threaten its fragile hegemony. Foucault also detected in these institutions the origins of a new discourse in which madness was perceived, experienced, and construed as a purely mental illness, no longer the psychosomatic disorder invented or discovered and treated by ancient, medieval, and Renaissance physicians. Thus the Great Confinement of the seventeenth century was, for Foucault, the institutional matrix for the classical and modern experience of and discourse upon madness—a mental and moral disorder that increasingly needed new methods (psychiatry) and new institutions (mental hospitals) in which to unfold. Such an analysis of discourse meant as well that Foucault often refused to deal with any underlying reality beneath or beyond the language in which madness was described. As powerful institutions, such as medicine and hospitals, shaped the language of madness, they necessarily shaped the experience and even the existence of madness.[9]

Some scholars have been so impressed, or so overwhelmed, by the philosophical power and cunning of Foucault's historical allegory that they have reacted by filling in the spaces that he left blank.[10] Others have praised his work in general while rejecting it in detail. One of these is Roy Porter, who in his exuberant history of English madness from 1660 to 1815 accepts at least Foucault's general notion of the asylum as the institutional basis from which the medical specialty of psychiatry arose, while disagreeing at many points with Foucault's picture of the way in which mad men and women were actually treated.[11] Similarly, Michael MacDonald's account of the protopsychiatric practice of an Anglican astrological healer recognizes the great value of Foucault's work in pointing to the ways that madness functioned as a mirror in which normal people saw their own image reversed and distorted; he calls Foucault's *Madness and Civilization* brilliant but plunges us into a world of suffering and healing very different from the repressive structures imagined by Foucault.[12] German scholars have also registered a set of nuanced reactions to Foucault's *Madness and Civilization* that recognize the importance of Foucault's remarkable project of providing a social, political, and institutional framework for understanding the excluding and repressive workings of our own reason but elect to ground that understanding in a substantially different history.[13] Some scholars have adapted Foucault's notion of discourse to imply that the question of historical reality is now passé, a relic of the old metaphysical quest for referentiality, that belief in a nondiscursive substance that "social scientists" might study "objectively." Foucault taught a postmodern relativism of competing discourses in which a search for "the facts" might evaporate. At their most extreme such theorists of discourse drifted far indeed from traditional efforts to create a social history of ideas. Because Foucault sometimes seemed to present himself (and was also presented by enthusiastic disciples) as a prophet, it is no wonder that most artisan-historians have despaired of implementing Foucault's program even when they have thought they understood it.[14]

In this work I will try to learn from Foucault's sensitivity to the sorts of discourse applied to the mad, whether medical, moral, or demonic, for example, but I will insist that these forms of discourse coexisted and competed with each other. I am less persuaded than some that there was a hegemonic or epistemic discourse that shaped the experience of madness for everyone in the sixteenth century, and I incline to doubt that there is such a hegemonic discourse even today. And while I will pay attention to the words and concepts used to capture the mad, I would not wish to imply that there was no underlying reality behind the texts I have examined.

Curiously, while there has been an outpouring of work about madness as a literary, medical, or philosophical category, we still suffer from a radical poverty of case histories of the early modern mad themselves. MacDonald and Porter have gone far, to be sure, toward filling in some of this picture for England in the seventeenth and eighteenth centuries.[15] But we lack adequate accounts describing the lives and the sufferings of women and men labeled and treated as mad by European society before 1600.[16]

MAD PRINCES

The study of mentally disordered princes from the Holy Roman Empire, from roughly 1490 to 1610, therefore has more than antiquarian interest. The records I have examined for this little book constitute perhaps the largest series of case histories and psychiatric opinion for any nation before the increasingly well-documented seventeenth century. Of course, these records were not all set down by a single hand, and so we do not have the signal advantages that MacDonald enjoyed in analyzing Richard Napier's voluminous records, covering thousands of patients. By the same token, however, we may be all the more certain that the tendencies to which I shall call attention were not merely the idiosyncratic creation of one solitary and fanatic record keeper. One aspiration of this book is, I hope, already clear: to present as fully as possible the case histories of several of the most unfortunate princes (and of a few princesses) from the age of the Renaissance. To be sure, these records document only the lives and miseries of the powerful, and we cannot simply extrapolate from them to the madness of ordinary people, whose experiences are so much harder to reconstruct. But from these histories we can at least descend from Foucault's abstractions and judge for ourselves just how adequately he and others have conveyed the flavor and the "experience" of Renaissance madness.

The dispersed and decentralized constitution of the Holy Roman Empire actually contributed to the process that accounts for most of the sources upon which this study depends.[17] That empire in the early sixteenth century consisted of an emperor, 7 electors (three archbishops and four secular princes), 50 archbishops and bishops, 21 secular princes (mostly dukes, margraves, and landgraves), 88 independent abbots and prelates, and 178 counts and sovereign lords, and roughly eighty free and imperial cities, to say nothing of the hundreds of free imperial knights.[18] Our story con-

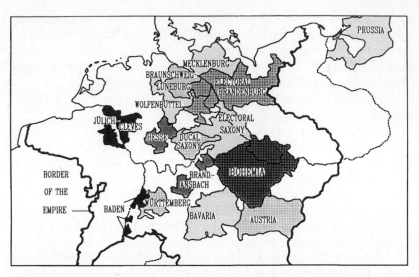

Principalities referred to in the text

cerns only the secular princes of the empire, but altogether there were about twenty-five sovereign principalities, scores of independent counties and proud lordships, and hundreds of secular princes. The most important of these maintained serious archives, and even the smaller dynasties kept up family archives that survive to this day, partly in private hands. The accumulation of paper is impressive by almost any standard.

When doctors treated ordinary private patients, their efforts usually went unrecorded, making it hard to tell at this remove how they proceeded, but when doctors treated the illnesses, and with them the mental illnesses, of ruling princes, their deliberations often became part of an official record. Their patients—as ruling princes, as dukes, counts, margraves, and landgraves—had a fair claim to being the real rulers of the German-speaking peoples. As such, their ruling houses could ill afford the more than merely personal disaster of mental illness. When a prince went mad, his whole principality trembled at the threat of civil war or of invasion by an unfriendly neighbor. Councilors, courtiers, and close relatives usually felt driven to intervene in order to circumvent the dynastic problems that could otherwise fester. Often sons seized power from their profligate or reckless fathers in coups d'état that remind us of *King Lear*. In such cases the historian can take the opportunity to uncover and analyze the social and medical responses to mental derangement among at least this privileged subgroup of German society. As we shall see, moreover, the Holy Roman Emperor was sometimes kept busy investigating and legitimating the emergency measures necessary to keep government from collapsing in the face of ducal insanity. This is a little-known but highly important function performed by emperors as different as Maximilian I, Charles V, and Rudolf II. In this way as in other, better-known ways, the emperors worked with some real effect to keep the rivalrous constituent parts of the empire from flinging themselves at one another's throats.

It is well known that there was no political Germany in the sixteenth century, but the Holy Roman Empire does not perfectly delimit the German cultural area either. Hence I have taken my subjects from all the German-speaking peoples, including the Duchy of Prussia, which lay far to the east of the empire but was distinctly German at least in its ruling classes.

Readers hoping to find broad ethnic generalizations might, I suppose, leap to the conclusion that the German nobles and princes were mentally more disordered than their English, French, or Italian cousins. Such a smear would be totally unjustified, I think, because the large number of princes I have studied is mainly an artifact of the excellent archives and dense antiquarian literature of Germany. As a percentage of all the German princes, I doubt that their numbers were unusual. Indeed, I suspect that most of our families today have one or more mentally disordered members who cannot be entrusted with major tasks or responsibilities. I have no doubt that the other countries of early modern Europe will display similar histories once scholars turn their attention to such sources.

Renaissance Medicine

Renaissance physicians were generally persuaded that mental disorders were the result of accidents (such as blows to the head), fevers (which could include phrenitis, or brain fever), congenital deficiencies (such as retardation), and humoral imbalances. The great bulk of medical observation and theorizing, both in the

Renaissance and in most histories of psychiatry, has always been devoted to the last-named category because the four humors or vital fluids corresponded conceptually with the four elements (air, water, fire, and earth), the four seasons, the four ages of man, and with the planets (Venus or Jupiter, the Moon, Mars, and Saturn); they were considered crucial to health as well as to disease. A well-ordered balance of the qualities associated with blood, phlegm, yellow bile (choler), and black bile (melancholy) determined a person's individual temperament or "complexion," one's general attitude or weltanschauung, one's energy level, and one's range of activities and interests. This ancient Greco-Roman system of health also helped to explain what went wrong when the daily regimen of food and drink and sleep, the daily exposure to air, heat, smoke, and humidity, and such contributing "nonnatural" factors as music, companionship, or sexual excitement combined to throw off the healthy balance of hot and cold, moist and dry, within one's body.[19] Humoral imbalances could produce the mental disorders of excessive anger, hilarity, torpor, or fear and sadness. If an imbalance continued too long, or if one lived immoderately, one of the natural humors (especially if excessive) might become overheated or roasted and thus degenerate into an unnatural (in other words, not inborn) sludge called "melancholy adust," or burnt black bile, whose consequences were frequently a severe mania, a raving melancholy combined with visual and aural hallucinations, raging, terrors, uncontrollable weeping, and a general madness that was increasingly difficult to treat. Much of this ancient theory was digested in the *Canon* of the renowned Arab physician, Avicenna (d. 1037), and was revived in the Renaissance.

Scholars have often assumed that this medieval way of understanding underwent a paradigm shift in the sixteenth century. Andreas Vesalius (1514–1564) has usually been taken to symbolize this dramatic transformation of medicine from a discipline of book-learning into an observational and empirical science. It can be shown that in some respects medicine (and especially anatomy) went through a revolution in the seventeenth century, but historians of science have exaggerated the extent of such a shift in the Renaissance. In the light of the best recent work, it now seems more helpful to emphasize that during the sixteenth century learned physicians actually improved and strengthened their grasp of the Greek sources of their medical theories and relied ever more heavily on Hippocrates and Galen. As scholarly medical doctors they worked to disaggregate the ancient physicians and began to undo the medical scholastic synthesis that had assumed, often enough, that disagreements among the classical physicians could be minimized or eliminated through the skillful deployment of clever scholastic distinctions. Renaissance physicians, in contrast to the medieval medical scholastics, began to emphasize the separate conclusions and points of view of Celsus and Aretaeus, of Rufus and Soranus, of Galen and Hippocrates. The result was a veritable publishing explosion as the whole corpus of ancient medical authorities was rushed into print. Editions and studies of Hippocrates and especially of Galen boomed, so that if it could be said that academic medicine had been Galenic in 1500, this was even more the case in 1600. But by 1600 it was a more authentic Renaissance Galen who dominated the citations of the academicians.

This revival of the medical classics went hand in hand with what could be called a Galenic and Aristotelian research program to continue the dissections and observations that Galen and other ancients had performed and to investigate the hidden or underlying causes of any anatomical connections or observed physiological patterns.[20] Even when its conclusions challenged the specific findings of Galen, however, this style of Renaissance medicine proceeded on ancient Aristotelian and Galenic principles. Thus Vesalius, the most famous Renaissance anatomist, contributed to the revival of Galen with an edition (1538) of a summary of Galen's anatomical and physiological teachings and with editorial work (1541) on an edition of the complete works of Galen. When he published his magisterial book *On the Structure of the Human Body (De humani corporis fabrica)* in 1543, he was not aiming to overthrow all of Galenic medicine (as some have thought) but rather to clarify and correct Galen on many a contested anatomical point.[21]

We need to keep this general reverence for and revival of Galen in mind if we are to grasp the aim of academic "psychiatry" (or medicine of the soul, to use a less anachronistic term), as practiced by university-trained German physicians in the sixteenth century. Such men hoped to emulate the ancients with their own shrewd and fundamentally Galenic observations. Their increasing command of ancient Greek made them into philologically competent natural philosophers rather than into a self-conscious vanguard of scientific and experimental revolution, the awkward position sometimes foisted upon them by modern historians of science and medicine. Thus they began to explore hitherto unnoticed complexities of black bile. Was it a kind of bile, or a separate substance altogether? How was natural melancholy different from melancholy adust? How could one tell the two kinds of melancholy apart? Was there anything to Aristotle's observation according to which all men of outstanding achievement (whether in poetry, the arts, philosophy, or statecraft) were melancholy?[22] These were serious questions in natural philosophy and in the academic medicine of the sixteenth century.

To understand Renaissance physicians and their patients we need to learn to take such questions seriously too, especially since it often happens that patients learn how to experience and present their illnesses from their physicians. If we do not master these subtleties, we will not be able to see why one medical remedy rather than another was employed, nor will we understand the often strained relations between doctors and preachers in dealing with the mad prince. If a troubled ruler thought of himself as lunatic, he may well have felt differently during times of the full moon. If he felt oppressed by excess black bile, purging and venesection may have given him relief. We need to consider that the Renaissance categories of medical analysis may have become the categories of experience and behavior.

As taught within the universities, learned medicine remained largely a scholastic enterprise throughout the sixteenth century, a fact nowhere more evident than in the proliferation of printed medical disputations from about 1570 onwards, especially in Germany.[23] In these works one finds a relentless concentration on just such questions as the nature of melancholy and the sicknesses of the mind or soul.

Well into the seventeenth century, the intellectual basis of the universities remained Aristotle. His writings provided not just a research program but vital connections and disjunctures among the disciplines, allowing for collaboration and cooperation. Physicians regularly respected the expertise and point of view of jurists and theologians because they all typically relied on Aristotle to mark their borders for them. We will see that, to a remarkable degree, court physicians could cooperate with lawyers and exorcists not so much because they were all Christians (even though that was true) but because Aristotelian categories kept them from interfering with each other. No wonder Protestant Reformers from Melanchthon on found it virtually impossible to do their work without preserving Aristotle in some serious form. Physicians felt just as strongly about the usefulness of scholastic (Aristotelian) categories and ways of explaining things. Without these ancient traditions most intellectuals felt lost.

One medical current, however, did challenge this philological and scholastic Renaissance medical practice: the theories and observations of the Swiss-born Theophrastus von Hohenheim, better known as Paracelsus (1493–1541). With roots in gnosticism and neo-Platonism, Paracelsus cultivated an alchemical, astrological, and self-consciously Christian medicine that paid attention to the whole person, body, soul, and spirit.[24] Much of Paracelsus's endeavor was explicitly religious and biblical, seeking to rescue medicine from the heathen. He aimed to set men right with God even as he treated the body with chemicals that violated the Galenic idea of humoral balance. Like Vesalius, Paracelsus has often been regarded as the prophet of a new and more scientific medicine, one that recognized the importance of natural observation and of chemical therapy. But in Paracelsus's case the argument is at best a strained one. It is true enough that his chemical remedies gradually made their way into the practice of orthodox medicine during the late sixteenth and early seventeenth centuries. In addition, Paracelsus's general approach did clearly influence the biological theories of Jan Baptista van Helmont (1579–1644).[25] By and large, however, academic physicians in Germany spurned Paracelsus's dangerously unprofessional blend of biblical religion and natural philosophy. By the second half of the sixteenth century, debates between Paracelsians and Galenists became common, and some scholars, such as Johann Albrecht of Wimpfen, began to suggest irenic ways of bridging the gaps between the two warring camps.[26] Even so, disciples of Paracelsus in the later sixteenth century continued to find it difficult to crack the academic world of orthodox Galenism.[27] Attacked and hounded from his position as city physician and lecturer at the University of Basel in 1527, Paracelsus himself had sought and found followers in nonacademic and often lower-class social circles. In a similar way, Paracelsians received a much warmer wel-come at the princely courts of northern Europe than at any univer-sity.[28] As we shall see, the rivalries of orthodox and Paracelsian healers reverberated in the controversies surrounding the proper care and treatment of princely insanity. Most physicians had an easier time imagining that an exorcism might be necessary in a seemingly impossible case than conceding that it was time to call in a "chemical physician."

On one point, however, these medical rivals were usually agreed: that madness was a medical condition that could and should be treated. They were Renaissance physicians, of course, and so they could have no inkling of what nineteenth-century psychiatry would try to understand as a moral malady, or as a purely *mental* illness, nor did they regard madness as a bestial condition that placed its victims outside the very limits of hu-manity and therefore beyond all therapy. Unlike certain Enlight-ened (eighteenth-century) physicians who, according to Foucault, maintained that madness was not even an illness requiring treat-ment, Renaissance physicians were sure that their patients were human beings in need of help.[29]

Court preachers and theologians sometimes challenged this medical judgment by suggesting that the prince was bewitched or possessed by a demon. Even if doctors agreed that demons *could* be at work in the world, this conclusion was not so eagerly accepted as our stereotypical assumptions about that supposedly super-stitious age might have it. It was usually hard to tell when the devil was involved in an ailment because he was known to be a master of disguise and also because he loved to exploit physical weaknesses. And so, if a demon intensified a melancholy sufferer's sense of despair, it was not always clear whether to begin by purging the excessive black bile, by purging the devil, or by offer-ing spiritual consolation. Nor was it easy to tell the difference between bewitchment and demonic possession, even though the-oretically one difference was that witches or sorcerers caused bewitchment while a demon might elect to obsess or possess its victim without any human help. Another important difference was that the charms of a witch might cause an ailment that looked and felt natural but failed to respond to medicine or other natural therapies; in contrast, possession by the devil had the external, unexplainable appearance and immediate, uncanny feel of the supernatural. In practice, though, these distinctions were not always of much use, and we will find the ritual of exorcism in use for cases of bewitchment as well as of possession.

THE SOCIAL DISTRIBUTION OF MADNESS AND MEDICAL CARE

The crucial question in the sixteenth century was not whether medical men regarded madness as a treatable illness but whether mad women and men would ever encounter a physician at all. Academically trained physicians remained a tiny elite among the mass of health care providers in Renaissance Germany.[30] Medical doctors were overwhelmingly urban but were also concentrated at universities and especially in the households of wealthy patrons. During the sixteenth century princes, in particular, proved eager to secure for themselves the reputed benefits of academically trained physicians.[31] But ordinary mad people, if they did not encounter a learned physician, might find that their relatives and custodians treated them as if they were not ill and merely confined them to keep them out of trouble, a confinement that bears some resemblance (except for its small scale) to the custodialism and *perception asilaire* of the seventeenth and eighteenth centuries. As we will see, it was not merely commoners or paupers who might lack the medical attention and perhaps, therefore, the medical label of mental illness. At the beginning of the sixteenth century mad princes, too, might through their dangerous irresponsibility virtually require the intervention of their relatives, and they were generally denied medical attention and treatment, even when they pleaded for help. Beginning in the 1530s, however, and rising toward the end of the century, princes were uniformly subjected to all the diagnostic labels and therapies a confident medical establishment could provide.

By the late sixteenth century these princes were treated to a range of healing efforts that were surprising not only for their inventiveness but for their tenacity. When one therapy failed, another was attempted, often one that ran theoretically counter to the one that had just been tried. We also find a remarkable range of healers employed in the increasingly desperate attempt to restore a prince to health. In these cases, examined here for the first time, we can find laid out before us something like the whole spectrum of therapy available in the late sixteenth century. It may be surprising to learn how easily "orthodox" therapies rubbed shoulders with the "heterodox," if not among orthodox physicians and theologians then among the sorely tested members of the princes' families. These energetic interventions stand in dramatic contrast to those from the earlier part of the century, when relatives of the prince took no other action beyond deposing and incarcerating him.

One way of telling this story would be to claim that princely madness was medicalized, that what had been simple incapacity became an illness or a medical disorder that demanded treatment. One could be tempted to describe this as part of the familiar story of progress or, alternately, as part of the Foucaultian story of increasing regimentation and repression, but a teleology would be clear in both instances. I prefer to see the story as something else, as that of the increasing deployment of ideas and therapies that were certainly available in 1500 even if they were not commonly used. We will need to wonder, therefore, why worried or despairing ducal councilors and relatives gave up sending an irresponsible prince to some cheerless mountaintop castle and took on instead the usually heartbreaking task of finding a cure for furor or melancholy.

It may well be that these cases point to a "domestication of politics," that is, to a growing realization that a mad prince did not just represent an adventitious problem that could be excised. As Ernst Kantorowicz pointed out, the king had two bodies, and even if the mad prince's mind could no longer control his disordered body (the source of his mental troubles), still his person continued to be essential to his other body, the body politic. In his political body, the king was a kind of god, immortal and incorruptible, and there might even dwell in that body politic "certain mysterious forces" that could remedy the weaknesses and imperfections of the king's fragile human nature.[32] That is what the lawyers of Shakespeare's England thought, but we do not yet know if the increasingly absolute rulers of Central Europe also exploited this notion. We do know that the ever more complex states of the sixteenth century depended in part on the august person of the prince for their legitimacy; the *princeps*, the *Fürst*, was imbued with an awesome authority. The history I have to tell suggests that increasingly it became symbolically counterproductive to stash the mad prince away, and assassinating him seems to have been out of the question. The prince in his physical body had become essential to the structure of authority, and so princely councilors, often frantic with indecision and desperate for a solution, found themselves more and more enmeshed and engulfed in the mental and physical problems of their masters.

The sixteenth-century state was also one that depended increasingly upon university-trained bureaucrats, and these men were far more likely to rely on experts, specifically medical experts, than their rough-and-ready counterparts of the late Middle Ages. In this way these cases may also illuminate the changing nature of statecraft and the early modern state.

In one major respect, though, these cases are disappointing. They do not do much to illuminate the possible differences between men and women. Nowadays it is common to note that certain kinds of psychiatric trouble are concentrated among women and that others are more common among men. Men and women may also experience the "same" mental illnesses differently. Unfortunately, the German cases I have collected and studied here were recorded in detail because they threatened some sort of state crisis. In most of these cases, the mad ruler was a man, and so we will have scant opportunity to examine the experience of women. We will in due course confront a couple of mad princesses, but that does not give us enough material with which to construct the woman's voice in Renaissance madness. There is one consolation. At least in Germany, the Renaissance medical language of melancholy and madness was not yet highly gendered, and except for hysteria (which was not thought to be very common) physicians expected to find roughly the same maladies among men and women.[33] In fact, women of child-bearing years were sometimes thought to be healthier (and mentally healthier) than men since they experienced a natural monthly purgation. With these qualifications, it seems that physicians were at least not deliberately imposing an asymmetrical understanding of mental illness upon their patients. Women did, however, enter into many of the cases under study here in another way, namely, as the wife or mother of a mad prince. With some regularity they found themselves locked in power struggles with the princely privy council, men who assumed that when a regency council needed to be set up, they were the men to do it. And so powerful women were often drawn into the constitutional crises prompted by the madness of men.

When the personal physicians of German rulers were invited to impose a medical therapy upon their masters, they generated piles of records that we can exploit in order to study the impact of the Galenic renaissance upon medical care. What difference did it make that learned physicians had become so much more attuned to the Galenic or Hippocratic complexities of melancholy by 1570 than they had been in 1490? Their interventions also document the growing power and prestige of the personal and court physicians (*Leib- und Hofärzte*), men who were increasingly impossible to ignore. Of course, physicians were not the only ones who imbibed Renaissance medical learning, for they served as instructors for all those whom they treated as patients. Then as now, doctors teach us how to develop a "medical" approach to ourselves, and so it is not too surprising that the ruling classes of Europe, at least in Germany, came to think in increasingly Galenic terms about their own mental health. Melancholy became a fashionable disorder and even an affectation by the time of Shakespeare, but it appears that it was popular only among those effectively (even if indirectly) exposed to Renaissance philosophy or medicine, and it is not yet clear how far down the cultural or economic hierarchy these doctrines spread. MacDonald notes that in England the number of Richard Napier's patients who described their troubles as melancholy dramatically increased in the 1620s, at least in part because of their reading of Burton's *Anatomy of Melancholy* (first published in 1621). Napier also redoubled his interest in "the technical niceties of humoral medicine" as a more precise way to describe the gloomy troubles of noblemen and gentry. "No other malady was so strongly linked to social class, and the evidence that gentlefolk were often diagnosing themselves suggests that the figures from Napier's notes are a measure of the diffusion of classical medical ideas among the educated elite."[34] The situation was similar in the German lands. As we shall see, Shakespeare's miserable and melancholy prince of Denmark had many a cousin among the imperial princes to the south.

PROBLEMS IN THE STUDY OF PRINCELY MADNESS

Before we undertake a survey of the mad princes of Renaissance Germany, however, a couple of disclaimers are in order. I have no intention of arguing that these princes (or that all of Europe's ruling houses for that matter) were somehow peculiarly prone to mental illness. We have no statistically reliable data on which to base any such conclusion. In fact, I am singling out princes for more intensive study precisely because they can be followed in the state archives of Germany, and of course they appear more often in these records than do commoners. As we will see, moreover, many of the mad princes and princesses of early modern Germany were related to one another. It would be natural to assume that so many of them were mad because they were related, but as I have noted above there were hundreds of German princes at risk, and I doubt that there were proportionally more mentally ill figures then than in any large, well-documented family of today. We certainly should not leap to the conclusion that the German princes' mental troubles necessarily had common roots in some supposedly defective genetic inheritance. Although modern psychiatry has identified genetic components for almost all disorders, it remains true that without much better information than we are ever likely to obtain, it is impossible to determine the inheritance of psychiatric disorders from four or five hundred years ago. Such caveats would not be necessary if historians had always handled their subjects with adequate discretion and distance.[35]

Another caveat concerns my methodology on a more sensitive point. If we try to study the "treatment" of "mad" princes, we must have some criterion that will allow us to tell which princes to study. The sixteenth century was, like every other century, full of odd cases, whom we might with some medical justification today regard as mentally ill. A wild duke of Württemberg, Eberhard II (1447–1504), for example, gave every sign of unreliability, willfulness, and tyranny—so much so that his short career as duke (1496–98) ended with the open rebellion of his estates and an imperially approved deposition.[36] Eberhard had such a defective personality that, in our modern terms, he must have suffered from a severe mental or emotional disorder. It is noteworthy, however, that his contemporaries did not, in the main, regard him as insane. At least they did not describe him as *furiosus, insanus,* or *melancholicus;* as *non compos mentis* or *wahnsinnig* (crazy) or *unrichtig.* Therefore, despite his nearly total ineptitude as a ruler, I will not deal with him. Similarly, I will not include the troubled margrave of Baden, Eduard Fortunatus (1565–1600), who spent so much money that he needed constant subventions from his cousins; he refused to pay his own officials, traveled widely throughout Europe but paid no attention to matters of state, ordered assassinations, and sold off some of his own Baden lands in an effort to pay his debts. Ejected from most of his margravate by Ernst Friedrich of Baden in 1594, he died from a drunken fall in his castle at Castellaun. Despite his reputation as a mad spendthrift and *tollkopf* (wildman, or, literally, a wild-head), Eduard Fortunatus was thought of by his contemporaries as irresponsible but not crazy.[37]

Even more dubious are such cases as that of the duke of Bavaria, Wilhelm V (1548–1626), who ruled his duchy from 1579 to 1597 with an ascetic piety that was a Counter-Reformation ideal. In 1597, overcome with sickness and cares of state, Wilhelm abdicated his throne in order to devote himself more fully to works of piety, to pilgrimages and the construction of churches, to charity and mortifications of his flesh.[38] Secular minds today might question Wilhelm's decision to retreat from the world and emphasize the mood of morbid melancholy at the Bavarian court.[39] This would, however, be a serious mistake, in my view, for it would open the doors to a psychiatric free-for-all, in which any behavior strange to us might be labeled mad or irresponsible. If Wilhelm's culture valued retreat from the cares of this world (as it did), then surely we will go wrong in thinking him deluded or morbidly depressed simply because he yielded to these values. Even more to the point, no one thought Wilhelm insane to have sought contemplative refuge from the world of peasant rebellions and state financial crises.[40] This does not, of course, mean that every prince who sought to withdraw from the world did so from purely pious motives, as we will see in the case of Emperor Rudolf II.

In several other cases, such as that of Count Ladislaus von Fraunberg, the last count of Haag (1505?–1566), I have found too little to go on. Although he was known as a stubborn and wrathful man, as a weird fellow (*seltsamer Kopf*), too little evidence survives to support the contention that he was regarded or treated as crazy.[41] In cases like these, therefore, we need to recognize that in sixteenth-century Germany, as today, one could be strange, eccentric, irresponsible, dangerous, willful, or just plain nutty without being judged crazy. The only sound historical basis for a consideration of mad princes in the Renaissance is that of early modern opinion. Using this criterion, we can construct a list of mentally disabled princes and princesses whose lives were lived so publicly that even their most troubled hours became part of the official record.

Modern readers will naturally wonder whether all of the princes labeled as mad and deposed from their offices were actually deranged. Could it not be that madness was simply a category used to get rid of an inconvenient father or uncle? As we will see, this suspicion was voiced in the case of Landgrave Wilhelm I of Hesse, but his case really suggests that it was more often the protest against the psychiatric label that was politically motivated. The surviving records make it clear enough that Landgrave Wilhelm was mentally incompetent but that his wife, Anna of Braunschweig, was unwilling to endure the fall from power that this implied.[42] There is, of course, no way to be sure that a mad prince was not driven mad by his confinement or deposition, and no way to be sure that personal physicians and other courtiers were recording their true impressions in the documents that survive, but my basic impression is that deposing a reigning prince was so drastic a step that the provocation had to be great. In many of the cases that we will examine it strikes me as remarkable just how long councilors and family members were willing to wait before they took steps to isolate or depose his princely grace.

THE DANGERS AT COURT

Even if we cannot today determine that the princely court of four hundred years ago was more mentally troubled or emotionally dangerous than in other times or places, sixteenth-century moralists were sure that the pleasures and temptations of court could easily drive a worldly prince to dangerous fantasies, to depression and melancholy sadness. In 1547, for example, a Benedictine court preacher and musician in Bavaria, Wolfgang Seidl (1491–1562), published a thirty-page pamphlet warning princes of the special dangers of sadness and "dangerous fantasy."[43] Aimed probably at Duke Wilhelm IV of Bavaria (1493–1550), the tract claimed that lords and princes could easily fall into depression and melancholy, those "bitter enemies of both body and soul." Some sadness was, of course, unavoidable, but a prince should be sure to allow time for amusements and diversions, for prayer and Bible-reading, for confession, for moderate food, drink, and sleep; and he should be sure to trust in God above all things, keeping servants and councilors on a tight leash and maintaining churches, abbeys, and charities in good order. Psychiatrically of interest is Seidl's concern that princes should seek out good advice and friendly companionship, rather than supposing they could.work out their fears and obsessions on their own:

> So when a prince is overcome by fantasies and falls into depression, he should at once reveal his problem to a trusted friend and not just trust himself. For if he trusts in himself and tries to dispute with himself alone, he will entangle himself; the longer his fantasies go on, the larger they become, especially in someone with a weak head, inclined to melancholy; for them a fantasy is like a fire that burns hotter the more one blows on it. So the more one tries to fight one's thoughts, the more firmly entrenched they become, until a man can't resist any longer.[44]

Quoting St. John Cassian (d. 435), one of the major monastic theorists of the sin of sloth, Seidl reminded princes that secret sadness is the devil's best tool for destroying a man and his faith. Steeped in Benedictine piety, Seidl's pamphlet was part of that large stream of literature called "mirrors for princes," but it was unusual in singling out the melancholy mental disorders that could disrupt a regime.[45] According to Seidl, a prince needed to preserve a certain "stillness and freedom of spirit" in order to meet his many obligations.[46] If stillness was required for a prince's tranquility of mind, then it is little wonder that moralists frequently regarded the court as a truly dangerous place of noise, excess, revelry, and constant temptation. Seidl and his fellow moralists did not urge melancholy princes to consult their physicians, but the court physicians of early modern Germany did argue that the princely court was the locus of specifically "court diseases" (morbi aulici).[47] While these writers concentrated on diseases such as gout, colic, obesity, and obstructions of the liver and spleen, they came in the course of the sixteenth century to accept Seidl's view that mental disturbances were another liability of life at court and drew the conclusion that medical care was necessary in such cases, too.

Sociologist Norbert Elias has pointed to another set of emotional pressures for the courtly society. During the Renaissance, he argues, ladies and gentlemen learned to repress their bodily functions and to develop a host of new shames and embarrassments.[48] He does not speculate on what might happen to those unfortunate enough to be caught in the contradictory commands and temptations of the Renaissance court, but at least in some cases it appears that the court could almost literally drive a ruler out of his mind. And when mental illness struck the prince, it required energetic measures to prevent catastrophe.[49]

A WORLD GONE MAD?

At least twenty major German princes and princesses of the sixteenth century were regarded as seriously mentally disordered, so mad that they needed to be controlled or set aside. Almost every major dynastic house produced a candidate for my list, and some contributed more than one. Because we lack detailed histories of the more numerous counts and counties, we can suspect that these lesser princely houses would contribute far more amply to this melancholy catalog if only we had more complete information. To get a sense of how such a situation may have appeared to princes of the time, let us examine the family of the mighty margrave of Brandenburg, Georg Friedrich of Ansbach (1539–1603), the son of Georg the Pious (see table 1).

While Georg Friedrich was not himself mentally ill, during the early 1570s he was appointed the guardian (custos) for his insane cousin, Albrecht Friedrich of Prussia. Because of the duties connected with this guardianship, he was unable to intervene very actively in the affairs of his mentally ill father-in-law, Wilhelm the Younger of Braunschweig-Lüneburg. At just about the same time, however, he was named guardian for his disturbed older sister Anna Maria, the widow of Duke Christoph of Württemberg and mother of Duke Ludwig. She was not the only mentally ill lady in his family, for his sister Barbara had fallen into a severe lovesickness and depression in the years after 1567. His aunt Elisabeth, who died before he was born, had had a father-in-law, Margrave Christoph I of Baden, who had fallen into so severe an insanity that he was deposed by his sons. Closer to home, Georg Friedrich's own

Table 1. Madness among the relatives and acquaintances of Margrave Georg Friedrich of Brandenburg-Ansbach

Princes and Princesses Known as Mad Are in Italics

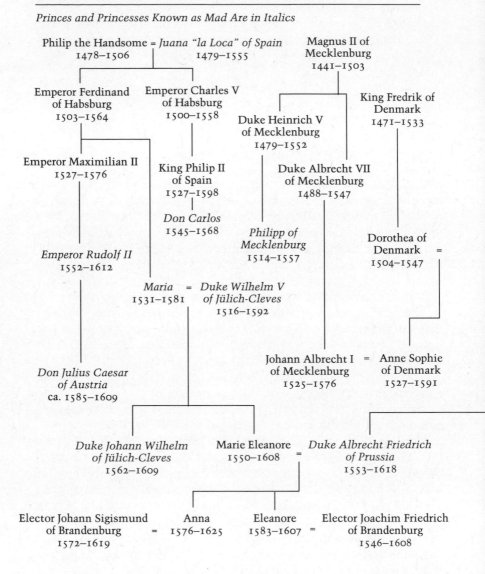

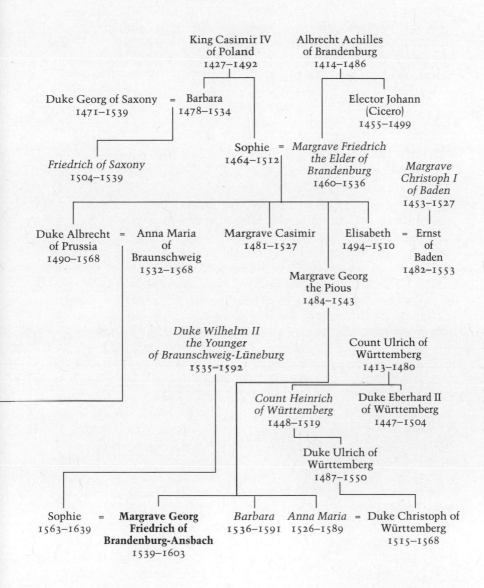

grandfather was the mad Friedrich the Elder (deposed in 1515), whose niece was married to the tyrannical and irresponsible Eberhard II of Württemberg (deposed, as I mentioned earlier, in 1498). This Eberhard in turn had a brother, the miserably afflicted Count Heinrich of Württemberg, who was so mentally disturbed that his cousin, the powerful Count (later Duke) Eberhard the Bearded, had him arrested in 1490 and imprisoned in the cold and inaccessible castle at Hohenurach for the rest of his life.

Margrave Georg Friedrich von Brandenburg-Ansbach had further contacts with the madness of princes through his ward, the mad Albrecht Friedrich of Prussia, for that duke had married (near the onset of his mental deterioration) the princess of Jülich-Cleves, Marie Eleanore. Her brother was the unfortunate Johann Wilhelm, the last duke of Jülich-Cleves, whose mental illness and marital incapacity, as we shall see later, changed the map and, indeed, the history of Europe. Marie Eleanore and Johann Wilhelm, for their part, were the offspring of a marriage in which both partners have sometimes been charged with serious mental affliction. The father, Duke Wilhelm V, suffered a major stroke in the 1560s and was not always mentally competent from then on until his death in 1592; and the mother, Maria of Habsburg, brings us at last into touch with the strain of mental illness that plagued the House of Austria from Juana "la Loca" (the mad mother of Emperor Charles V) down to Emperor Rudolf II and his illegitimate son, Don Julius (Giulio) of Austria, who were both widely regarded as mentally deranged. Margrave Georg Friedrich of Ansbach was also distantly related to the princely houses of Mecklenburg, Hesse, and Saxony, which all produced further entries in my list of mad princes.

When Georg Friedrich went north to Königsberg to take charge of Prussian affairs, he must also have learned (if he did not indeed already know) that just across the Baltic Sea the Swedish nobles, led by Johan Vasa, had recently deposed and imprisoned the mad King Erik XIV (1569), whose brother, Magnus, had also gone insane.[50] In Hungary, Princess Elizabeth Bathory (1560–1614) provided another sad and disturbing spectacle of mental deterioration.[51] It would be of interest to learn whether Margrave Georg Friedrich concluded that his whole world had gone mad, but at the moment we know too little about his personal weltanschauung to say how he felt about his extraordinary links to many of the mentally incompetent rulers of his day. I have sketched the world of his relations only in order to make the now obvious points that mental illness was a well-known problem for early modern princely dynasties and that this problem prompted such severe dynastic crises that they could on occasion alter the course of German and European history.

PART

I

FROM DEPOSITION TO TREATMENT

1

The Early Sixteenth Century

Having taken a bird's-eye view of the whole century, let us take a closer look at these mad princes. For the sake of clarity, it will help if we divide them roughly into three groups, corresponding to the early, middle, and late sixteenth century. In contrast to cases from the 1570s onwards, the mentally ill princes of the late fifteenth and early sixteenth century left very few records of their illness behind, for reasons we will soon understand.

Count Heinrich of Württemberg

Count Heinrich of Württemberg (1448–1519), for example, had by all accounts led a life of uncontrolled excess, but the traumatic event that seemed to send him off the deep end was his experience of an unusually harsh imprisonment at the hands of Duke Charles the Bold of Burgundy, during the years 1474–77. Charles had threatened Heinrich, so that he lived in constant fear of being immediately beheaded.[1] Historians from that time on have repeated the story that this threat was so terrifying that it accounts for Heinrich's subsequent madness.[2] Without trying to deny for a minute the horror of this episode in his life, few of us today would rest content with a theory of mental illness that seems to rest upon a single trauma. We would probably want to emphasize the fact, which did not escape Heinrich's contemporaries, that he was already an unsteady and foolish man years before his Burgundian captivity. In any event, all of the sources agree that after his release from captivity Heinrich became stranger and stranger until

1489, when, without apparent provocation, he had his men shoot their crossbows at Jacob von Rathsamhausen, wounding him and taking him captive.[3] The noble Rathsamhausen was at that time in the service of the mighty Rhenish Palatinate and was even wearing Palatine colors at the time he was wounded, and so the incident threatened to become a major diplomatic embarrassment for Württemberg. Rathsamhausen declared a feud against Count Heinrich and against the head of the Württemberg dynasty, his cousin Count Eberhard the Bearded. Count Palatine Philipp succeeded in keeping these warring parties apart and summoned them to his court (Hofgericht) in Heidelberg for a hearing on 27 February 1490. Instead of sending his excitable and scattered cousin Heinrich, Eberhard the Bearded dispatched an altogether more imposing figure to Heidelberg, his famous humanist councilor Johannes Reuchlin. But at the hearing, Reuchlin evidently could think of no appropriate defense or excuse for Heinrich's behavior. Apparently it did not occur to him to plead insanity on behalf of the count, perhaps because such a plea might have had most unpleasant consequences for Heinrich. And so, with no credible explanation for his wild attack, Heinrich was condemned to pay four thousand gulden to Rathsamhausen, a large sum of money.[4] Under these conditions poor Heinrich's debts were now so overwhelming that he felt driven to extract forced loans from his own officials and courtiers, loans that he obviously could not repay. His troubles grew so deep that he made plans to turn over part of his patrimony (the lordship of Reichenweiher) as a fief to the electorate of the Palatinate. Such a move threatened to increase yet further the pretensions of the Palatine Wittelsbachs along the middle Rhine. Here was the point beyond which most family members refused to remain idle spectators; when these concessions came to the notice of Count Eberhard the Bearded, he struck swiftly. Heinrich was calmly invited to come down to Stuttgart, just for a visit, but once there Eberhard arrested him. Strong men "wrestled him away in a draped carriage and took him up to Hohenurach," to quote the description handed down to Heinrich's son Georg, who was born at Hohenurach seven years after his father's capture.[5]

In the months after the hearing in Heidelberg, Eberhard the Bearded strengthened his acquaintance with the insanity defense and with the law relating to custody. His councilor, Reuchlin, composed a short legal brief concerning the Roman law of insanity, and at first sight one might hope to gain from this autograph work of the then thirty-five-year-old humanist some glimpse into how his mind worked on legal questions. Unfortunately, on closer inspection the two-page memorandum turns out to be a simple summary and translation of two passages from Justinian's *Digest*, which do not speak, technically or literally, of mental *illness* but, rather, of *furiosi*, that is, of madmen.[6]

As we will see in other contexts, *furor* and *furiosus* (madness and madman) were not yet specifically medical terms in 1490 or 1500. Physicians did not usually employ such vague and legally charged terms unless they modified them with a medical or anatomical term, such as *furor uterinus* (uterine madness). It seems that *furor* still had basically biblical, legal, and philosophical implications. One could speak of God's *furor*, of a poet's *furor*, and of a wild criminal's *furor*, without implying that they were sick.[7] And so when we ask how Count Heinrich's contemporaries regarded him, we cannot say for certain that they thought him sick. He was a wrathful, excitable, mad, moody, dangerously unreliable and unpredictable prince, but our sources do not speak of him as mentally *ill*. Reuchlin's translations from Justinian speak of nonsense (*unsinn*), of being out of one's wits (*entsetzung des gemüts*), and of lack of all understanding (*mangel aller verstentnis*), but these were mainly legal or commonsense terms with no current medical content. Other contemporaries described Heinrich as *lunaticus* (lunatic), *taub* (literally "deaf" but by extension "uncomprehending"), and "so corrupt in the head that he periodically, according to the phases of the moon, was not himself."[8] The city councilor of Stuttgart, Sebastian Küng, described his mental condition as a "lack and a deficit," as a "weakness" that aroused in others the fear that he might "harm himself or others."[9] Here, then, were concepts such as lunacy, madness or wrath, and (bodily) weakness. It seems characteristic of the cases from the late fifteenth and early sixteenth century that observers did not naturally turn to such technically medical terms as *morbus* or *dementia*, *mania* or *melancholia*. Judging from these records we cannot tell if anyone thought Heinrich was sick. The opinions of doctors were not solicited or recorded.

If no one thought Heinrich mentally or physically ill, we can perhaps explain why he received almost no medical treatment.

During the first bitter months of what would turn out to be a long imprisonment in Hohenurach, Heinrich's wife, Eva von Salm, and the appointed bailiff both requested various concessions, such as a second shirt or a specific father confessor. In one important passage from these letters the bailiff wrote that Heinrich "desired that I should allow him to have a barber who could bleed him," a request that Heinrich's cousin Eberhard approved.[10] Heinrich evidently saw himself as in need of a bloodletting, but to conclude from that that he perceived himself as ill might be stretching our little text too far. Bloodletting was, after all, a common practice employed to maintain general health. Chained, shackled, or locked up in a castle overlooking the cliffs of the Swabian Alb, Heinrich never once (in the admittedly rather sparse surviving correspondence) definitively spoke of his mental disorder or *illness*, nor did his observers remark any condition that required specifically medical attention. We can, therefore, ask the at first apparently silly question: was Count Heinrich, despite his madness, really regarded by those around him as mentally or physically *sick*?[11] Certainly medical doctors would have tried to treat his condition medically if such doctors had been consulted; but it seems significant that, so far as we know, doctors were not consulted. Another explanation for the curiously nonmedical language used to describe Heinrich might derive from the low social status of princely physicians at that time, who were perhaps not given to high falutin Greek or Latin phrases. Or we might choose to emphasize the popular character of late medieval medical culture, a culture that was not yet thoroughly permeated with the Greek *termini technici* of Galen. Perhaps in this way we could explain why Heinrich to all appearances was never treated by a physician and why his madness was never once described in the expert language of academic medicine. The simplest explanation would seem to be that Heinrich's guardians, his bailiff, his wife, and other observers simply did not see him as "sick."

Margrave Christoph I of Baden

We can probably draw a similar conclusion in the case of Margrave Christoph I of Baden (1453–1527). Like Count Heinrich, he suffered increasing difficulties with his relatives, in this case several

Margrave Christoph I of Baden, by Hans Baldung Grien. (Courtesy of the Kupferstichkabinett, Staatliche Museen zu Berlin, Mende no. 28)

of his sons, Christoph the Younger, Ernst, and Bernhard. In 1505 their situation had grown so tense that the father arrested and jailed his son Christoph in order to force his obedience.[12] In 1510 Ernst went so far as to publish printed threats against his father and to hang them up on various church doors. In angry reaction Christoph made plans to disinherit Ernst. The third son, Bernhard, did not escape these problems, and Christoph had him arrested and threatened to disinherit him as well. He was banished to Brussels. By 1515 the sons had had enough and decided that it was their turn. Favorite son Philipp was now also alienated and joined a cabal with the disgruntled Ernst to seize control of the government and lock up their father in the ruined castle called Old Baden. The old man, now sixty-two, dictated and duly signed an act of abdication that was supposed to last for four years. On 15 January 1516, however, Emperor Maximilian intervened with his own declaration, stating that old Christoph was so weak and incompetent to rule that he would have to give up his government. Little information exists about the state of Christoph's mind, but the imperial edict says explicitly that Christoph's "decrepitude of body and the other defects of his reason and of his capacities under which he suffers" could cause serious damage to the principality of Baden.[13] It is probably from about this time that we should date a miniature portrait of old Margrave Christoph, supported by St. Christopher. The old man is represented as decrepit, weak, and probably senile.[14] In the standard (and usually reliable) entry on Margrave Christoph in the *Allgemeine Deutsche Biographie* Arthur Kleinschmidt wrote that after 1518 Christoph I fell into total insanity, but unfortunately Kleinschmidt failed to cite any source.[15] The fact remains, then, that we have no contemporary evidence that anyone thought of Christoph as sick. The sparse records contain nothing about medical treatment or physicians for him.

Margrave Friedrich the Elder of Brandenburg-Ansbach

In the same year that Christoph fell from power (1515) the sons of Margrave Friedrich the Elder of Brandenburg-Ansbach (1460–1536) seized control of their father.[16] On 26 February they struck, deposing the fifty-five-year-old man at the height of the shrovetide Fasching festival (Carnival), a time of heightened tension because of the frequent role reversals and serious jesting that went along with the holiday.[17] They imprisoned him in the strong castle of Plassenburg, whose high towers overlook the town of Kulmbach. Margrave Casimir and his brother Johann took this step partly to save the state finances of Ansbach, for their father had developed the frightening habit of living well beyond his means. But the two brothers also aimed, obviously, at seizing control of the government for themselves. Evidently they feared the possible political problems that might flow from their coup d'état, for they immediately undertook a full-fledged propaganda war to explain why their father had become incompetent to rule. Rumors had, in fact, been circulating for some eight years that the old man was irrational. Indeed, like many another Renaissance prince, Friedrich was having trouble living within his means. He fathered a large brood of children (by 1515 he had eight living sons and five living daughters), and his court festivals were known for their tendency to become bacchanalia. In 1509 he admitted to his estates that he felt old (he was forty-nine) and that he was resolved to cut back on his elaborate household expenses, pay off his debts, and dedicate five of his sons to positions within the church. By 1512, with the death of his mother and of his wife, a sick and weary Friedrich seemed ready to allow his ambitious son Casimir to share in his government. This arrangement proved difficult for the autocratic Friedrich to absorb, however, and soon he was thinking of remarriage and of regaining full, personal control of the government, a move opposed by his sons Casimir and Johann. Friedrich reacted with fury, and the sons prepared to take steps that would cut off Friedrich's personal and political plans.[18]

When they actually seized power, however, Casimir and Johann tried to disguise their act of force by getting their father to sign a declaration, which they published, stating that Friedrich was *voluntarily* transferring his government to his sons. Friedrich admitted that his territory had already "suffered not just small but large damages and disadvantage" and that he, "because of evident necessity and the weakness of our body," had decided to give up governing.[19] In this declaration he euphemistically spoke only of the weakness of his body, assuredly because a valid act of abdication could only be made "legally and reasonably, with deliberate mind and careful consideration."[20] And yet the two sons, Casimir and Johann, also declared that their father was mad. Margrave Casimir explained to the shocked estates of Brandenburg-Ansbach that he had liberated them from the rule of a "mad tyrant," who had abdicated "owing to the debility of his grace's mind."[21] Logically and legally speaking, this was a complicated position, for a valid abdication required the full command of one's reason and yet, if Friedrich had been in full command of his senses, his deposition would not have been necessary.

Despite these irregularities, Friedrich was incarcerated under miserable conditions within the strong walls of the Plassenburg castle. He was permitted neither to receive nor to write letters; he could accept no presents or gifts; and he was allowed no visitors without Casimir's permission.[22] The Ansbach estates agreed that the old margrave had to be imprisoned "in order to prevent further damage to himself, to the young lords, and to the whole land, and guarded so carefully that his princely grace may not escape." The estates also ordered the old prince confined in what they hoped would be a "well-appointed princely chamber" and insisted that he be allowed "to hear Mass daily and other divine services at appropriate times, and to have a bath and other necessary rooms connected with each other." The young princes were to permit "reasonable and trustworthy persons to attend his grace by day and by night and to provide him with service, food, drink, clothing," and other necessities. In these provisions for the now deposed margrave, the careful researcher can find not a hint of Friedrich's madness or irrationality, except perhaps in the words "in order to prevent further damage to himself." But even these formulaic phrases, although they may suggest his mental disorder, say nothing of a mental *illness* or of a sickness of any kind. To be sure, Friedrich needed "a pious, learned man," that is, a priest, and he was to "suffer no lack of such nourishments and necessities as befit a prince."[23] But during the whole period of his confinement in the Plassenburg, from 1515 to 1528, the records contain not a trace of doctors or medicine.

These are the grounds on which Reinhard Seyboth has recently tried to erect an explanation of the deposition and imprisonment of Friedrich as a pure act of political force. Seyboth is surely right to emphasize that the various parties who declared Friedrich mad had their own vested interests tied up in that diagnosis.[24] This fact does not, however, mean that Friedrich was therefore an innocent victim, imprisoned unfairly and illegally. It seems much more likely that Friedrich the Elder was actually seriously mentally disturbed. Otherwise we would have a hard time understanding the words of some of those who attended Friedrich. Captain Conrad Possen, for example, wrote a letter three months after the coup d'état of 26 February 1515, asking that Friedrich be permitted a little money for gambling so that his old master "might play with his attendants from time to time for heller or at the most for pfennigs, and thus perhaps drive out many an illusion" ("dadurch villeicht mancherlei fantasei vertreyben").[25] The captain here obviously based his recommendation on the fact that Friedrich was suffering from a dangerous or disturbed fantasy, perhaps from delusions of some sort. Later on in the same letter he requested that Friedrich be allowed a mirror and some pictures, especially a picture of Emperor Maximilian; he remarked that depriving his lord of such "entertainments" would not "reduce his grace's fantasy."[26]

These remarks are also consonant with the ordinances regulating the guards for Friedrich. The authors of these regulations were so clearly in awe of the rage of the old margrave that they decreed that his meals should be delivered to him through a small hole in his door.[27] Nor was it only Friedrich's political enemies who depicted him as mad. The distant but more impartial *Chronicle of the Counts of Zimmern* also presented him as crazy: "for many know that the pious prince was somewhat deranged in his head from too much (horse-)racing and jousting."[28] Even Seyboth concedes that Friedrich was probably distrustful and given to rages, vehement, furious, and disturbed, suffering from what he calls "a certain psychic instability."[29] In the end, however, he doubts only that Friedrich had succumbed to "a totally uncontrolled behavior resulting from a thorough mental illness." Such a defense of Friedrich the Elder seems unfair to me, for it sets the hurdles of historical justice too high. And, after all, it is not our first duty as modern historians to adjudicate the coup d'état of 1515. We are obliged instead to try to understand the assessment of Friedrich by his contemporaries. For this purpose it is noteworthy that no one in his day, whether his ally or enemy, portrayed him as psychically *ill:* deranged yes, and not right in the head, feeble of mind, and foolish, but not sick according to the technical terminology of sixteenth-century medicine. And so we find descriptions like "deranged," "not right in the head," "fragile of mind," "silly" (*zerrüttet, nicht richtig im Kopf, gebrechlich im Gemüt, blöd*), but none of the technical terms we find in the Galenic study of disease. There is only one exception, so far as I am aware. It appears in the *Chronicle of Heilsbronn* by Abbot Sebald Bamberger, an inveterate enemy of Margrave Friedrich the Elder. In his contemporary account of the coup against Friedrich, Bamberger remarked that the old prince had grown so hard or unbending in his evil black bile that he could no longer be cured.[30] Here at last, and significantly in Latin, one hears the medical language of the sixteenth century, but Bamberger turned it to the purpose of showing that medical treatments were now useless. Medical terminology could thus sometimes be deployed to exclude medical intervention. In this case of madness in the house of Hohenzollern, we can see that early-sixteenth-century men had fully accepted the idea that mad princes should be deposed, but physicians played no role in determining the condition, prognosis, or possible therapy of the prince. In fact, in the cases that have come to our attention laymen did not even describe insanity as sickness of any kind. Doctors had no role in these early cases.

The best proof of this apparently extreme conclusion is the procedure adopted by the estates of Ansbach at their diet in 1528 when they wanted to determine whether Friedrich, now sixty-eight, "has come to competence and to decent reason according to his grace's age and situation" ("nach seiner gnaden alter und gelegenheit zu vermöglichem wesen und schicklicher vernunft kummen sein").[31] Although high-ranking personages and Margrave Georg the Pious (who had succeeded his ruthless brother Casimir) held the view that Friedrich the Elder had now "returned to full competence and reason," the estates insisted on their right to verify this conclusion. Evidently they trusted no experts, no physician or committee from a medical faculty, with this investigation. Instead, they decided to send a representative of each estate to live with and to observe Friedrich for a whole month under the guise of servants or guards. In Plassenburg castle they were instructed to attend him but especially to observe him, "without telling him of their purpose." Apparently this plan went off as hoped, for as a result Friedrich was allowed to return to Ansbach after thirteen years of confinement. He returned, to be sure, not as a ruling prince but nonetheless as a distinguished lord, who wanted now to "complete his life in divine services to the salvation of his soul."[32] To my way of thinking it is highly significant that the estates could think of no better procedure for testing the true mental and moral condition of their old ruler than to send their own observers personally for a whole month. This difficult and time-consuming procedure speaks volumes for a general lack of confidence in expert physicians at that time. It is, of course, also evidence for just how politically sensitive the release of the old man still was.

LANDGRAVE WILHELM I OF HESSE

We cannot be sure whether the picture I have sketched, based on the princes of Württemberg, Baden, and Brandenberg-Ansbach, can be generalized to apply to all of the cases of mentally disturbed princes from the late fifteenth to early sixteenth century. When Duke Friedrich of Braunschweig-Lüneburg-Calenberg (d. 1495), for example, fell into madness or severe mental decay, his contemporaries evidently did call him sick (*krank*), but that medically tainted designation did not obtain any sympathetic care for him. He was deposed by his brother, Wilhelm II of Braunschweig-Lüneburg (1425–1503), and kept harshly imprisoned until his death.[33] Concerning Landgrave Wilhelm I (the Elder) of Hesse (1466–1515), to take another example, we know hardly more than the simple fact that in 1491, when Wilhelm was returning from a pilgrimage to Jerusalem, he began to show signs of mental disorder. By 1493 his advancing insanity had gone so far that he was forced to turn over his government to his brother Wilhelm II (the Middle) (1468–1509) and to retreat to his castle at Spangenberg.[34] His friends and relatives called him "weak" and "sick," but they apparently ordered no medical therapy for him. Instead, he was taken on numerous pilgrimages, although in other respects he was badly neglected. During the turbulent confusion after the death of his brother in 1509, supporters of Wilhelm I tried to restore him to an independent position as ruler of at least half of Hesse, declaring that he had recovered his mental health and was again competent to rule.[35] To settle this question Wilhelm's wife, Anna of Braunschweig, did not turn to expert medical opinion, as we might today. Instead, in January 1511 she invited representatives of the towns of Hesse to come to Spangenberg to see for themselves how healthy and mentally competent Wilhelm I was.[36] Knights, too, were to send their own observers.

We know, however, that all was not well with Wilhelm because Anna had been trying for years to get him a doctor.[37] In February 1510 Caesar Pflug reported to his master, Duke Georg the Bearded of Saxony, that he and other Saxon councilors had visited the old landgrave at his castle. While there, Anna of Braunschweig had "brought in a priest who supposedly was experienced in the art of casting out the devil, and he practiced [his art] in our presence. We, however, were not able to determine that the landgrave was possessed with the evil spirit; and although this brought no results, the old landgravine [Anna] appealed to us councilors that we should send the monk again and also personal physicians in order to see if he could be helped."[38]

This report from the Saxon Pflug reveals that Anna was evidently desperate to improve Wilhelm's mental state and that in the absence of doctors she had turned in vain to exorcism. At Strasbourg in April 1511 representatives of old Wilhelm presented their case to Emperor Maximilian, claiming that the landgrave was, in fact, competent to govern but that the regents of Hesse with their Saxon allies had seen to the arrest of Wilhelm's councilors and had mistreated Wilhelm himself. They alleged, for example, that Wilhelm had not been given a bath for fifteen years, that he had been given no fresh linen or clothing, and that he was regularly treated with contempt and forced to eat from common bowls of wood or pewter while the regents dined off fine silver.[39] In reply to these charges the Saxon lawyers insisted that Wilhelm was still clearly unfit to rule, although they did not deny that he had been badly treated for a long time.[40]

In an effort to settle the highly complex issue of who was to govern Hesse both in the short and in the long run, Emperor Maximilian determined at Cologne in September 1512 that Wilhelm I was to remain in the custody and care of the Saxons until God might restore his health. All manner of financial and dynastic questions were settled here, and Maximilian explicitly ordered that Wilhelm, "who at this time is burdened with debility of his body," should obtain the attention of doctors "as soon as it is necessary." In fact, a personal physician was to be attached to his household.[41] The emperor recognized that Wilhelm had been badly abused during his madness but was obviously unconvinced by the claims of Anna of Braunschweig that her husband was actually in good health and fit to rule. In her view, though, these judgments were all the product of vested political interests. Naturally the regents labeled Wilhelm as crazy, she wrote to Maximilian on 9 August 1512, "for even if he were as wise as Solomon, he would still have to appear incompetent to them so that they could stay on longer as lords."[42] Psychiatric diagnoses could obviously be abused for political purposes five hundred years ago, just as they can be today, but this fact does not empty all diagnoses of their medical content and validity. It is of great interest, of course, that an attempt was made to debunk an unwelcome judgment of madness with the claim that the diagnosis was nothing more than political propaganda. Such a claim was extremely rare in the sixteenth century, and never successful.

In contrast to the other cases we have looked at so far, we must emphasize that Wilhelm I of Hesse was obviously regarded (by some) as sick. Physicians were recommended; an exorcist was called in. But the general impression remains that Wilhelm suffered from severe neglect and from contemptuous treatment, judging his case not by our standards but strictly by the standards of his time.

LANDGRAVE WILHELM II OF HESSE

Oddly enough, Wilhelm I's younger brother Wilhelm the Middle also endured madness, together with medical mistreatment. Although he took over the Hessian government in 1493, he too had increasing mental troubles, which evidently began when he fell victim to the newly rampaging epidemic of syphilis in 1504.[43] In 1508 he complained at great length in a remarkable and well-known writ of grievance against his own councilors that he had not been given the medical attention he deserved. Rather, his councilor Konrad von Waldenstein had done just those things that Wilhelm was sure would keep him crazy (unvernunftig, onsinnig). Against the advice of doctors the councilors kept him confined to his room even in good weather, causing him to fall into such excessive melancholy and sadness that "we have been totally robbed of our reason, strength and bodily abilities."[44] Instead of allowing him the use of the good room he had set aside for himself as a sickroom, they ignored his pleas and stuffed him into a cold room with a broken stove that filled the room with smoke. Doctors had recommended that he be allowed to gamble, using gold coins and jewels, in order to pass the time, but, as with Friedrich of Brandenburg, here too in Hesse this diversion was forbidden as too costly.[45] Wilhelm was especially vexed that his councilors ignored his requests for medicine and physicians, taking "our health and reason into their own hands." Coarse servants made sport of Wilhelm, poking his wounds and banging him into the walls, chairs, and tables. They took his cap and tried it on themselves; they held up their fingers behind his head, making fool's ears or ass's ears at his expense; their antics and rough treatment seemed calculated to drive him mad.[46] He never got the fresh air he craved, air and sunshine that he was sure had life-preserving qualities even for those who were given nothing to eat or drink. But his food, for that matter, was also all wrong; what he wanted he never received, and what he disliked he received daily. "Whatever we are given to eat we have had to eat like a senseless animal, tearing [the food] apart with our hands and fingernails as if we were mad or as if we were a werewolf."[47] Although his councilors treated his every word as fantastic nonsense ("vor ein fantasei"), they still came to him for fiefs and legal favors, as they sought to enrich themselves at his expense. The list of such offenses went on for eighteen pages.

Wilhelm II and his doctors knew that the syphilitic landgrave was sick in both mind and body. Despite his claims that he received no medical treatment, fragmentary medical records survive in the Marburg state archive, suggesting that he was treated by at least two doctors, one of whom evidently prescribed pomegranates.[48]

Both he and his brother Wilhelm the Elder regularly used the phrase "weakness of body" to describe their madness, unreason, and mental disorder. While these men and their wives sought and valued medical advice, the regents and councilors who took over the government of Hesse during the debility of the landgraves apparently did little for their care. Did they fear that proper medical attention might restore their lords to good health? Or, as seems more likely, were they mainly concerned to discipline, ridicule, and contemn their former masters?

Summary

Time and again there are signs of dramatic family conflicts surrounding the deposition and guardianship of such mentally incompetent princes. In the case of the most powerful dukes and landgraves of the empire, we can often reconstruct case histories in some detail, but in the case of more obscure counts or lords, such as Count Philipp of Ysenburg, we are often left grateful for a few crumbs of information. A thorough investigation of princely or noble family archives would doubtless turn up scores of further examples, but it is in general clear enough that insanity as a family problem was more disruptive of dynastic ambitions than either death or minority rule.[49] Summing up the situation of the late fifteenth and early sixteenth century, we can see that mentally incompetent princes were decisively removed from their high honors and deposed from office. There was nothing new in that.[50] Advisers and family members spoke of weakness, folly, debility, and the condition of not being "right" (*Blödigkeit, Schwachheit, Unsinnigkeit, Unrichtigkeit*), and occasionally of furor, or melancholy, or sickness. We citizens of the twentieth century have been conditioned to expect the devil everywhere in the supposedly superstitious late Middle Ages and often read that demonic possession was the standard description for what we now recognize as mental illnesses. But such a notion rests on a large exaggeration. So far as we can see in these late medieval cases, only Anna of Braunschweig thought of demonic possession as a diagnosis, and so it should not surprise us that only she tried to get an exorcist to drive out the devil from her husband, Wilhelm I of Hesse. The striking truth is that irate and frustrated councilors and family members did not in general avail themselves of any therapy for the princes whom they ousted. Altogether Heinrich of Württemberg, Christoph of Baden, and Friedrich of Brandenburg were incarcerated for fifty-four years without an echo of therapy—a long and unexplained silence in the archival record, if in fact therapeutic efforts were being made. It seems easier to interpret the silence to mean that no efforts were made on their behalf. In Hesse the landgraves Wilhelm I and Wilhelm II complained in vain that they could not receive the medical care they desired.

It is not my claim here, as Michel Foucault has written of madness in the eighteenth century, that such persons were regarded as mad but that they were not seen as mentally ill or as having a disordered medical condition because (in his view) the category of *mental illness* did not yet exist. We should have little doubt that if a physician had been assigned to these princes, he would have found illnesses to treat, and perhaps even "mental illnesses."[51] Foucault's point was, however, that in the world of confinement medical doctors were not allowed to exercise their therapeutic arsenal; instead the new perspective of the asylum dictated a discourse of discipline, control, and correction. This Foucaultian conclusion actually seems applicable to the very early sixteenth century. Here, too, doctors worked within a medically therapeutic perspective but were not regularly summoned to the chambers of princes who had begun to exhibit signs of mental disorder. Councilors and close relatives, by way of contrast, focused more upon removing the troublesome ruler from positions where he could cause trouble. Under these circumstances it cannot surprise us that these princes were not regarded as mentally ill. Had doctors been summoned, the situation would have probably looked different, and certainly if exorcists had been regularly assigned to these cases, demonic possession, too, might appear more regularly as an official diagnosis. In modern or secular terms, possession provided medieval men and women with a category that could discriminate functional mental disorders from the brain fevers, intoxications, and cerebral lesions of organic or somatic disease. Churchmen were often warned not to use the label of demonic possession for cases that could be explained in physical terms. So, in a certain sense, the notion of possession described a form of strictly *mental* illness inasmuch as it was a category of "mental disorder without apparent physical origin" and was thus a religious form (or perhaps *the* early form) of immaterial, nonorganic, mental illness.[52] Despite our modern prejudices, however, demonic possession was not very common in the late Middle Ages. We do know that the categories of melancholy and of demonic possession obviously existed in 1500 and 1520, but these diagnoses were not applied to ruling princes in Germany with any regular therapeutic consequences in the early sixteenth century. Even the few cries for therapy that we can overhear from five hundred years ago met with almost no response. As we shall see, though, the time would soon come when both doctors and exorcists were more commonly summoned to the private chambers of the mad prince.

2

MID-CENTURY:
THE TURN TO THERAPY

From the central decades of the sixteenth century there are a number of mostly rather poorly documented cases of mental disorder among the ruling houses of Germany. As usual, there is little information to be had concerning the minor houses of the empire, but we do know that a certain Count Sighard V went mad in the middle 1550s.[1] From such instances we can begin to detect a changing attitude toward the madness of princes. They also illustrate further the kinds of constitutional and religious crisis provoked by mental disorder in the heir apparent. We now find mad princesses, as well.

ANNA MARIA OF WÜRTTEMBERG

One example is Anna Maria of Brandenburg-Ansbach, wife of the pious Protestant Duke Christoph of Württemberg. She was born at the end of 1526 and married at the age of seventeen. The mother of twelve children, she was widowed at the age of forty-two, in 1568. Apparently her grief, combined with the temptation of remarrying, produced such mental conflict that in the spring of 1571 she fell into a deep melancholy. She dreamed, hopelessly, that young Margrave Georg of Hesse, then only twenty-two, would marry her. She tortured herself with agonies of yearning and doubt over him, painfully sighing in May 1571, "I can't do or think otherwise, and I know that if my cousin will not have me, I must die or go crazy" ("von Sinnen kommen").[2] She further tormented herself with the thought that she should remain faithful to her former husband, although she remembered that in his last months he had urged her to remarry.[3] She was also aware that at her advanced age she was no longer a young beauty and that she was weak from grief and from so many births, but she kept up her hopes.[4] Her daughters, appalled at their mother's romantic delusion, tried energetically to talk her out of it. Evidently this is why she protested that her affections were "not just pretending or melancholy" ("kein angenommenes Ding oder Melancholey"), but family members were sure that she was mad.[5] They conducted her to her widow's residence, the Castle at Nürtingen, and kept her confined there (with minor interruptions) until her death in 1589. The state archive in Stuttgart preserves twelve folders of material concerning Anna Maria, including detailed reports on her last illness and death.[6] While there are ample financial records to document the contents of her household and the expenditures of her servants, nothing survives to suggest that physicians tried in any way to treat, or even to comment on, her lovesickness and melancholia. Separated forcibly from the world of power and politics, she could be ignored, and so her voice, her suffering, and her treatment (if any) are beyond our ken. Feminist scholars have contributed much to our understanding of the way that a patriarchal culture silenced and repressed women, but in cases like this one it may be useful to remember that dropping out of the surviving records meant mainly that a woman was being treated to the same documentary neglect (and perhaps to the same medical neglect) enjoyed by all the other men and women of her time who had no political power or financial independence.

DUKE PHILIPP OF MECKLENBURG

We know that some princes, however, were beginning to obtain serious medical attention. We are relatively well-informed about the illness of Duke Philipp of Mecklenburg (1514–1557), the son of Duke Heinrich V the Peaceful (1479–1552). At the age of twenty-two the young prince took part in a tournament celebrating the wedding of his sister, during which he received a sharp blow from a lance to the side of his head. His condition developed into a weakness and mental debility that lasted until his death twenty years later. In Philipp we have the first case of a mad prince with a lengthy medical paper trail. More than one hundred years ago Ludwig Spengler published the seven most important medical *consilia* and recommendations regarding Duke Philipp's condition, and so we are unusually well placed to evaluate the nature and intensity of the care he received. These *consilia* range in date from 1537, shortly after the accident, to 1549, and are characterized by a surprising variety of views as to what the basic trouble was.

The first sort of treatment Philipp received was more a sort of nontreatment, as Duke Heinrich's personal physician seemed content merely to observe the prince. Soon, however, Heinrich consulted Dr. Gregor Koppe from Kalbe (perhaps the Kalbe fifteen miles south of Magdeburg), who responded in some detail to the lengthy written description he had been sent. For Koppe the crucial problem seemed to be Philipp's state of labile melancholy. He warned that the young man should never be left alone for fear that he might fall "deeper and deeper into thought," until he became "depressed and anxious" ("swermutigs . . . und forchtsam"). Almost as important was keeping the prince from anger, for his easily excited wrath could damage his health. Koppe recommended nine to ten hours of sleep each night, herbal baths, the music of stringed instruments, and soothing foods and drinks. These included larks, finches, veal, young rabbits, and capon, with wine to drink, but Philipp was to avoid such foods as old beef, smoked and pickled meats of all kinds, venison, wild boar, and all water fowl along with "other birds that live in swamps or reeds." Heavy beers and strong, sweet wines were forbidden. He needed happy servants to cheer him up, "but his princely grace should keep away from women for now."[7] Koppe also sent along some herbal medicines, as well as recipes for herbal baths and for lettuce salads "for strengthening the head."[8]

During 1538 Duke Heinrich received learned opinions from two other doctors, one the famous polymath Jodocus Willich (1501–1552), and the other an unknown doctor, whose opinion was transmitted to court by the Lutheran statesman Simon Leupold (1517–1583?). Let us look at Willich's opinion first. A prodigy as a philologist, Willich had become a physician and distinguished himself in theology and musical studies as well. One of his scholarly interests was (pseudo-)Aristotle's *Physiognomy*, which he translated into Latin, and so it is perhaps not too surprising that he put this kind of learning to use: "From his physiognomy and from the urine of Duke Philipp I conclude that he is of a choleric complexion with which a certain amount of the phlegmatic is mixed in."[9] Willich did not exactly agree with Koppe that young Philipp suffered mainly from sadness and depression. Instead his disease was "what the old Greeks called *eroticos* and is a special insanity or madness (*abwiczung odder unsinnigheit*) that arises from love." In his case the choleric humor had been roasted, producing "the third kind of melancholy, for which reason he is mostly out of his mind."[10] Philipp slept poorly and was still overexcited, anxious, and depressed, Willich said, agreeing here with Koppe's observations of the previous year; but Willich suspected syphilis and directed that "that part which is ignoble by nature" should be tested to see if it was "still strong enough to expel the dangerous excess fluid." Philipp evidently needed to be purged not only from his head but from his genitals. Willich included with his recommendations a set of recipes for purges, foot baths, and head poultices, all with special attention to the adjustments necessary during the hot, sultry, dog days of late summer.[11]

In the autumn of 1538 an unknown doctor submitted a cure for Philipp that emphasized yet another therapeutic option: sweat baths in a cubicle suffused with the smoke of laurel berries. Philipp was directed to sit for one and a half hours in such a room until he had sweated out his impurities and excess fluids; then his head was to be washed and a poultice of hot oatmeal bread steeped in brandy bound to his head, and he was to be laid in a warm bed. Like Koppe, this doctor recommended a light diet of young, tender meats and the avoidance of venison, pork, and dried fish. We do not know what effect these measures had, of course, nor do we even know whether they were tried, but we do have the summary remarks of the feeble young duke, in his own handwriting, in the margins of this *consilium*. Dating from about the same time are a couple of notes from Philipp to his father, Duke Heinrich, one claiming that he was now, thank God, "fresh and healthy," but the other asking him and others to pray that God would "restore me to reason and to my soul's salvation." Evidently Philipp's condition went up and down, but he showed no real improvement.

In 1539 the court of Mecklenburg received yet another learned opinion, this one from Dr. Martin Boler, the personal physician of the duke of Braunschweig-Lüneburg. Like the previous physicians, Boler was concerned that Philipp eat properly, avoiding smoked and salty foods, and keep a proper schedule both for meals and for bedtime (allowing twelve hours for sleep). Every morning his head was to be warmed by rubbing it with fine cloths, "and especially the back of the neck, for his memory is suffering." Baths and massages needed to be carefully calibrated to the phases of the moon, suggesting that Boler thought of Philipp as possessed by lunar spirit, or, literally, a lunatic. By now Philipp's memory was increasingly defective, a point that later opinions confirm.

Duke Heinrich continued to seek help for his son throughout the 1540s. The recommendations of three physicians survive, from 1545, 1547, and 1549, and for all we know there may have been others. In 1545 Dr. Stephan Wild wrote a lengthy *consilium* emphasizing the now familiar advice about food, drink, and sleep. In Hippocratic fashion Wild also recommended that Philipp's air be closely monitored, that it not be too hot or cold, and that it be spiced with seasonally adjusted odors.[12] Philipp was also told to take moderate exercise, walking or even hunting, and that his mind, too, should be exercised, not with fear, anger, or sadness (for this would only make him more melancholy), but with games, happy diversions, and the music of stringed instruments or of song. By now he seemed to have recovered from his erotic mania, and Wild even suggested that he could occasionally be allowed to visit with the ladies of court.[13] Along with the pills, purgative draughts, and digestives that Wild prescribed was another recommendation of warm baths thrice weekly, "for the bath is the strongest cure of melancholy, as Galen himself writes."[14]

In 1547 Dr. Barthold Sandow wrote to Duke Heinrich that he had recently visited Philipp, who was now in his thirty-fourth year; to Sandow the prince's chief symptom seemed to be feeble memory. In other respects he was much improved, but he needed to be bled from the head in the hopes of restoring his memory.[15] Oddly enough, none of these early medical opinions mentioned Philipp's tournament accident and the blow to his head. All these physicians dealt with his disorder as if it was an internal problem of his physical complexion and his humors, perhaps indicating how strong and conceptually irresistible the Galenic theory of humors was.

But in 1549 Duke Heinrich consulted the famous city physician of Hamburg, Dr. Jakob Bording (1511–1560), originally of Antwerp, who evidently pleased the duke so well with his consultation that Heinrich hired Bording as his personal physician and as a distinguished professor at the University of Rostock.[16] In Bording's frank opinion there was very little one could hope for. Poor Philipp was, in his view, perhaps congenitally retarded, and the blow to his head had only made his poor condition worse: "Ex stupido factus est fatuus" ("From being merely stupid he's become a fool"). Over and over, Bording emphasized the wound to Philipp's head and the shock and fear induced by the accident. Summing up his gloomy impression he wrote: "As far as curing him goes, I am forced to confess that I know of nothing to cure this sick man or of any rational doctor who would either cure or even try to cure him completely."[17] Still there were foods and drinks that could moderate Philipp's lamentable state, and here Bording joined the established tradition of medical palliators, who had, as we have seen, sought to soothe Philipp's rages and depressions.

One matter worth remarking here is the obvious seriousness with which Philipp's father and the whole Mecklenburg court tried to find remedies and strategies to heal the prince. His is the first case in which we have full documentation of the strenuous medical efforts that could be taken to cope with mental disorder. For twenty years the young man troubled this north German duchy with his feeble state of mind, but unlike many of the other, earlier cases to whom we have devoted our attention, in this case the doctors were encouraged to do their best. As staunch Lutherans, no one at court suggested pilgrimage or exorcism. In fact, there is no hint in the surviving records that anyone saw Philipp's problems in other than medical terms, but that is perhaps to be expected from documents so exclusively medical in origin.

Philipp died at forty-three. His father, Heinrich, who had earned his sobriquet "the Peaceful" because of his unwillingness to join the militant Protestant cause against Charles V, had already died in 1552, five years before Philipp. Judging from the frequent succession crises prompted by madness in the other major hereditary lines of German princely houses, we might have surmised that Philipp's condition would have an unsettling effect upon the dynastic politics of Mecklenburg. But this was not really the case. Mecklenburg was jointly governed by two dukes, who kept separate residences (at Schwerin and Güstrow) but who had not separated their territory into two independent duchies (a measure that finally came in 1621). After young Philipp's tournament accident in 1537, Heinrich the Peaceful had placed all his dynastic hopes on his son Magnus, whose marriage to a Danish princess unfortunately remained childless. The final blow to Heinrich's hopes came with the premature death of Magnus in 1550. Now desperate for a competent heir, Heinrich married again (for the third time) in 1551 at the age of seventy-two, but he died the very next year, whereupon the whole duchy of Mecklenburg fell into the hands of Johann Albrecht (son of Heinrich's brother Albrecht), who continued the odd and often tense policy of joint rule among brothers.[18] Inconvenient, and sad, as the mental incapacity of Duke Philipp doubtless was, the system of shared rule in Mecklenburg guaranteed that his debility could not, in and of itself, throw the duchy into dynastic chaos.

FRIEDRICH OF SAXONY

Panic and chaos, however, did erupt in Saxony, which had been divided in the late fifteenth century by the brothers Albert and Ernst. The trouble arose in Albertine Saxony, which was in the hands of Duke Georg the Bearded (1471–1539), a staunch opponent of Luther's reforms in the neighboring lands of Ernestine Saxony. Georg had grown up partly at the imperial court in Vienna and totally under the influence of his anti-Hussite mother, Sidonia, the daughter of George (Jiri) Podebrady of Bohemia. Intended first for a life in the church, Georg obtained a decent education in Latin and theology before he was recalled to secular rule in place of his father. Famous for his resolute opposition to Martin Luther from the Leipzig Disputation of 1519 onwards, Georg was also a zealous church builder and religious disciplinarian, a reformer of monasteries and patron of humanists. His court in Dresden was brilliant, and the university at Leipzig flourished under his careful attention.

Duke Georg came to understand the whole goal of his life as the preservation of Catholicism in a region that seemed to be sliding bit by bit into Protestant infidelity. His Ernestine Saxon cousins were, of course, the worst offenders, but there were problems even closer to home. In 1533, for example, Georg felt compelled to force eighty burghers of Leipzig, solid taxpayers, to leave his territory because of their stubborn adherence to Luther.[19] Then, in 1537 his own brother Heinrich, the so-called Pious, sick in body, fat and self-indulgent, finally gave in to the insistent urgings of his energetic wife, Katharina of Mecklenburg, and began to introduce the Reformation in his lands, centering on Freiberg in Meissen.[20] To make matters worse, Georg's firmly Catholic son, Johann the Younger, died in that same year, and Johann's widow, Elisabeth of Hesse, also introduced Lutheran reforms in her widow's territory of Rochlitz. All that Georg had lived for now seemed to depend on the only one of his five sons who survived, Prince Friedrich, his youngest, who had been born in 1504.

Unfortunately, Friedrich was mentally incompetent and had long been regarded as an impossible successor to his father. But Georg now took steps to have the estates of his duchy of Saxony declare that they recognized Friedrich as his legal successor. On 4 May 1537 the estates, meeting in Leipzig, accepted Friedrich on condition that he be surrounded and controlled by twenty-four regents, a permanent committee of the estates consisting of two counts, two prelates, two burghers, two university professors, and sixteen knights, three or four of whom were to attend Friedrich at all times.[21] This step would secure the continuance of Catholic rule after Georg's death, to be sure, but since Friedrich was not married, it was only a half-measure. Georg began, therefore, to cast about for a suitable wife for his poor, sickly, and mentally disturbed son. By the end of 1538 he had settled upon Elisabeth, the daughter of Count Ernst II of Mansfeld. A quiet wedding, with the twenty-four regents in attendance but with only a small celebration, was planned for 27 January 1539.

The only hitch in these dramatic, not to say desperate, measures, was the anxious advice of Friedrich's doctors, who had warned ever since 1537 that the prince was in no condition to undertake marriage. Some physicians even declared that marriage might kill him.[22] Friedrich himself was eager to marry, however, and had pestered his father's chief councilor endlessly about which princess it was to be and when the wedding itself would take place.[23] Naturally, no one thought of soliciting Friedrich's views on such important matters of state.

On 27 January 1539, and for the week thereafter, Friedrich and Elisabeth's wedding was celebrated. A tournament was held, with racing and ring-lancing, in which the elderly Duke Georg himself took part. But Georg also took advantage of the meeting to confer with the assembled regents about the future succession and the need for his territories to remain firmly opposed to Protestant innovations.[24] Unfortunately, we do not know how Friedrich and Elisabeth managed during and after the wedding, but the dire warnings of his doctors turned out to have had substance. Just three weeks later the Dresden court celebrated Carnival, with more horse races and tournaments, in which even Friedrich took part. Two days after that, on 22 February, Friedrich complained that he didn't feel at all well. On the 26th he felt slightly better and took nourishment. The famous court physician Dr. Sebastian Roth of Auerbach (1493–1555) prescribed a medicinal drink that the prince refused to take until told that his father had ordered him to drink it. Moments later he cried out, "Oh, doctor, how bad I feel! What kind of drink did you give me?" Within hours he was dead, and rumors circulated that he had been poisoned.[25] What had the doctors prescribed? One could suspect an assassination plot engineered by Lutherans or Ernestine Saxons, but there is no evidence to support such suspicions. And after all, Friedrich had been sick for years: it may well be that the excitement and exertions of his wedding and four-week marriage were enough to tilt the balance. But, of course, this is speculation, however irresistible such thoughts may be.

Duke Georg now felt defeated in all his efforts, and within two months he too was dead. The Saxon succession subsequently went to Duke Heinrich the Pious (1473–1541), who slowly introduced the Lutheran Reformation and began the process of turning all of Saxony into a thoroughly Lutheran land. The dynastic crisis in Saxony was not like that of Baden or Brandenburg-Ansbach, in which a ruler needed to be removed, nor was it so peaceful as in Mecklenburg, where other family members of an acceptable religious conviction stood ready to take over. Instead, the madness or debility of Friedrich meshed with Reformation politics to produce a bitter end to Catholic rule in one of Germany's most important duchies.

ANNA OF SAXONY

Women rarely had the chance to produce, through mental illness, this kind of dynastic crisis, although the case of Queen Juana ("la Loca") of Spain, mother of Charles V, has received a fair amount

Princess Anna of Saxony, by Abraham de Bruyn. (Reproduced from *Nassauische Annalen*, vol. 53 [1934])

of attention.[26] Another such case almost wrecked the plans of William of Orange, who was married to Anna of Saxony, daughter of Moritz of Saxony and thus a granddaughter of the aforementioned Heinrich the Pious. She was born in 1544 and spent her earliest years in Dresden. At nine she lost her father, Moritz, who had been distant in any case, and at eleven her mother, Agnes, the daughter of Philipp the Magnanimous of Hesse. Anna grew up as the only surviving child of the great Moritz, much indulged, secluded, and encouraged to develop a strong sense of her own importance.[27] She was a "difficult child" in difficult circumstances, and her stepfather, Elector August of Saxony, together with her grandfather, the landgrave of Hesse, determined that she should marry early. She was promised a glittering dowry and was widely regarded as the wealthiest catch of all the German princesses of her day. Her marriage to Prince William of Orange solved William's pressing financial problems at a stroke. The lavish wedding, in August 1561, was described as breaking all the current records for consumption and excess. Some fifty-five hundred guests celebrated for a week, consuming thirty-six hundred buckets of wine and sixteen hundred barrels of beer.[28]

Despite such glorious festivities, however, the marriage was troubled from the very beginning. By 1564 Dutch and German courtiers were tittering and smirking in their letters about Anna's uncontrollable moods, her outbursts, and her disobedience. She was rude to Regent Margaret of the Netherlands, unkind and uncaring to William's children from his first marriage; she was passionate, haughty, and distinctly odd.[29] She called down upon herself the gossip and disapproval of her whole society, although it is possible that a modern feminist reader could see in her behavior a vehement struggle against the patriarchal conventions of her day. Why, indeed, should she obey and show herself a "manageable" wife? Even if this line of interpretation has something to be said for it, as it may, the struggle cost Anna dearly. In 1566 Anna cut loose from her husband to travel to Spa, southeast of Liège, where she filled the air with complaints and derisive comments aimed at her husband. She consorted with "lewd fellows," bringing dishonor upon herself and all her relatives.[30] She even publicly ridiculed William to his face, heaping contempt on his social standing and openly laughing at his sexual inadequacy. Her first two children, daughters, died in infancy, but a son, baptized at Breda amidst euphoric celebrations, also seemed to bring no joy to her life. She began to express thoughts of suicide and despair, secluding herself for days on end in a darkened room illumined only by candles, receiving no visitors, and refusing food. Fits of gaiety alternated with drunken bouts of melancholy gloom in which she voiced the fear that her husband was trying to poison her.[31] Her Hessian cousin, Landgrave Wilhelm, wrote to her in February 1566, hoping to temper her lust for drink and dishonorable company, urging her to return in faithful obedience to her husband and to dismiss the heavy thoughts that made room for the devil and could drive her to desperation.[32] As time passed, however, her Saxon relatives began to show less and less enthusiasm for helping her. She had gone too far. From 1568 onwards William did not live with her, and Anna plunged into a life of increasingly grotesque extravagance and intemperance in Cologne.[33] In 1570 she gave birth to a daughter, Emilia, who later in life experienced extreme difficulties in living, was arrested as mad, went through bouts of screaming at her attendants, attempted suicide, and died in 1629.[34] Historical eugenicists might say, "What else could you expect from such a mother?" But the defenders of nurture could as easily reply that the conditions under which such a child was reared were hardly conducive to mental health. Here again, we are too far removed from the issue to decide the matter.

By 1570, her mother, Anna of Saxony, had retreated from her censorious society to a country house in Siegen, located in the rough, mountainous country between the Westerwald and the Sauerland, east of Cologne. With her went a bourgeois lover, Johannes Rubens, a Calvinist refugee magistrate from Antwerp who also left his wife and four children in Cologne. Their romance was all too public, and William's younger brother, Count Johann of Nassau, decided to take matters into his own hands, arresting the flagrant couple in 1571 and transporting Rubens back to the family castle at Dillenburg. In Siegen Anna denied any wrongdoing, but her unmistakable pregnancy and her loquacious lover both testified to her infidelity. Anna then broke down and asked William to execute them both, a plan that appealed but little to Rubens. But William decided to spare them, perhaps influenced by the persistent and passionate intervention of Rubens's wife.[35] On 22 August 1571 Anna gave birth to a daughter, whom she named Christine. William refused to recognize her as his child. The Rubens family, now reunited, was sentenced to local exile in Siegen, where six years later Rubens and his wife became parents of the prodigious Peter Paul.

As for Anna, William divorced her in 1571, and she was held in custody, first in Siegen, then in Beilstein, until 1575, when she was sent home to Dresden. There she was confined to two rooms whose windows were bricked up and whose doors were provided only with a small, iron-grated aperture. She died in December 1577, at the age of thirty-three.[36] Her last years were filled with violent outbursts, hallucinations, and filthy talk of things that "reasonable women of innate modesty and restraint keep secret." She contradicted herself, claiming to have killed her own children, and declared that her daughters had committed incest with their father.[37] To her Saxon custodians it was clear enough that she was "crazy in the head" ("im Kopfe verrückt"). Her malice had produced a "melancholy or total derangement," which doctors needed to examine in order to determine whether it was melancholia or mania and whether she should be treated with medication or with punishment.[38]

This put the problem in a nutshell, for it was never fully clear to her custodians that Anna was simply sick. Her behavior was so reprehensible, her speech so shameless and malicious, that so far as we can tell she was never treated by doctors. Right up to her death, the court preachers were trying to extract a truly repentant confession from her, trying to break her of a "stubborn, petrified malice" that horrified all who observed her. It had been obvious at least since 1570 that Anna drank too much, but then as now it was not clear whether this was more a physical or a moral-spiritual problem.[39] It took a surprisingly long time for her family to conclude that she was steadily going mad. In October 1572, for example, it was decided that she should not be reading "worldly" books, whereupon eleven "novels," including *Amadís de Gaula* and the "Cento Nouelles" (probably the *Cent nouvelles nouvelles* from the late fifteenth century), were confiscated. Anna was told that she should be devoting herself to the Bible, not to books that could drive her to levity and wantonness. At Beilstein preachers were ordered to deliver sermons to her twice weekly in her room, as if she could still be expected to respond with Christian repentance. Other measures, though, suggest that she was also regarded as irresponsible and ill. She was not to be left alone; knives were to be taken away from her after meals. And yet there is no hint in all the surviving records that Anna was ever seen by medical doctors.

By 1575, as her physical and mental condition worsened, she began complaining bitterly about inadequate food. She dosed herself with vast quantities of olive oil, perhaps following the advice of one of the popular medical manuals she kept near her, and she began demanding to see a "doctor from an imperial city," which perhaps reflects the current high status of city physicians in Germany's most important towns.[40] Her custodians noted that she now talked nonsense "as if she were crazy," trembling and foaming at the mouth. By November 1576 the captain of Zeitz reported that Anna had attacked him with knives and was "raging and foolish as if she were possessed."[41] Remarkably, still no one sent for a doctor or an exorcist, and so when she was near death, as we have seen, it was not clear to her contemporaries what her medical condition actually was. Should she be treated medically or punished further?

The question was still unanswered when Anna died. Her case allows us to modify our emerging conclusion somewhat. We cannot simply say that medical care for mad nobles was unusual in the early sixteenth century but commonplace by mid-century. The sad case of Anna of Saxony shows that when madness was seen as a major moral lapse, and when no dynastic issues were at stake, a princess, at least, could be harshly treated and medical care could seem irrelevant or peripheral. It may well be that because women were held to a stricter standard of domestic morality, they presented more acutely difficult problems when it came to deciding whether a particular case was one of immorality or of sickness, and so whether opprobrium or hellebore was appropriate.

DUKE WILHELM THE YOUNGER OF BRAUNSCHWEIG-LÜNEBURG

The last case from what we can regard as the middle decades of the sixteenth century moves us back into the world of major state crises. The duchy of Braunschweig in northern Germany was no stranger to problematic princes. In the late fifteenth century Duke Friedrich of Braunschweig-Lüneburg had been abruptly set aside and harshly treated because of his mental disorders.[42] But the madness of Duke Wilhelm the Younger of Braunschweig-Lüneburg (1535–1592) had far greater ramifications, touching off a long, tense, governmental crisis that began in 1577. Wilhelm was the youngest son of Duke Ernst the Confessor and Sophie of Mecklenburg, sister of the incompetent Duke Philipp of Mecklen-

Duke Wilhelm the Younger of Braunschweig-Lüneburg shown with the palace in which he was later confined. (Courtesy of Bomann-Museum Celle)

burg, whom we have already met.[43] When his two oldest brothers died in the 1550s, Wilhelm and his remaining brother, Heinrich, decided to rule this small duchy in common, and Heinrich probably even agreed not to marry, so that problems of dynastic succession might be avoided.[44] Although Heinrich did marry later, the dukes of Braunschweig-Lüneburg nevertheless had established a tradition of cooperative joint rule that gave the principality almost a hundred years of dynastic peace, in sharp contrast to the harsh competition and territorial splitting that characterized so many German princely houses of the sixteenth and seventeenth centuries.[45] This was all the more necessary because Wilhelm's marriage in 1561 to Dorothea, daughter of King Christian III of Denmark, was amazingly prolific. Altogether eight daughters and seven sons survived their father, numbers large enough to have destroyed the duchy if each child or even each son had demanded a separate slice.

The Reformation had made an early and deep impression on Braunschweig and its court at Celle. From Urbanus Rhegius in the 1520s to the ten years (1611–21) when Johann Arndt was general superintendent of the territorial church, Braunschweig-Lüneburg seemed to foster a deep Lutheran piety. A new church ordinance, judicial reforms, and a new code of "police ordinances" all appeared in 1564, and the pious Wilhelm also worked hard on a new statement of the Lutheran faith, published in 1576 as the *Corpus doctrinae Wilhelminum*. Between 1559 and 1578 the chapel of the ducal palace was transformed into one of the masterworks of German Renaissance architecture.

The first signs that not all was well with Duke Wilhelm emerged in 1577 when he was getting ready to embark on a visit to his brother-in-law, August of Saxony, who was himself then dealing with the terminal madness of his niece, Anna of Saxony, as we have just seen. Before Wilhelm and his entourage set forth, he fell into a major confusion, marked by crying, indecision, too much late-night drinking, and an inability to sleep. Fatigued, he suddenly fell asleep in the middle of a lengthy dinner. He started off toward Gifhorn, only to return in confusion.[46] Dorothea was clearly upset to see how excitable and disordered her husband had suddenly become. Lower Saxon historians from that day to our own have suspected that the pious duke ruined his health with too much drink, a habit that the court preacher Eilhard Segebade could not even ignore in his funeral eulogy.[47]

Regardless of the cause, the consequences of such irrationality in a ruling prince were serious. When Wilhelm began to ignore affairs of state, paying no attention to his councilors and refusing all visitors, the councilors decided to call in Wilhelm's closest friends and relatives to provide a government that could relieve the duke. A regency council of six to eight men was formed, whom Wilhelm was to appoint during a peaceful, lucid moment. Although the councilors decided not to call for the help and intervention of Emperor Rudolf II, Elector August of Saxony (who was married to Dorothea's sister, Anna) sent word to Rudolf on his own and obtained the sage imperial advice that Wilhelm was to be given peace and quiet so that he might come to his senses; or if God had given Wilhelm this heavy cross to bear, then measures must be taken to protect both Wilhelm and his duchy. Some relatives, notably Duke Julius of the neighboring duchy of Braunschweig-Wolfenbüttel, expressed their anger that so personal a matter had become public gossip, but as we have seen often enough, cases of this sort were hard to conceal.[48]

By January 1578 the prescribed rest may have been having the desired effect, for Wilhelm seemed to be his old self again and even proposed that an apparatus be set up in case he should fall ill again. For four years, things went well enough, but in 1582 he fell into violent rages again, running up and down in the streets at night, shooting off pistols at random. Rumors spread in Celle that even though he was obviously sick, no one was ready or brave enough to help him. In the densely half-timbered houses of Celle and in the taverns, local gossip had it that "any drunken peasant" would get help in a case like this, "but the way they are treating his princely grace is a disgrace to councilors, courtiers, and servants alike."[49]

Duke Wilhelm, however, certainly did not make it easy for those who might try to help him. He threatened to shoot or imprison anyone who touched him. In an earlier day, a Casimir of Brandenburg would have seized power, but conditions now were different. It is perhaps a sign of the growing awe with which the prince was treated that Wilhelm's council felt stymied. In their view they needed a firm order from Wilhelm's relatives before they could act; they evidently felt that they were at the center of a legitimacy vacuum. And so they decided to wait to see what God would do. Dorothea again persuaded Elector August to intervene, and August predictably concluded that Wilhelm should be put under arrest, but still the council hesitated. By June Wilhelm was "worse than ever," and the council's lieutenant (*Statthalter*) was persuaded to call a meeting of the noble *Landräte*, a body of ducal advisers midway between the estates and the duke.[50] They ordered Wilhelm, who was evidently still roaming the countryside, to return to Celle. They also set up a rotating group of five or six ministers and nobles who would stay with their duke at all times and at least ward off the accusation that the duke's councilors were simply allowing Wilhelm to crash about the duchy with no supervision. Two days later Wilhelm suddenly reappeared in Celle, furious to learn that the *Landräte* had met without his knowledge. Again the timid council hesitated to arrest him, and Wilhelm left town, headed north to Holstein. Dorothea was beside herself at the condition of her husband and at the agonizing inaction of the council. With the help of her relatives, Elector August and Duke Ulrich of Mecklenburg, Emperor Rudolf II was persuaded to appoint a regency council consisting of Eberhard von Holle (the bishop of Verden and Lübeck), Duke August, and Duke Ulrich. These princes in turn appointed five others, including two professors from Rostock, to make up an imperial commission that was to meet with Duchess Dorothea and the council to determine how to pacify the duke and restore order to Braunschweig.[51]

As the summer of 1582 wore on, Duke Wilhelm's behavior grew odder and odder. He ran out into the streets of Celle half-dressed, offered odd gifts, spoke unintelligibly, gesturing weirdly, "until anyone could easily see that his princely grace was out of his mind."[52] Finally, at the end of August the council ordered Wilhelm confined; the city gates were closed, a special chamber was constructed for him, and Wilhelm was to be fed according to the instructions of the court physicians, who now begin to appear regularly in the official records. Even so, the council was still astonishingly reluctant to capture Wilhelm, confined as he now was in his palace, until word came that he was attacking Dorothea with a tailor's shears, furious at her for obtaining the aid of a princely and imperial commission. A small prison cell was prepared for him, but now Dorothea herself refused to cooperate, finding the room, with its iron bars and little hole for food, too harsh. With stoic tenacity the commissioners tried to reason with Wilhelm, insisting that he follow the advice of his doctors and preachers and blandly assuring him that his majesty and rights to rule would not suffer but that he had to get some peace and quiet so that he could recover and return to rule his duchy.[53] On 27 August Wilhelm agreed to be a good patient, to moderate his food and drink according to his doctors' advice, and to wait "until dear God helps restore us to our natural peace and right understanding."[54] Although the imperial commissioners suspected that Wilhelm needed close confinement in the small prison cell, they agreed to these looser arrangements as an experiment for a month. Soon we learn that twenty special guards had to be brought in, for Wilhelm forgot his agreement and insisted on free-ranging travel again. Under close confinement Wilhelm really did improve, however, and by November he seemed to be back to normal. The commissioners agreed that he could rule again but insisted that procedures be set in place should he suffer another relapse.

For five years things went rather well, but in the fall of 1587 Wilhelm fell into madness again on returning from Franconia, where he had visited his daughter Sophie and her husband, Georg Friedrich, the margrave of Brandenburg-Ansbach. This time Wilhelm lost all confidence in his council, favoring instead the advice of one man, the Grossvogt Gabriel von Donop, governor general of the district of Celle. Historical rumors have spread for centuries that this man was the evil genius of Wilhelm's last years, the worm of dissent and discontent in the Braunschweig council.[55] In the midst of chronic indecision, von Donop seemed all too eager to take charge. What is uncontested is that the council now split into factions, and Dorothea knew not whom to trust. Although confined to his splendid palace, Wilhelm ate and drank to gross excess, attacked his servants, and ignored his doctors. Instead of imprisoning the mad duke, the council again adopted milder measures, sending in the court theologians and physicians to urge Wilhelm to listen to the Word of God instead of giving over his heart to gluttony and drunkenness (citing Luke 21:34, an apocalyptic passage), habits that would give Satan access to his soul. His doctors were less upset by Wilhelm's filthy language than were the ministers, but they insisted that he needed a "moderate and regulated life," with normal mealtimes and enough sleep.

From about this time onwards the Lower Saxon state archive contains masses of material regarding the medical care Wilhelm received. In sharp contrast to those early cases from Baden, Württemberg, Ansbach, and Hesse, we are now overwhelmed with so much information that we could easily lose all perspective and go on indefinitely. Let me summarize.

A regime of medicines, bloodletting, and warm baths appeared to calm and restore the duke in early 1588, but not permanently or completely. And so, late in 1588, the council consulted other doctors, paying special attention to Dr. Johannes von Schroeter (1513–1593) from the University of Jena, personal physician to the duke of Saxony-Weimar and known throughout Germany and Italy as one of the best diagnosticians of his day.[56] Schroeter was a great believer in the therapeutic value of warm baths, having published a treatise on that subject thirty years earlier, but he was also a convert to the new Paracelsian remedies that used strong chemicals, such as antimony and *vinum ellaboratum* (wine mixed with hellebore). The duke's personal physicians, Hektor Mithob and Johann Mellinger, were frightened to use these risky medications. Such a dispute among the physicians actually opens for us a most welcome window into the psychiatric thinking of high medicine at the time, for normally we are treated only to the finished product of formal recommendations and treatises or *consilia*, in which everything is made to appear clear and certain. Here we can see just how much discussion and debate, especially about the new Paracelsian methods, actually went on.[57]

We even possess unique daily notes and reports on how the duke spent his day, from October 1588 to January 1589, written by his personal physician, Johann Mellinger, a man who also made a name for himself as the pioneering cartographer of Braunschweig.[58] His amazing mass of detailed observations allows us to get about as close to the mental patient and his doctors as any sixteenth-century source will ever permit. We learn much about the daily routine at court as well, a social situation that can otherwise be hard to reconstruct. It seemed to matter a great deal to Duke Wilhelm in exactly which room he took his prescribed baths: sometimes it was the "golden room," but he often preferred the "green room" or "Catherine's [his daughter's] room."[59] His doctors and advisers continued to have a hard time controlling Wilhelm's lust for alcoholic drinks. Baths were often ordered for the afternoon, and after an hour in a hot tub Wilhelm would be put into a warm bed for a nap. His doctors often pronounced themselves satisfied with his progress if the outcome was nothing more than a calm, restful period. The implicit theory seems to have been that Wilhelm's mind was so disordered from too much excitement that above all he needed peace and sleep. He also took regular and modest meals that were calculated to soothe his system. But these records also make it plain that the Galenic physicians had no monopoly over Wilhelm's therapy. His Lutheran court preachers were doing their share, too, for Wilhelm heard sermons daily and with enthusiasm ("mitt vleiss"), and also enjoyed the singing of the new cantor and the music of his organist.[60] He whiled away some of his vacant hours playing games with his advisers or with visiting noblemen.

Wilhelm's day usually began early, at five or six o'clock, when his servants awakened him. In the morning he often took one of his hour-long baths and the nap that followed. Then came the first sermon of the day, and Wilhelm usually took Holy Communion at this time, too. At noon he lunched, often with a few of his councilors, and received other visitors. His doctors allowed him to eat very little, but they concocted a special herbal wine that he especially relished.[61] In addition to such medications, Wilhelm underwent almost daily cupping (phlebotomy) to expel whatever noxious humors were responsible for his deranged mind. By four in the afternoon, following Dr. Schroeter's bathing regime, Wilhelm often took another hot, hour-long bath and heard his second sermon of the day. After supper the duke retired to bed around nine or ten.

Although Duke Wilhelm seemed to get better from mid-October to mid-November, things then went downhill again. On 15 November, for example, Dr. Mellinger reported to the duchess that her husband had started to break down his door. His guards, the doctor told Dorothea, feared that he might break through "and from there [obtain access] to your princely grace's own chamber." Despite nine to eleven hours of sleep at night and a tightly regulated life, Wilhelm had become highly agitated again. Regardless of efforts to reinforce the door, it appeared on 17 November that he might soon break through and be on the loose. It was a delicate situation, for Dr. Mellinger was well aware that confining Wilhelm to a secure jail cell might simply drive him to wilder despair. Dorothea, on her part, called for other medical opinions.

At times such as these Wilhelm often refused to take his medications, which were therefore mixed into his food. Instead of constantly changing his therapy, however, the doctors were frequently unwilling to use force and were much more inclined to wait for the right season before beginning any new therapeutic initiative. After all, Hippocrates had said, reassuringly, that changes in chronic diseases were more likely in the spring or fall, and so one could always justify delay. Wilhelm often asked for permission to walk at large or to spend more time in the green room, but when his doctors explained that these were political decisions for the council to make, he became verbally offensive with much "immodest language." The duke also demanded Hamburg beer, which Dr. Schroeter allowed over the objections of Dr. Mellinger. The careful records of Dr. Mellinger also permitted Wilhelm's doctors to observe that "his grace has always been fairly content for two or three days before the new and the full moon, so that we have repeatedly hoped for a recovery; but as soon as the new or full moon has arrived, his princely grace suffers a relapse."[62] This description strongly suggests that Dr. Mellinger had diagnosed Wilhelm's insanity as a form of lunacy, the mental condition of being possessed or overly influenced by the moon.

Having had so little success, the doctors turned to other cures after the spring of 1589. Now the records are full of references to pills that were supposed to act as cathartics. Wilhelm was regularly bled, cupped, and treated with leeches. We hear of clysters, of soda and niter pills, and of antimony, as well as of fierce arguments among the attending physicians. Indeed, one way that Paracelsian remedies entered the regime of orthodox medicine was the claim that chemical preparations would actually purge the body of noxious humors more effectively than galenicals. So here Paracelsianism could insert itself pragmatically, without its theoretical baggage of macrocosmic correspondences and unorthodox Christian theology. In one way after another, then, the doctors were united at least in trying to rid the duke of his excessive and harmful humors.

The records now become so voluminous that they are almost impossible to summarize, an embarrassment of riches that stands in stark contrast to the documentary silences of fifty years earlier.[63] One of the most fascinating reports from the period is of the detailed hearing held in June 1589 before Emperor Rudolf II's princely commissioners, who came to Celle to investigate Wilhelm's condition and the state of the Braunschweig government. One of their major concerns was that the Grossvogt von Donop had taken on too much power, but they were also disturbed at reports that the local physicians were reluctant to consult with foreign doctors on the grounds that such consultations just led to

arguments and confusion.[64] Apparently the intrusion of the famous Dr. Schroeter was still resented months after his return
home to Jena. His dangerous Paracelsian recommendations of
antimony seemed both irresponsible and heretical to the more
orthodox Hippocratic-Galenic physicians at court. During Schroeter's visit they had catered to his recommendations, but they were
not converted to his schemes.

For the remaining three years of Wilhelm's life his medical
condition continued to fluctuate. We hear of better times, when he
was released to walk and exercise (under guard), and of further
consultations with physicians from Wittenberg. Politically, however, the biggest upset was his brother Heinrich's decision to
obtain a part of the Braunschweig inheritance for himself, a problem that Emperor Rudolf II again settled peacefully by means of an
imperial commission in 1590.[65] Dorothea continued to be hopelessly alienated from the ducal council and was for a long time
under the influence of the Grossvogt. The councilors showed,
time and again, that they lacked the force, the courage, or perhaps
the authority to solve the long constitutional crisis caused by
Wilhelm's illness. As model bureaucrats they displayed an amazing and relatively new dependence on experts of all sorts.

We note, moreover, that despite the years of regencies and
committee rule, Wilhelm's sons remained patiently in their loyal
places. It seems possible that their respect for the duke's body
politic kept them in awe of his person as well. Moreover, Rudolf II's intervention and his imperial commission with its powerful members probably made it unthinkable that anyone would try
a naked grab for power. Certainly, the lack of religious differences
in this thoroughly Lutheran land removed one possible motive for
forceful intervention. Perhaps most noteworthy, however, is this:
no one seems to have doubted that the old duke was sick and that
the best medical advice should be sought. This case thus ex-
emplifies a dramatic shift in priorities from the harsher days of the
early sixteenth century.

Seeing madness as a medical problem did not, of course, cause
political problems to melt away. In fact, the intrusion of medical
authorities served in some ways to make the problems of handling
a deranged monarch that much more complicated, uncertain, and
time-consuming. Now there were experts and authorities to be
consulted. And the basic problems of hereditary succession re-

mained, even if the prince was given the most scrupulous medical attention. If the prince did not beget a legitimate male heir, his dynasty and sometimes the religion of his territory might be subject to abrupt change. It is true that the duchies of Mecklenburg and Braunschweig-Lüneburg mitigated these dangers by arranging for fairly harmonious cooperation among the various branches of the immediate family, but these arrangements did not depend upon the novel idea of treating the prince's insanity as a therapeutic dilemma. Hereditary succession was always so precarious that ruling dynasties were well advised in any event to try to foresee and forestall squabbling and wrangling among the interested parties.

We have also begun to see the fallout from the Paracelsian heresy in sixteenth-century medicine. While orthodox physicians could keep the occult doctrines and holistic ideology at bay, once their own remedies had flopped, they could not easily resist the appeal of new and promising Paracelsian therapies. Princely courts were one of the major entry points for Paracelsian medicine, and we will see that such a medically heretical invasion was always an occasion for determined Galenic resistance.

PART

II

THE AGE OF THE
MELANCHOLY PRINCE

3

DUKE ALBRECHT FRIEDRICH
OF PRUSSIA

With Anna of Saxony and Wilhelm of Braunschweig we have begun to deal with figures from the 1570s and 1580s. Whereas Anna was treated to a steady stream of sermons, Wilhelm got a mixed diet prepared not only by theologians but by physicians and even musicians. This turned out to be the emerging pattern for the last decades of the sixteenth century and the first decades of the seventeenth. These decades also saw the emergence of the full-fledged melancholy prince.

Albrecht Friedrich of Prussia (1553–1618), son of the famous first duke in Prussia, Albrecht of Brandenburg, had a hard time of it even as a child. He seemed overly sensitive and was notably difficult.[1] Before his fifteenth birthday, he lost both his parents on the same day in March 1568. His father, Albrecht, the former grand master of the Teutonic Order, the Lutheran reformer of Prussia, and the energetic architect of a new secular duchy under Polish suzerainty died at the ripe old age of seventy-seven and had been in ill health for years. There were unsavory rumors, however, that Albrecht's estranged and extravagant wife, Anna Maria of Braunschweig, had been poisoned, for she had enjoyed reasonably good health, so far as we can tell at this remove, and was only thirty-five years old at the time of her death.[2] The trauma of this dual loss cannot but have left its mark on the emotionally delicate Albrecht Friedrich.

The regency council that had managed affairs of state in Duke Albrecht's declining years proceeded to maintain an iron grip over young Duke Albrecht Friedrich. The duchy of Prussia was already under the heavy influence of her nobles, who had won very consid-

Duke Albrecht Friedrich of Prussia, by an unknown copper engraver. (Courtesy of the Stadtmuseum Düsseldorf)

erable rights for the territorial estates in 1542. The prospect of a
continued regency during the minority of the duke could thus
only strengthen the reputation of Prussia as an "aristocratic re-
public," or *Adelsrepublik*.[3] In fact, the ensuing regency brought to
the surface most of the simmering tensions in Prussia: between
members of the highest nobility (the lords) and the lesser nobles
and knights; between those who favored closer ties to the king of
Poland and those who were eager to keep him at arm's length; and
between orthodox Lutherans and those willing to consider or tolerate the deviant views of theologians such as Andreas Osiander.[4]

Many Prussians must have been relieved, therefore, when in
1571 young Albrecht Friedrich reached the age of eighteen and
could begin to act on his own behalf. It is not clear just how fully
he managed to assume control of his government, however, for he
had already begun to exhibit signs of mental disorder. As plans
were drawn up for his marriage to Marie Eleanore, the daughter of
Duke Wilhelm V of Jülich-Cleves, rumors of Albrecht Friedrich's
instability may well have unsettled Duke Wilhelm in distant Düsseldorf, for he sent his renowned personal physician, Reiner Solenander, on ahead of the slow-moving bridal party to Prussia in the
fall of 1573. From Königsberg, both before and after the wedding
on 14 October, Solenander reported in some detail on what he
thought was the surprisingly good physical and mental condition of Albrecht Friedrich.[5] To be sure, the prince had behaved
strangely and with some hostility even during the wedding festivities, refusing to get dressed in the prescribed costumes, refusing to eat or to attend church with his guests from Jülich, and
responding, when asked why he was so unfriendly to his new
bride, "That is not my bride; my bride is all burned up."[6] For
reasons that may be linked to Solenander's evident desire to return
to Düsseldorf, the Jülich physician conveyed a far too rosy picture
of Albrecht Friedrich's mental condition.

From the diary of the Prussian court historian Lucas David,
however, we can glimpse the physical and mental disorders of
the young prince at the end of 1572 and for the better part of 1573,
well before Solenander arrived with the express purpose of observing him.[7] From David's pages emerges a sad and detailed portrait
of princely madness. In late November 1572, for example, Albrecht Friedrich could hardly sleep because he feared that the
court preacher had poisoned his wine, insisting that he had seen

the poison swimming in his cup.[8] These paranoid fears, which gave way to bouts of crying and self-accusations, may have been rooted in the rumors surrounding his mother's death three and a half years earlier.[9] He nursed his fear of venom to the point that he suspected even the eucharistic hosts had been poisoned.[10] When his personal physician and his chancellor spoke friendly, encouraging words to him, they often received no reply. Soon they, too, were among those he suspected of plotting his death. He complained often of stomach pains, for which his doctors prescribed baths and a special white medicinal powder that he had inherited from his father.[11] By 13 December these measures produced an intense sweating that evidently made Albrecht Friedrich feel much better for several days.[12] Despite returning fears of poison, the prince had moments in early 1573 when he begged permission to attend dances and masquerades, and with drinking and dancing his mood could lift for a time.[13] Still, his troubles kept resurfacing, and by April the regents were demanding an official report from the physicians as to what was the matter.

Poor Albrecht Friedrich felt abandoned and betrayed by all his closest advisers, and especially by the conservative Lutheran clergy. The hyperorthodox "Gnesio-Lutheran" followers of Flacius Illyricus had seized control of the Prussian church following the defeat of the Osiandrian party (first in 1552 and emphatically in 1566), and Albrecht Friedrich complained bitterly that all they preached about was whoring knaves and dissolute polluters of Prussian morals. "I learn nothing more from them," he claimed.[14] In particular, Albrecht Friedrich could not stand the preaching of Tilemann Heshusius, the vehement, controversial, and often exiled Flacian Lutheran bishop of Samland, whose bitter attacks, on supposedly immoral theater pieces and on suspected Calvinists, had led to his recent expulsion from Magdeburg and his enthusiastic acceptance as bishop by the estates of Prussia in 1573. In Königsberg, however, he again became the center of further acrimony as he moved to claim rights of appointment and censorship over the university and to denounce Philippists (followers of Melanchthon) and Calvinists throughout the Prussian church and especially among the nobility.[15] Heshusius also used his time to develop a speculative anti-Calvinism that bubbled out of his study and into street fights in Königsberg, until eventually his doctrine was condemned by a local synod and he was expelled from Prussia in 1577.[16] No wonder Duke Albrecht Friedrich had his troubles with the preachers to whom he was subjected, especially since it appears that he was religiously attracted to the condemned doctrines of his father's favorite theologian, Andreas Osiander.[17] In addition, Heshusius objected so strenuously to the reform-Catholic leanings of Duchess Marie Eleanore's father (Duke Wilhelm of Jülich-Cleves) and to her own tolerance of Dutch Calvinists on her estates that in 1576 he refused to baptize a daughter of Albrecht Friedrich and Marie Eleanore.[18]

Certainly such contentions did not contribute to Duke Albrecht Friedrich's equanimity, and he often refused to go to church services, whereupon his pastors visited him in his chambers and preached to him there.[19] At least twice Albrecht Friedrich attempted suicide, and he seems at times to have repudiated the Reformation, tearing down the pictures of Luther, Melanchthon, and Jan Hus and replacing them with likenesses of the duke of Alba, Philip II of Spain, and the cardinal of Lorraine.[20] To his Lutheran advisers, such Catholic sympathies must have appeared totally insane. He often slept in his clothes because "Turks and Muscovites were about to overwhelm Germany" and refused to change his shirt. Amidst periods of moody introspection he occasionally burst out in unexpected flights of violence. He refused periodically to cooperate with his doctors and handlers, withholding the urine they wanted to examine and pouring his medicines on the floor.[21] He also refused to meet with an official delegate sent by Emperor Maximilian II, hurling a clock and the delegate's beretta to the ground.[22] He spoke to persons not present and seems to have gone off into a world of his own. His three personal physicians tried faithfully to purge his melancholy and to elevate his moisture with baths, while other physicians recommended more adventurous Galenic cures, such as the application of the entrails of a freshly killed snow-white dog to the duke's head or the similar application of a black hen, freshly killed and split. Or perhaps he should ingest a portion of powdered pearls or a roasted concoction of bean straw and vermouth.[23] Obviously, the normal orthodox remedies were giving way to experiments of a livelier sort.

During the week of 19 November 1573, one month after his wedding, official hearings were held regarding Albrecht Friedrich's health and especially regarding the origins of his severe melancholy.[24] A report to the elector of Brandenburg concluded from these investigations that Albrecht Friedrich had shown serious retardation from early childhood on: "The good lord was born into the world with no discretion or judgment and has always spoken and written miserably . . . repeating and imitating like a parrot."[25] But the danger was that he would not simply remain childish "for now a raving madness is breaking out. God Almighty knows what will come of this. It's a horrible spectacle, in which the duke's childishness gets worse every hour."[26]

Among the theories offered to explain the young duke's condition, we find that Hofmeister von Lehnsdorf blamed, first, the wrath of God and, second, the fact that, given the early loss of his father, Albrecht Friedrich had had to grow up too quickly and thus "the reins controlling him were relaxed too soon."[27] In addition, many seemed ready to blame the evil ministry of Heshusius or of Johannes Weidmann, or the prince's fears that his mother might have been poisoned, or Albrecht Friedrich's excessive drinking. But court physician Dr. Stoy emphasized that in his view the young duke had been retarded and temperamentally melancholy from the age of three or four onwards.[28] His servants and teachers, Stoy claimed, had badly mistreated their young charge, prompting him to complain that he had been driven out into a wilderness and abandoned. Mocked and contemned, he "became ever more melancholy and more addicted to drink."

Dr. Stoy was ready to admit, however, "that this is not simply melancholy but something demonic as well."[29] Here we find the familiar mixing of physical with supernatural reasoning that was so common in the late sixteenth century. Especially in difficult cases it was normal to discount even one's own specialty and profession and to admit that another order of reality (and another order of professionals) might have to be recognized. But Lutherans generally thought of exorcism as superstitious Catholic priestcraft or magic. In Lutheran Prussia, therefore, one could no longer call in the exorcists, and so Stoy recommended simply "that some theologian help out, admonishing the duke to be pious."[30] Somewhat ironically, according to the court preacher the infighting at court over Calvinism and crypto-Calvinism had helped drive the duke mad.[31]

When Dr. Valerius Fiedler was interviewed during the hearings, he steered a course back to the world of natural explanations. The prince's problems came not from the stars but "from the blood of his mother and father" ("ex sanguine materna et paterna").[32] In his view the young prince had inherited many of his mother's worst characteristics: her love of leisure and "ignoble deeds" ("non multas laudabiles actiones"), her vacillation, and her Osiandrian sympathies. She had been "distrustful, cruel, and bloodthirsty. When pregnant she had torn the heads off her swans. The young prince [therefore] loved wars and magical spells." His diet, however, had also left much to be desired. He refused to follow medical instructions and "had been tormented by the coarse beer" available in Königsberg.[33] But in Fiedler's view, "the most prominent and highest cause" of Albrecht Friedrich's madness "was that His princely Grace was an enemy of the preachers and the ministry," and especially of the pure doctrines of Wittenberg. No wonder God had seen fit to punish him.[34]

Another physician, Dr. Titius, confirmed that under his care Albrecht Friedrich had as a child shown an "imbecillitas ingenii": he had been slow to walk and talk and to learn all sorts of things. He was unable to speak until well into his third year and had had constant head colds and more dangerous diseases.[35] When the ducal councilors tried to investigate Dr. Stoy's suspicion of witchcraft and demonic influence, however, Fiedler and all the other courtiers and servants could provide no evidence. The most anyone could recall was that at some point the duke had begun to curse and to pray that the devil would remove his enemies.[36] Similar efforts to determine whether medical malpractice—the antidotes given the prince for his fleshly lusts—might have made him worse also came to nothing.

The hearings in November 1573 were extraordinarily long and thorough. It seems that everyone from the duke's tutors to his cleaning maids was interviewed, and the general conclusion appears to have been, as Dr. Adrian reported on 26 November, that Albrecht Friedrich had been somewhat retarded from birth but that God and nature were now conspiring to punish him with a raving madness. This was the man whom Princess Marie Eleanore of Jülich-Cleves, probably suspecting little or nothing, had just married.

The court doctors were obviously trying to do their best, but when it became obvious in 1574 that orthodox academic medicine was having little effect, irregular and unorthodox healers were called in. It is not always clear from the abundant records who actually called in such persons, but the old Königsberg archive (now in Berlin) is full of reports and critiques over the next several years, detailing the extraordinary range of therapies tried out on the unfortunate Duke Albrecht Friedrich. The first to try his hand was Leonhard Thurneisser (1530–1595/96), the celebrated Paracelsian physician and alchemist, who was sent a specimen of Albrecht Friedrich's urine in March 1574.[37] He had already proved his value to the Hohenzollerns by relieving the sickness of Sabina, the wife of Elector Johann Georg of Brandenburg, and had been employed as that elector's personal physician, working up an enormously successful consulting service that kept ten to twenty secretaries busy just with correspondence. As H. R. Trevor-Roper has recently pointed out, Paracelsians, although reviled by most court physicians, often found a warmer welcome at princely courts than anywhere else in Europe between 1560 and 1650, and this was surely true of the Brandenburg courts at Berlin and Königsberg.[38]

Before he got down to the details of Albrecht Friedrich's urine, Thurneisser began his analysis with Paracelsian observations on the place of man in God's order. Man was the noblest creature of all, he said, because (1) he had an eternal and immortal soul; (2) he had understanding, reason, and sense; and (3) he was made in God's image.[39] The skilled physician could discover much more about a person from a urine sample than just his physical condition, and Thurneisser duly pointed to parts of the specimen that showed that Albrecht Friedrich was suffering an "internal fear and horror together with bitter bad temper and deep contemplation." Other aspects of the urine prompted him to conclude that the prince's blood had been overcooked and had become thick, black, and choleric. This accounted for Albrecht Friedrich's bitterness and mad melancholy ("desipientalische Melancholia unnd aberwitz"), which in turn caused lack of appetite, trembling, shivering, heart palpitations, and the overburdening of his spleen, so that he could no longer regulate his excess of melancholy humor, and this in turn led to the prince's sadness and fear. Obviously no one organ was at fault here, but a regular schedule of proper food, drink, sleep, and exercise was bound to help. One could not, however, rest content with such physical remedies. "Truly, there is a spiritual weakness here. . . . And so it must be helped from the ground up: the spirit and mind must be cured with medicines just as much as the body."[40] Here was the authentic note of Paracelsian medicine, the emphasis on a holistic approach that would treat man in his humanity rather than reducing him to a composite of physical humors. This was a pure draught of Paracelsian theory, in contrast to the frequently pragmatic, chemical cures sponsored by the less ambitious "chemical" physicians. But writing from Berlin, Thurneisser did not extend the hope that at such a distance he could do much good. He seems to have visited Königsberg at some point, but in 1574 he hoped that perhaps Albrecht Friedrich could come to Berlin for therapy, even though it would be better if he were treated where he lived.

Evidently Thurneisser's advice was neutralized by the academically orthodox Galenic court physicians in Königsberg, although the records are so thin for 1574 that we cannot be sure what therapy was actually employed. In 1575, however, another outsider and medical panacea-monger was consulted, a man with the appropriate name of Johann Fortuner, who treated Albrecht Friedrich from 2 June through 26 August with a colorful bouquet of herbal remedies that used quantities of juniper, camomile, lilies, fennel, veronica, agrimony, mint, and crushed coral. This time the forces of orthodoxy brought formal charges against the interloper, and Fortuner was arrested on 16 September, with the injunction that he was to stop behaving so shamefully and to leave off heavy drinking.[41] We do not know exactly what trouble Fortuner had gotten himself into, but heavy drinking was a well-known problem at the ducal court in Königsberg. In late October 1575 Fortuner was still in custody, complaining that despite his medical success with a "considerable number of your princely grace's male and female servants," he was now unable to fulfill his duties and was suffering also a loss of honor owing to his imprisonment. He asked for a passport to leave and for payment of his fees. Some accommodation must have been worked out because Fortuner simply drops out of sight.

The intrusion of so unorthodox a quack seems to have prompted both the regency council and Albrecht Friedrich to solicit a broad range of advice from the best physicians in Germany and abroad. It is worth noting that Albrecht Friedrich signed much of this correspondence himself; he was at least formally participating in the search for the best therapy. Far from being merely pushed aside by power-hungry relatives and councilors, the prince knew that he was sick, or at least deferentially accepted the judgment of his doctors that he needed help. Indeed, my impression is that in the sixteenth century most of the so-called mad princes were actually suffering from a serious mental disorder, rather than from a politically inspired label, and that, like Albrecht Friedrich, they tried to use their lucid intervals, if any, to secure help.

The first clue that orthodox medicine was organizing a systematic examination of the options may be the treatise, dated 13 August 1575, bearing the title "Discursus in melancholia cuiusdam illustrissimi principis."[42] This wide-ranging, anonymous work combined a general account of the origins of Albrecht Friedrich's madness and of the possible therapies with a learned assault on Fortuner, whom the author blasted as "destitute of sane reasons" ("Fortunerus ille sanis rationibus destitutus").[43] Perhaps most interesting were the author's observations on the heavy burden of inherited madness in the young prince. The author located mental troubles among three of Albrecht Friedrich's blood relatives: his paternal grandfather Margrave Friedrich the Elder of Brandenburg-Ansbach, whom we have already discussed; his maternal grandmother, Elisabeth of Henneberg, whose piety had been so tinged with sadness that she fell into a morbid melancholy; and his mother, Anna Maria of Braunschweig, to whose spendthrift fantasies I have alluded and who fell into what was now called a "choleric madness" shortly before her mysterious death.[44]

In addition, according to the "Discursus," Albrecht Friedrich had suffered as a child from convulsions that often lasted three or four hours. This was an epilepsy, the author thought, that was exacerbated by the storms and turbulent air of the first months after his birth and that had slowly, under the adverse influence of Saturn and of comets, turned into melancholy.[45] Satan only made these astrological and physical difficulties worse, producing cold weather and storms that defied God's ordinances and ruined the prince's health.[46] In a short section on the action of poisons, the author considered not whether Albrecht Friedrich had been poisoned but what herbs and drugs (namely, aphrodisiacs) he might be given to strengthen his seed and his genitals so that his marriage might be fruitful.[47] (Whether the aphrodisiacs were tried or not, the duke and Marie Eleanore did produce two sons and five daughters, but unfortunately for local Prussian hopes for an autonomous existence the two boys died before their first birthdays, and the succession passed to electoral Brandenburg through two of the daughters.)

In the last section of this "Discourse on the Melancholy of a Certain Most Illustrious Prince," the author took up the question of how excessive black bile was produced in the body. Albrecht Friedrich suffered from no simple humoral excess, its author claimed, but from the roasted, adust sanguine humor that was corrupted by the malfunctioning of heart, liver, and spleen. Trying to specify the cerebral action of adust melancholy, he cited Gilbertus Anglicus for the view that "mania is an infection of the anterior cell of the head with a lessening of imagination," while "melancholy is [an infection] of the middle cell with a lessening of reason," and "phrenesis is [an infection] of the nets that are in the middle ventricle of the brain."[48] Because the duke needed regular bleeding, it seemed to his scholarly doctors that he really could benefit from artificially induced hemorrhoids, a therapy on which the Greek, Arab, and Latin authors all agreed. Even the celebrated Andreas Vesalius provided new and useful information on how to bleed such difficult cases. In the end, however, the pious author reminded his readers (probably the regency council) that despite the best of our natural knowledge, it was God who was finally in charge.[49] Another hand (apparently that of Valerius Fiedler) appended a note to the effect that it was to be feared that Albrecht Friedrich's infantile epilepsy and youthful melancholia had created the conditions for an unavoidable adult mania. "May God have mercy upon us."[50]

In the wake of the Fortuner scandal and the bleak implications of this anonymous "Discourse on the Melancholy of a Certain Most Illustrious Prince," plans went ahead for extensive consultations. On 14 October 1575 (Albrecht Friedrich's second wedding anniversary) the court physician Valerius Fiedler submitted a report to his superior at court, the Hofmeister Erhard von Kunheim, on why the prince was so hard to treat ("De impedimento curae"). Starting with a blistering attack upon phony doctors and healer-priests ("Agyrtes") such as "that mad Fortuner" ("Fortunerus ille insanus"), Fiedler described the duke's condition in exactly the same terms and with many of the same source citations as the "Discourse" of the previous August. The similarities are in fact so extensive that we must conclude either that Fiedler was relying heavily upon the earlier text or that he was perhaps its author.[51] It

seemed obvious, Fiedler wrote, that Albrecht Friedrich was suffering from a stubborn and complex "melancholy made from the
roasting of his blood," but it was less obvious what should be done
about it. Fiedler agreed that the duke's stopped-up hemorrhoids
had allowed a superabundance of "materia melancholica," but the
harsh medicines used by Thurneisser and Fortuner were too dangerous. Among the milder remedies he strongly recommended
chicken soup. Clearly, these Galenists were making no concessions to the Paracelsian remedies that were popular at some other
courts.

Two months later a wide-ranging search for other expert opinions was well under way. Albrecht Friedrich reported to Emperor
Maximilian II that he planned to send Dr. Severin Göbel and
his secretary Enoch Baumgartner throughout Germany to gather
advice from "the most famous, most learned, and most eminent
physicians about my condition."[52] It was evidently not always
easy to track down the desired expert physicians, however, for
Göbel and Baumgartner reported in mid-December that they had
traveled to Nuremberg, Augsburg, Regensburg, Ansbach, Marburg, Leipzig, Jena, and Dresden without always finding whom
they sought. But they did attach two *consilia*, one a short memorandum by Valerius Fiedler summarizing yet again his views on
the importance of herbal drugs, bleeding, and diet to counteract
the duke's melancholy inheritance. Dr. Paul von Stein (de Lapide),
however, another of the duke's personal physicians and thus not
really one of the foreign experts that Göbel and Baumgartner were
looking for, reported in much more detail. In his *consilium* he
agreed that Albrecht Friedrich was mad from a combination of bad
inheritance, infantile epilepsy, and bad air compounded by lack
of exercise, a lack of baths, the wrong food and drink, and even
a botched marriage (it is unclear what Stein thought had gone
wrong). Even demons were involved, he thought, for Avicenna had
held that the devil was attracted to melancholy. Of course, Christians knew that God was the ultimate source of all disease, and
God had plenty of reasons to be angry at the sins of the Prussians, but Stein referred this topic to theologians. He was certain,
though, that a major problem had been the repeated consultation
of phony doctors, such as "a certain Paracelsian, Thurneisser,
[who was] totally ignorant and a pseudomedicus."[53] This continuing hostility to unorthodox medicine surfaced in another report of

Severin Göbel ridiculing the repeated consultation with such persons as Thurneisser, Fortuner, and a certain Johann Philipp Paleologus.[54] Obviously, someone at court, perhaps the regency council or the Duchess Marie Eleanore, had been continuing what was almost a tradition in Königsberg of inviting self-proclaimed experts to solve those problems (whether medical, theological, or political) that academic orthodoxy was having trouble with.[55] University-trained physicians reacted with a mixture of scorn and scandal at this tendency.

By early 1576, however, the expert opinions of orthodox medicine were pouring into Königsberg. A list compiled (or begun) on 7 March listed fifteen *consilia* altogether that had been received. Perhaps the most prestigious and weighty was the *consilium* of the imperial physician Johannes Crato von Crafftheim, who began by observing that it was only the (learned) *medicus* who truly knew what to do in cases of disease, for he knew not just the name but the essence of melancholy. He agreed about the diagnosis of infantile epilepsy and its likely transformation into melancholy madness. On the subject of treatment, he also agreed on the use of clysters to provoke hemorrhoids, but he urged the use of black hellebore and lapis lazuli and cautioned against the use of anise. His recommended therapies also included the ample and traditional use of such syrups as borage, mint, oxtongue, apples, and "manna," as well as the application of the oriental magical bezoar stone. He thought that placing a warm, fresh calf's liver on the duke's head might help, and that a compress of hot bread soaked in butter might also serve to warm and moisten the duke's wits. While warning against the use of sweet or strong wines (especially after meals), Crato said that he often had good success with pepper, juniper, and cannabis (hemp or hashish).[56] Well aware that Albrecht Friedrich's fertile imagination could seize upon the slightest suggestion of conspiracy and danger, he cautioned that the duke's doctors and councilors should avoid all talk of poison as if it were poison itself.

Throughout 1576 Albrecht Friedrich continued his quest for further expert opinions, negotiating hard to obtain the help of Caspar Naevius, professor of medicine at Leipzig, who sent a *consilium* and promised to come in person in 1577, but only if large sums of money for himself, his servant, and his horses were forthcoming.[57] All in all, though, these professional opinions seem to have persuaded the official doctors at home in Prussia that the duke was incurable. On 21 December 1576, his three personal physicians summed up the accumulated evidence and presented an anonymous treatise entitled "The Reasons Given by Doctors Why the Duke of Prussia Cannot Be Cured."[58] It is an interesting document, for it tries to explain why the Prussian and foreign doctors had had so little success. Unlike the usual physicians' treatise, this one emphasized that, as Christians, these three doctors recognized not only natural causes (as even the heathen did) but supernatural causes of illness as well. It was sin and God's resulting wrath that brought disease into the world, and so any proper therapy should start with God.

Unfortunately, God had all too many reasons to be furious with Prussia. The list was impressive. (1) Duke Albrecht, father of mad Albrecht Friedrich, had allowed Osiander's "blasphemies" to fill the land, and Albrecht had actually supported them. Everyone knew that the sins of fathers could be visited unto the third or fourth generation, and so these blasphemies from twenty-five years earlier might well be a cause of Albrecht Friedrich's illness. (2) Duke Albrecht had also allowed blasphemous Calvinists to obtain noble rank and official positions in Prussia. (3) Duchess Anna Maria, too, had fallen for Osiander several times, and, it was claimed, for unexplained venal purposes. (4) Both princely personages had sinned gravely against the second table of God's law. (5) Duchess Marie Eleanore's father, Wilhelm V of Jülich-Cleves, had fallen from God's Word back to the papacy.[59] (6) Duke Albrecht Friedrich showed contempt for God's Word, His Sacraments and servants, and especially for [Gnesio-Lutheran Bishops] Joachim Mörlin and Georg Venediger. (7) Albrecht Friedrich had blasphemed in song and in reading, and by mocking God's Word. (8) He abused the holy Sacrament horribly when he accused the court preacher of poisoning both the host and the sacramental wine. (9) "For many years he has practiced unmentionable, secret vices, even when married, and [they are] still continuing."[60] (10) He had began his marriage with thoughts of prideful magnificence rather than with humble prayers. (11) He had tolerated the sins and blasphemies of others, especially of Calvinists, while refusing to listen to the sermons of Bishop Venediger and stubbornly objecting "that he wouldn't listen to any Flacian."[61] (12) He had actually sought the aid of the devil by employing a Catholic "witch"

(*Zeuberin*) from Ressel in Polish Pomerania, who had evidently tried to expel demons from Albrecht Friedrich. (13) He had invited the "blasphemous" Calvinist Fortuner to Königsberg.

These charges suggest what we have seen already, that the regency council and the personal physicians of Duke Albrecht Friedrich had adopted a hyperorthodox Flacian Lutheranism by whose standards any compromise with Calvinists counted as hideous blasphemy. We now learn that Calvinism had been one of the problems with the irregular Fortuner in 1575, too. But we also learn that the duke, or perhaps his wife, had gone so far in searching for unorthodox cures as to try out a folk exorcism at the hands of a Catholic woman. It is a pity that the records contain nothing more about this presumably surreptitious and desperate effort. This whole section, which concerns the spiritual causes of illness, reminds us, moreover, that it was not only Paracelsians who could deal with the whole person, body and soul. These Galenists invoked Lutheran moral theology to deal with spiritual matters, although it must be said that the effort involved an appeal to totally ungalenical principles. Indeed, the Paracelsian advantage in such matters, if there was one, was that the theory of mind, and soul, and spirit meshed systematically and smoothly with the theory of the body. No wonder Galenists usually left such questions to the theologians.

When they turned to the natural sources of Albrecht Friedrich's madness, however, his official physicians had to deploy a set of assumptions, those of academic medicine, that were completely alien to Lutheran theology. But in these terms, too, there was little reason to hope for relief. First and foremost, there was the duke's inheritance of mad influences, and here the list was considerably expanded from that presented in the "Discourse" of August 1575. By December 1576 the physicians had compiled a list of mentally disordered relatives that implicated not only his grandparents but also even his heroic father, Duke Albrecht, who could not safely be charged with mental illness but who, it was now emphasized, begot Albrecht Friedrich when he was sixty-two years old—too old, they implied, for a healthy outcome. Albrecht's mother and grandmother were now both alleged to have been mad, along with two of Margrave Georg Friedrich's sisters. On his mother's side, the physicians now listed not only Albrecht Friedrich's mother but her sister, Elisabeth, who married in 1543 Count Georg Ernst, the last of the Hennebergs; his mother's grandfather, Duke Wilhelm II of Braunschweig (1425–1503); and Wilhelm's brother, Duke Friedrich of Braunschweig (d. 1495). Anna Maria of Braunschweig's mother, Elisabeth (1510–1558), had suffered from a kind of "hysteria" (a mental disorder thought to be the result of a disordered womb); her maternal grandmother, the Electress Elisabeth of Brandenburg (1485–1555), born a princess of Denmark, the daughter of King Johan I, was allegedly mad from 1535 to 1539, when she recovered under the care of Martin Luther.[62] The entire world around Albrecht Friedrich had apparently collapsed into an insanity that no physician could do more than palliate. Add to that the sickly youth and naturally weak head of the young duke, driven crazy by Osiander, by bad diet, an ill-planned marriage, bad medicine, bad timing, and foreign doctors. His case was hopeless.

When Galenic medicine gave up, the ducal court turned elsewhere. In December 1577 Albrecht Friedrich and his handlers consulted the barber-surgeon, Hans Markhauser, who, while apologizing that he was not a learned man, produced a recommendation that emphasized, perhaps predictably, the anatomical basis of Albrecht Friedrich's troubles. No one should feel too guilty, he urged, that all therapies had hitherto failed, for medicine only worked when God wanted it to. It might well be, he told the duke, that God kept him in such a miserable condition not because of his own sins (as the *Medicorum rationes* of 1576 had suggested) but because of Prussian sins more generally.

According to Markhauser, the physical root of Albrecht Friedrich's "heavy, depressed, sad, and deep melancholy thoughts along with heavy temptations [*Anfechtungen*]" lay in the blockage of his "ascending and descending pineal net" ("nezlin pinea ascendens et descendens wie die Wund Arzt solches nennen").[63] When it functioned properly, this membrane had a hole or holes that allowed spirit to move up and down as necessary, but when it was blocked, the patient displayed little understanding, answered questions poorly, and suffered from twitches or tics of the head. His "sense" and his thoughts were so separated that he talked to himself. So the solution was to open up the reticular membranes of the pineal body, which, despite his lack of the learned jargon, Markhauser proposed to accomplish on the strength of "my art and experience," using an electuary composed of pearls, amber, "Rodon abbatis," sweet moss, and "manna" to shock the head, heart, and stomach and strengthen them against both heavy melancholy and moist choler. A second recipe combined the flowers of violets, water lily, verbena, and sweet clover with barley and lettuce seed, camomile, human breast milk, and hemp root. A proposed salve for the duke's head mixed mushroom spores, mandragora, saffron, and vinegar. A poultice to be wrapped around his head every evening contained goat's milk, saffron, white clover, and opium.

Once again the three personal physicians of the duke felt their competence challenged; doctors Valerius Fiedler, Paul von Stein, and Severin Göbel responded promptly to the inexpert ramblings of the barber-surgeon, whom they attacked as totally lacking in experience of such matters. His talk of the "netzlein pinea" was a dream, a pure fabrication "never found in any person, as can be shown from the most experienced anatomists old and new."[64] His recommended cures were not just useless but positively harmful, they charged, staunchly defending their turf.

At some point Albrecht Friedrich also consulted the Paracelsian doctor Alexander von Suchten, the noted chemist and poet from Danzig, who complained in an undated letter to the duke that despite his successful treatment of Albrecht Friedrich's wounded thigh, he had been steadfastly opposed by the ducal physicians, who claimed always to know better than he what therapy to employ. "Your Princely Grace surely knows what envy they have for me. Even were I an angel or Christ Himself I couldn't do the right thing, for envy always finds something to villify even in the saints of God. And Your Princely Grace will rightly apprehend more in these words than I write."[65] Of course, if Duke Albrecht Friedrich really did want to take "the medicine that Galen taught," as prescribed by his academically orthodox physicians, the alchemist Suchten would not stand in the way. "But if Your Princely Grace wants to use the medicine that Theophrastus of Hohenheim [Paracelsus] brought out into the light again, it is reasonable that I will be attacked as the enemy by that faction. . . . Woe to the sheep whose guardians are wolves!"[66] Because of the opposition to Paracelsian medicines that used chemicals and coral mixed in wine, Suchten prescribed a preparation made only of "common herbs," namely, comfrey, hole wort, calamus root, periwinkle, rhubarb, sanicle, vinca, and "mummy."[67] Suchten here suggested a concoction of such commonplace elements that Galenic orthodoxy would raise no murmur, and in the process he confirms our impression that the personal physicians of Duke Albrecht Friedrich kept a tight rein over the therapies to which he was exposed even when the duke or someone else close to him managed to consult unorthodox healers.

The last hint of such ongoing struggles between orthodoxy and more adventurous cures comes from November 1581, when the village mayor of Upper Ufgaerden, a certain Hans Frese, wrote to report that the authorities had investigated the claims of a "witch [*Zauberin*], who claimed that she could restore the mad duke to health." We cannot tell whether the ducal chancellor and the ducal comptroller would have invited her to try her arts or would have instead punished her as a magician, but when interrogated she (perhaps prudently) denied any special therapeutic knowledge and was sent home.[68]

In 1587 Duchess Marie Eleanore gave evidence once more of her continuing concern for her husband, writing to Emperor Rudolf II personally for help in obtaining Turkish bezoar stones (the concretions formed in the digestive tracts of certain goats and ruminants), for she had learned that "they are supposed to be excellent and useful for all kinds of diseases."[69] Bezoar stones were widely believed to have semimagical properties, especially as an antidote to poison, but also against the plague, pox, epilepsy, fainting, heart palpitations, worms, and bloody dysentery.[70] It is of interest to note that Rudolf, with his well-known occult interests, might be asked for assistance in getting a Turkish variety, but unfortunately we do not know whether he was able to help. We can suspect, however, that this was yet another effort on the part of the court to go beyond the orthodoxies of academic medicine.

Even the orthodox could disagree amongst themselves, of course, and the records contain an echo of an especially bitter dispute from 1590, when Dr. Severin Göbel, whom we have seen acting as personal physician, brought legal charges of malpractice against a Dr. J. Montanus because of his prescription of sleeping pills and sleeping drops for the mad duke. In his defense Montanus maintained that none of these charges had been proved.[71] Obviously, doctors were still trying to help Albrecht Friedrich nearly two decades after his troubles became so severe that the regency council and Margrave Georg Friedrich had found it necessary to take matters into their own hands. But by 1590 the issue no longer had the burning interest it had enjoyed in the 1570s and early 1580s, when all manner of therapies and therapists were employed in a sometimes reckless, even desperate, effort to cure the duke. Such early efforts may well have had the backing of the Prussian regency council, who clung to the notion of the duke's fundamental capacity to rule in order that they as councilors could retain a right to govern and thus keep Prussia independent of interference from the Hohenzollerns of Ansbach and Berlin.[72] In the end, though, this fiction was as unavailing as the regents' other attempts to keep Margrave Georg Friedrich of Ansbach at a distance. Although they had enjoyed a momentary success in 1573–74, the powerful margrave negotiated separately with King Stephen Bathory of Poland and obtained the official title of Dux Prussiae in 1577, along with the full authority to govern Prussia until Albrecht Friedrich should recover his reason.[73]

Politically speaking, therefore, the campaign to find an effective cure for the ducal madness was much more in the interests of the Prussian estates and the regents than in those of Margrave Georg Friedrich, and the frenzied efforts of 1574–77 seem to reflect just this desperation. Once Georg Friedrich was firmly in the seat of power, from 1578 onwards, the regents and the estates turned their attention to a direct confrontation with this princely newcomer. Unfortunately for them, Georg Friedrich was a powerful and decisive politician, who recognized immediately that the weakness of Duke Albrecht Friedrich and the divisiveness of the Prussian regents and estates had left Prussia with a series of problems that he, as a man of ruthless vision, was unwilling to tolerate. Within a few years of his triumphal return to Prussia in 1578, Georg Friedrich had raised new taxes to pay off large outstanding ducal debts; established a general visitation of all ducal estates and resources; ordered a new state seal displaying his own personal authority as duke; fired the previous administrators and employed new (largely Franconian) ones; reestablished the central court (Hofgericht) on a new basis; settled the ongoing religious uncertainties by accepting the 1577 statement of Lutheran orthodoxy, the Formula of Concord; and, finally, met the challenge of his rebellious estates, who with mounting fear and frustration had appealed to King Stephen in 1582 in the hopes of maintaining their authority and autonomy.[74] Georg Friedrich showed himself a master of diplomacy in disarming the estates' rebellion by enlisting the Polish king's authority on his side against the estates, for Polish kings had traditionally supported the estates precisely in order to weaken the rule of the Prussian duke. In addition, King Stephen found in Georg Friedrich a reliable and much-needed ally for his wars with Russia and in his planned campaign against Sweden; the king ordered the noble dissidents of Prussia to pay their taxes and obey the duke he had placed over them.[75] Despite ongoing flare-ups of opposition, the rebellion of the Prussian estates was essentially over by 1585, and although they may well have continued to hope that poor Albrecht Friedrich would recover his mental health, it is no surprise, really, that the more firmly Georg Friedrich was in power as "Dux Prussiae" the less we hear of efforts to find a cure for his mad cousin.[76]

At the acme of the estates' power, when the regents were riding high, however, the panoply of therapies opened up for Albrecht Friedrich had been truly impressive. We have seen, in a sense, everything a pious and desperate Protestant regime could do, the whole arsenal of therapies ranging from traditional Galenic baths, diet, drinks, and compresses to more adventurous Galenic efforts using the freshly slaughtered entrails of various animals in an effort to moisten the wits and perhaps influence the duke's spirits. The court had twice tried Paracelsian therapies, once in a fully theoretical form and once in the more common pragmatic and chemical form. And finally, the desperate court had turned to the unorthodox recommendations of a barber-surgeon, a folk exorcism by a Catholic laywoman (a "witch"), and to the controversial remedies of itinerant healers. In addition, orthodox Lutheran preachers had bombarded the unwilling duke with countless sermons. In these efforts we can sense the new importance of the dynastic prince to the legitimacy of the early modern state, a legitimacy that was slowly shifting from feudal contract to true dynastic right.[77] If the early modern German state depended on the person of the prince in a new way, no wonder he could not simply be locked up and forgotten. At least while political hopes survived, therapy had to be tried.

Not that it counts as an official part of his therapy, perhaps, but we must also note in conclusion that Duke Albrecht Friedrich evidently loved to play with coins struck at his newly founded mint and enjoyed a recreational collection of approximately one hundred thousand imperial pfennigs.[78] So on this score, too, the Prus-

sian Hohenzollern was treated with more respect than was shown
to his unfortunate grandfather, Margrave Friedrich the Elder of
Ansbach, whose request for coins with which to play had been
refused. It is also pleasant to think that perhaps Albrecht Friedrich
was among those in the princely audience who enjoyed early
productions of Shakespeare's plays, performed at the Königsberg
court by traveling players well before such productions were à la
mode throughout Germany.[79]

By the time he died in 1618, though, he was a lonely relic of a
bygone day. His wife, Marie Eleanore, had died in 1608. Margrave
(Duke) Georg Friedrich had died in 1603, but without direct de-
scendants, so that control of Prussia now fell to Albrecht Friedrich's sons-in-law, Hohenzollern princes from the electoral Brandenburg (Berlin) branch of the family. First one daughter (Eleanore,
1583–1607) and then another (Anna, 1576–1625) ascended to the
electoral dignity, guaranteeing Brandenburg's claims to Prussia
and the continuation of the direct electoral line.[80]

A venerable historiographic tradition congratulates only the
Austrian house of Habsburg for its successful marriage diplomacy
("Tu felix Austria nube"), but it must be said that even the future
house of blood and iron knew well how to secure its diplomatic
base and its plans for territorial expansion through the cunning
use of marriage. In early modern Germany, and for that matter
throughout early modern Europe, with so much dependent on the
smooth hereditary transition of power to legitimate heirs, it is no
wonder that princely families insured themselves against the all
too frequent assaults of impotence and madness upon the patriarchal lineage.[81]

4

The Last Dukes of Jülich-Cleves

Six hundred miles to the west-southwest of Königsberg, around the same time, madness was also taking its toll on the house of Jülich-Cleves, a dynastic union of the three duchies of Jülich, Berg, and Cleves, together with the counties of Mark and Ravensberg and the lordship of Ravenstein. Although small and splintered, these principalities had, through their wealth, densely urban population, and strategic location on both the right and left banks of the lower Rhine, a far greater importance than their small size alone might lead one to expect.[1] Combined for the first time by a marriage in 1510 between the houses of Jülich-Berg and of Cleves-Mark, the dynastic union was necessarily fragile for the first few decades, and all the more so after Duke Wilhelm V, the Rich, lost the short but expensive war of the Guelders succession to Emperor Charles V.

Wilhelm the Rich

In the Treaty of Venlo in 1543 Wilhelm was compelled to concede to the victorious Charles V that he would not allow the introduction of the Reformation in his lands. Both the expenses of the war and the religious concession were unpopular with Wilhelm's estates, which took up a position of steady opposition to any policies that smacked of ducal autocracy or "despotism." Many towns and noblemen of the lower Rhine (with major exceptions in Jülich) had already by 1540 or 1550 gone over to the Protestant Reform, and the Protestant movement only accelerated after that. For his part, Duke Wilhelm showed a remarkable moderation in religious matters, inspired in part by his Erasmian education at the hands of Conrad von Heresbach.[2] He continued, despite his pledge to Charles V, to support outright Protestants at his court, such as his personal physician, Johann Weyer, or his court preacher, Gerhard Vels; and three of his daughters were raised Protestant and married Protestant princes.[3] His apparent stance of evangelical humanism (or as some suspected, covert Protestantism) also found expression in his steadfast support of taking the eucharist under both species (both bread and wine) and his opposition to witchcraft trials. Apparently following Weyer's advice, he did not approve or confirm a single witch's execution, although he did evidently reintroduce the controversial "water test" for witchcraft in 1581, a procedure in which those accused of witchcraft were dunked in a pond to test their claims of innocence. Most orthodox theologians agreed that the test was an unacceptable revival of illicit judicial ordeals, but Wilhelm's councilors may have seen the test as a way of proving a suspect's innocence. In general they seem to have doubted normal witchcraft accusations: "It is an impious abuse that afflictions and burdens [cruces] are thought to be imposed by the devil or inflicted by the spells of evil persons."[4] So the court at Düsseldorf was one of the surviving centers of late Erasmian skepticism.

Unfortunately, Wilhelm the Rich fell victim to a series of eleven strokes in his fiftieth year during and after the imperial diet at Augsburg in 1566, and as a result lost control of his government from time to time over the next twenty-five years.[5] Many scholars have noticed that Wilhelm's policies began to shift toward the orthodoxy or zeal of Catholic hard-liners from 1567 onwards. Though he had not given up his government, he was increasingly under the influence of fervent Catholic councilors, especially, perhaps, Wilhelm von Waldenburg. There were, of course, other and more practical reasons, too, why any government on the lower Rhine might try to be or to appear more Catholic from the late 1560s on.[6] First and foremost among these reasons was the presence of the duke of Alba and his Spanish troops in the neighboring Netherlands, beginning in 1567. And during the 1580s Jülich-Cleves was drawn into the Cologne War (1582–84), which broke out when Archbishop Gebhard Truchsess von Waldburg tried to convert his archbishopric to Lutheranism. Spanish troops occupied portions of Wilhelm's territories and might well have been even fiercer than they were if Wilhelm had not turned in a more

Catholic direction. No one doubted, however, that he retained a warm affection for reformers and mediators, and so the pro-Catholic party, including the papal nuncio, Ottavio Frangipani, placed their hopes on Wilhelm's only surviving son, the fanatically Catholic Johann Wilhelm.[7] This growing influence of a predominantly Catholic council could only agitate and threaten the increasingly Protestant estates of Jülich-Cleves, who responded to perceived threats by increasingly insisting on their prerogatives, on their rights to raise taxes and resist the Spanish, to retain Calvinist preachers, to enjoy a generally free exercise of religion in fact, and to refuse all nonnative participation in any of the upper echelons of government.[8] Thus the political constellation of forces was such that any weakness in the duke would result in a bitter contest between the ducal councilors and the estates, and might well draw in the emperor and the potentially competitive contenders for succession to the combined duchy, if the heir apparent, Johann Wilhelm, should die without heirs.

Weakness in the old duke was unfortunately a growing fact of life. It is not fair to claim that he was mad or totally incapacitated from 1566 onwards, but he was indeed paralyzed on his left side and suffered a permanent slurring of his speech. His motions and gestures evidently became more rigid and lacking in spontaneity. An extraordinary examination conducted by Dr. Heinz Schweitzer in 1954, when the ducal crypt was reopened, determined, moreover, that Duke Wilhelm the Rich also suffered from an osteoporotic collapse and compression of his spinal column that must have made standing or sitting for any length of time a real torture for him.[9] For unknown reasons, he also occasionally fell asleep at meals or while sitting in conference. Even the portraits of Wilhelm in his old age reveal a fragile and decrepit man, overburdened with physical and perhaps also mental troubles. Although he still undertook long trips in the early 1570s, such as the wedding journey to Königsberg in 1573, by the late 1570s his travels were over. And during the 1580s, saddened by the premature death of his elder son Karl Friedrich (in 1575 at the age of eighteen), Wilhelm fell more and more often into paroxysms of unconsciousness or perhaps mental illness.[10]

Right up to his death in January 1592, however, Wilhelm remained a figure to contend with. His councilors took over almost all of the daily business at court, and yet they did not succeed in

Duke Wilhelm the Rich of Jülich-Cleves-Berg, by Wilhelm Swanenburg after
Johann Malthain. (Courtesy of the Stadtmuseum Düsseldorf)

setting up a regency or "curatel" for him, and in his last years they
had to watch, helplessly, as Wilhelm fell out with his only surviving son, Johann Wilhelm (1562–1609). He continued to take communion under both species and to impress Ottavio Frangipani, the
shrewd papal nuncio, with his stubborn competence. In 1591 Wil-

helm's daughter Sibylla repeatedly remarked on her father's mental decline, but she saw it more as part of the frailty of old age than as madness. Therefore, although the general histories of Jülich and Cleves are full of vague remarks concerning the madness of Duke Wilhelm V, it appears to me that his episodes of mental debility were sporadic and certainly not serious or long-lasting enough to require a regent or guardian.[11]

Wilhelm's historians, however, have looked hard for signs of insanity and have therefore quoted the detailed account of his last days by his personal physician, Reiner Solenander, as if it supported such a conclusion. As Wilhelm grew sicker and weaker around Christmastime of 1591, Solenander reported in great detail the physical weakness that kept the old duke confined to bed. On the day of Wilhelm's death, 5 January 1592, Solenander reported that the duke was "still of sound mind [*noch bei gutem verstandt*] and more cheerful and animated [*mehr ermuntert und erleuchtet gewesen*] than I had seen him in any day for the last several years."[12] Such a statement is hardly reliable evidence, in my view, that Duke Wilhelm had been insane or mentally ill in his last years; it only confirms that he had been weighed down with cares and worries and that now, on his deathbed, he could joyfully give his peaceful blessing to his son and take leave of this world.[13] It is indeed surprising how steadily the older literature used to indict and impugn Wilhelm's mental health when we consider the fact that none of Wilhelm's advisers or observers actually tried to confine, control, or depose him; no one even seized the political opportunity to call him crazy. Solenander also conducted a thorough autopsy that described Wilhelm's cerebrum and cerebellum as "unharmed, without any blot and well formed," so that the origin of any of Wilhelm's physical and mental troubles lay not in the conformation of his brain but in his occasional intemperance. Solenander did find a quantity of "syrupy liquid" under the brain that had, he thought, come up from the duke's lower parts.[14] But we are entitled to doubt whether Wilhelm the Rich was ever fully or irretrievably mad.

JOHANN WILHELM

No such doubts are possible in the case of his surviving son, Johann Wilhelm.[15] We can never be sure how much of his mental constitution was determined by his heredity, but contemporaries remembered that Johann Wilhelm's paternal grandfather, Johann III (1490–1539), had been nicknamed "the Simple." A visitor to Johann's court in 1537 noted that, quite apart from an evident enthusiasm for splendid clothes, he seemed to have "little brain."[16] Johann Wilhelm's great-grandfather, Johann II (1458–1521) had also earned a derisive title, "the Babymaker" (proletarius), because he was said to have fathered sixty-three illegitimate children before settling into a marriage with Mechtild of Hesse at the age of thirty-one. Aside from the undeniable drain these children made on the treasury of Cleves, however, we have no evidence that Johann Wilhelm's lusty ancestor was mad. On the Jülich side of the family, contemporaries of Duke Johann Wilhelm could point back to his great-great-grandfather, Duke Gerhard II of Berg and Jülich (ca. 1417–1475), who had lost his mind in 1455 and had been declared incompetent to rule.[17] But as we have remarked earlier, such examples would perhaps nowadays count more as "risk factors" in the inheritance of Duke Johann Wilhelm, rather than as direct and sufficient causes of his mental troubles.

For contemporaries, though, or at least for his male physicians, the more blatant hereditary burden seemed to lie on his mother's side. Maria of Austria had apparently suffered from depressions in the years before and after giving birth to Johann Wilhelm in 1562, and observers have been all too quick to conclude that she had simply inherited the madness of her Spanish grandmother, Juana ("la Loca") of Castile (1479–1555). If it were all so simple, however, we would have to explain why Maria's fourteen brothers and sisters retained their mental health, at least so far as we can tell.[18] Feminist scholarship has sensitized us to the possibility that women were more regularly blamed for madness than men, but from these sources it is impossible to tell whether this tendentious suspicion resulted from a gender bias concerning mental illness or from a prudent reluctance to blame the ruling lineage. As in Prussia, though, the plain fact is that the ducal physicians of Jülich-Cleves strongly suspected that their difficulties in curing the young duke were traceable to his congenitally corrupt constitution. When called on to evaluate his illness in the fall of 1589, the three ducal physicians, Reiner Solenander, Lambert Wolf, and Galenus Weyer explained that the young duke was "by nature and complexion melancholy and depressed [melancholisch und swermutig]" and that not just his mother but both his parents had contributed their share to his troubles "for his complexion is inborn; he is this way by nature from his father's seed and his mother's blood [*ex paterno semine et materno sanguine*]."[19]

This phrase has been much quoted but will not bear all of the weight that historical eugenicists have placed upon it. The doctors explained what they meant by noting that "when he was begotten, his father was still weak from a long bout of fevers, at first continual but then quartan [every four days], and from scurvy; at that time he therefore had a swollen spleen" that failed to purify his body of "coarse, earthy, melancholy humors; and so the inborn natural weakness of his complexion was multiplied."[20] The doctors declined to speculate further on what might have corrupted Johann Wilhelm's mother's blood, but there is no hint here of Juana la Loca's curse. Rather, it seems that these physicians, like those in Prussia, were thinking very specifically of the exact circumstances under which the prince had been conceived in the fall of 1561.

For whatever reason, Johann Wilhelm had a childhood of disease and weakness. Overshadowed by his more gifted older brother, Karl Friedrich (1555–1575), he was elected at the age of nine by the cathedral chapter of Münster to be the coadjutor (and probable successor) of the bishop. Shortly before his twelfth birthday the chapter in fact postulated him as bishop, but within a year his golden brother's death of smallpox in Rome thrust the young, untested, and retiring youth into the forefront of international diplomacy and speculation.[21] He was now the sole legitimate male heir of Wilhelm the Rich.

In preparing his son for the episcopal office of Münster, Duke Wilhelm had employed the strongly Catholic Werner von Gymnich as tutor for young Johann Wilhelm, and so when it came to choosing a wife for him, Johann Wilhelm required a firmly Catholic marriage. Princess Jakobe of Baden (daughter of Margrave Philibert) seemed to measure up beautifully, for she had received an exemplary Counter-Reformation education at the Bavarian court of her cousins in Munich. The wedding was celebrated in 1585 with a level of official festivity and consumption that eclipsed anything ever seen before on the lower Rhine.[22] Sadly, the marriage seems to have been troubled right from the start, in part because Duke Wilhelm never fully accepted Jakobe as his daughter-in-law (her critics said that she came to Düsseldorf with

Duke Johann Wilhelm of Jülich-Cleves-Berg, by Wilhelm Swanenburg after Johann Malthain. (Courtesy of the Stadtmuseum Düsseldorf)

expectations of a continuous round of parties and luxurious fri-
volities), but also in part because the old duke jealously guarded
his right to rule throughout his duchies. He began to exclude the
increasingly ambitious Johann Wilhelm from his deliberations,
going so far as riding out into the countryside with his closest
councilors in order to avoid his son whenever he had to make a
major decision.[23]

Johann Wilhelm began to impress even fervent Catholics as a
fanatic who could not be trusted with delicate political affairs. But
although some observers indeed criticized him in 1586 and 1587
for foolish and undigested thoughts, he showed no convincing
signs of mental illness until 1588. By 1589 Johann Wilhelm, still
childless, was plagued by a deepening religious depression, feeling
under attack by the wrath of God and gradually coming to fear that
his father's Protestant physicians and apothecaries were trying to
poison him. He also began to voice the fear that he might be the
last of his line. Already in the summer of 1588 he and Jakobe had
traveled to the legendary spa at Ems, whose waters were then a
well-known cure for infertility. It appears, moreover, that Johann
Wilhelm and Jakobe may have engaged in increasingly frantic sexual intercourse in a continuing effort to conceive a child. In addition, the depredations of Alessandro Farnese's Spanish troops sta-
tioned nearby depressed Johann Wilhelm, as did the misery of his
people and the giddy desire of Jakobe for amusement.[24] Through
the summer of 1589 Johann Wilhelm was periodically mad, but
the permanent break in his mental health came in October of that
year.

Our chief source for Johann Wilhelm's condition in late 1589 is
a medical report dated 18 October and signed by the three ducal
physicians, Reiner Solenander, Lambert Wolf, and Galenus Weyer.
They commented that the twenty-seven-year-old heir apparent
was weak in body, to be sure, but that his real problem now was a
"weakness of mind" ("blödigkeit des gemueths") and a melancholy, "which we also understand as a depression," a melancholy
that had its origin in his bodily constitution but was triggered by
his unreasonable way of life.[25] His madness had reached such a
level that when his father died, Johann Wilhelm would not be able
to take up his princely duties. The doctors pointed to defects that
the young duke had inherited from both his father and mother
(here is the famous passage about his father's seed and his mother's
blood that we have already noted).[26]

The result was that Johann Wilhelm exhibited the classical symptoms of melancholy: excessive and unrealistic fear and sadness, a depressive suspicion, and a miserable, afflicted sense that he was under constant threat of death. This Renaissance "melancholy" as described by the doctors was no mere sadness; it was a disabling condition. The young man was so worried about his father's disregard that he feared his father would have him executed. As good Galenists, the three physicians ordered immediate changes in the young duke's diet, sleep, exercise, games, music, and society. He needed cheerful servants "who can refresh their master with pleasures." He needed medicines, including opium, that could be slipped into his food should he refuse such pharmaceutical remedies. He should calm himself with drafts of sweet milk. But Johann Wilhelm also needed a less active sex life, "for it is not advisable that he have constant cohabitation with his wife in his room." Thus, riding and travel out of town were recommended not just as exercise and diversion but also "in order that the cause of his constant intercourse [stetigen bywohnen] may be removed." Such unremitting sexual congress, they argued, weakens the body, disperses one's energies, and "fails to retain the male seed long enough that it can become ripe and useful for fertility." Especially for melancholy persons such an immoderate sexual life was dangerous, for their heads and brains were already disturbed and their senses confused. "Now it is clear and well known that frequent intercourse and cohabitation especially weaken the head," which is why Hippocrates called orgasm "a small epilepsy, which is to say, a disease of the head."[27]

The doctors were also sure that Duke Wilhelm could do something to relieve Johann Wilhelm's fear of paternal censure by writing to him lovingly and forgivingly. Indeed, that very day Johann Wilhelm's younger unmarried sister, Sibylla, wrote: "I can hardly describe to you just how pleased our father is with you. He hopes sincerely that a trip will help you feel better and wants to know how you are doing." And on the next day Duke Wilhelm wrote the kind of letter requested of him: all was forgiven; Johann Wilhelm should just ride all around Jülich and amuse himself.[28] These reassurances and a letter from Jakobe seemed to cheer the young duke up momentarily, but by 20 October he had fallen back into despair. Since many of his complaints were of a religious nature, it seemed prudent to enlist the opinion of Hubertus Fronhoven, the court chaplain. Near the end of October the chaplain responded that it was especially appropriate to consult a cleric because Johann Wilhelm's fear of poisoning inhibited him from taking any of the medicines prescribed by his physicians. From Fronhoven's point of view, however, there was "little help to be found among men for such weakness of mind," and so Johann Wilhelm should distribute alms and ask for the earnest Christian prayers of all his subjects.[29]

The duke's specific madness seemed to present itself in three forms. He evidently was ashamed that he had no "power" and did not yet have children; he experienced despair that he was falling into disfavor with the king of Spain because his father seemed to favor the Dutch rebels (Johann Wilhelm felt worthy of imprisonment and death because of this infidelity); and, third, his over-scrupulous conscience plagued him for faults he was sure had enraged his father. Despite frequent absolution, Fronhoven found that "when the melancholy, which recurs in intervals, comes on, his princely grace falls back again into remembering this." The most solemn assurances of God's mercy did seem to console Johann Wilhelm, however, and Fronhoven concluded that he was "not truly threatened with despair [the spiritual offense] but with melancholy thoughts [which were more a medical matter]."[30]

Exactly how Johann Wilhelm behaved or how he was treated for the next two months is unknown, but rumors and news reports spread rapidly that he had gone mad. In January 1590 Philip II of Spain alerted Duke Alessandro Farnese of Parma to be ready to intervene in the combined duchies in order to prevent their takeover by Saxon or other Protestant forces. The duke of Parma proceeded with plans to build a floating bridge across the Rhine at Wesel so as to facilitate the movement of troops if necessary. The Catholic duke of Bavaria kept himself well informed about events in Düsseldorf, as did the emperor, Rudolf II.[31] On the Protestant side, rumors flew among the princely sons-in-law of Duke Wilhelm V (the so-called *Interessenten*, or "interested parties"). Landgraves Ludwig and Wilhelm IV of Hesse joined Margrave Georg Friedrich in nervous speculation over what would happen if Duke Wilhelm V of Jülich died leaving the now incompetent Johann Wilhelm as his only male heir.[32] By late January 1590 these parties all learned the troubling news that Johann Wilhelm had fallen into such a rage that he had been disarmed and confined to a secure room under guard. By then the young duke was so agitated that he refused to undress at night, had let his hair grow wild and unkempt, neglected mealtimes and bedtimes, and had grown so suspicious of even his own personnel that it was no longer safe to be around him. He had attacked and wounded several of his closest servants.[33]

In early February the ducal physicians composed an elaborate Latin treatise on the proper therapy for Johann Wilhelm.[34] They agreed that the case was urgent; fasts and vigils were rapidly destroying what was left of the young duke's health. He needed a firm Galenic and Hippocratic regimen. In academic fashion they considered each of the six "nonnaturals" that affected human health and concluded that everything needed change. His air should be calm and pure, perfumed perhaps with the odors of rose water, apple peels and citrus bark. The light in his room should be neither too bright nor too dark. Humid, smoky, fetid air was to be purged. The room temperature, as well, needed to be kept neither too hot nor too cold, and simple tapestries with pictures of flowers and fruits might encourage good cheer and modest dancing. So much for "air," the first nonnatural.

His food also needed radical changes in order to avoid the gross, dense, glutinous, feculent substances that encouraged the production of black bile. In particular, Johann Wilhelm should abstain from the flesh of stags, wild boar, hare, swine, swamp birds, starlings, quail, and fish that had no scales. His cooks should refuse to prepare foods that were hard to digest, such as sauces, old cheese, animal feet, cartilaginous or visceral meats, and brain, as well as any foods that might burn the blood or degenerate easily into melancholy adust, such as foods fried in butter and spicy or sweet foods (including most desserts and pastries). He was to avoid onions, radishes, mustard, crocus, vegetables such as cabbage, herbs such as thyme or marjoram, and most sausages as well as foods cooked in milk, for they were notorious for obstructing the liver and the spleen. The best foods for the young duke were juicy, easily cooked dishes that would contribute to the production of healthy blood. Bread was excellent (if well-risen and well-baked), as was the flesh of young animals such as kid, deer, rabbit, and indeed most farm and game animals except boar. Recipes for these dishes included ample dollops of borage, rose water, and bugloss (oxtongue).

Johann Wilhelm, it was now suggested, should not be confined to his room. He needed a walk before meals and "liberal," honorable amusements and exercise. But his main problem was sleep, the third nonnatural: Johann Wilhelm did not get enough, and the danger was that his current condition, worrisome enough as it was, could consequently deteriorate into mania or some bestial delirium. Medications and the right foods should be employed to produce eight or nine hours' sleep, and *at night*, for "sleep moistens the brain."[35] Thus he should not go to bed right after the evening meal, but only after a three-hour delay to avoid any digestive disruption of his sleep.

The young duke should be sure to keep all his fluids flowing. A light sweat induced by massage or exercise was good. His bowels and bladder should be emptied regularly. And under the rubric of the fifth nonnatural—repletion and excretion—the doctors recommended a mild sexual regime: "Love is relevant here, so long as it is moderate and tempered by reason." Doubtless it was best if times were chosen when Jakobe was equally eager for intercourse, but care had to be taken to keep it from becoming too frequent. "Moderate sex is healthy for melancholiacs."[36] By then, however, the problem may have been that Johann Wilhelm did not desire sex at all.[37]

The sixth nonnatural was "affectus," emotion, a topic on which one might have expected pages of analysis, but these Galenic physicians contented themselves with blandly and briefly recommending the removal of all external causes of fear, dejection, and morose depression. Preachers and confessors should bring Johann Wilhelm to embrace true piety while teaching him the dangers of such superstitious practices as excessive fasting. Games and honest jokes had their uses here as well.

These medical recommendations represent well the Galenic emphasis on somatic or physical remedies for what might seem like mental troubles to us. And yet it is clear that the recommended therapy was not purely or obsessively somatic. On 13 April 1590, however, the physicians presented an even more detailed set of recipes for foods and medicines that would purge excessive black bile, temper the humors, and moisten the brain. By this stage the three ducal physicians, Solenander, Wolf, and Weyer were joined by Heinrich Botter, who was apparently Jakobe's personal physician. Their chief concern was to prevent a burning (adustion) of Johann Wilhelm's humors that would produce mania. A full cure was difficult, they conceded, but far from impossible. The duke should undergo venesection on his left side to relieve his overburdened spleen, and hellebore was now prescribed, that famous ancient purgative for black bile.[38]

Johann Wilhelm's father joined the physicians in hoping that the young duke could be brought to a more moderate way of life. An undated copy of a letter survives from this period, cosigned by Solenander, in which Duke Wilhelm urged his son to let his hair and beard be trimmed in order that his sweat pores might drain properly. He should also undress before going to bed, like other princes and lords. "Take off your boots and spurs, for it is uncomfortable and unusual" to keep them on at all times. Get eight or nine hours' sleep a night with your clothes off. In the morning, wash your face and head, partake of divine services, and pass the day moderately, with a balanced mix of food, exercise, and light work. Bathe regularly. Wilhelm urged his unfortunate son to take care of himself, for he would soon be duke.[39]

Duchess Jakobe also did what she could for Johann Wilhelm's health. Although her detractors objected that her addiction to luxury and frivolity kept her from caring about her husband, it seems that at least for a couple of years she continued to have sexual intercourse with him "not too often but every three or four nights and otherwise when requested. . . . If it would have helped him, I'd have gladly stayed away from him not just for a month but for a full quarter of a year."[40] From the tone of her response to questions it seems clear that Jakobe had been accused of engaging too frequently in sexual congress with her deranged mate. Soon she was to stand accused of adultery, and by 1597 she was dead, amongst dark accusations that she had been murdered by ducal councilors who were eager to maintain control over the united duchies even as Jakobe strove, clumsily, to secure some considerable control for herself.[41] Inasmuch as these scandals and intrigues do little to illuminate the history of madness, we need to pass over them, fascinating and pathetic though they are. But in the early 1590s it seems clear enough that Duchess Jakobe was taking an active part in caring for her husband.

The ducal advisers were not content with medical advice alone. As in the previous October so again in February 1590 the opinion of theologians was requested, and a full-fledged *consilium* was produced, signed by six divines. Their immediate task was to

Duchess Jakobe of Jülich-Cleves-Berg, by Crispin de Passe. (Courtesy of the Stadtmuseum Düsseldorf)

evaluate a cure proposed by Pastor Cornelius Ingenhoven, which mixed together physical and spiritual approaches.[42] He contended, for example, that if a vial of Johann Wilhelm's urine failed to foam up when it was placed over a fire, it was a sign that the young duke was bewitched. On the assumption that Johann Wilhelm was bewitched or possibly possessed by an unclean spirit, Ingenhoven had also proposed administering holy water and consecrated hosts on which novel exorcisms and passages of Scripture were written. The theological consultants included two ducal chaplains (Hubertus Fronhoven and Winand Thomasius) and four other priests, who unanimously pronounced their disdain for the proposed cures. Their chief objection was that Ingenhoven's procedures had no scriptural basis: they could only be used "by those who have either an explicit or a hidden pact with the devil." They were gross superstition or even witchcraft. Ingenhoven wanted to combine natural and supernatural remedies, but the theologians were eager to avoid such illicit mixtures. If Johann Wilhelm were truly possessed by an evil spirit, a possibility they did not reject out of hand, there were good old, tried-and-true exorcisms that could be administered by "unsuspected and pious priests."[43] The Jesuits in Cologne evidently agreed that Ingenhoven's proposals savored of manifest error. To orthodox theologians such a mixing of natural and supernatural could be as offensive as fully Paracelsian remedies were to orthodox Galenists. For both orthodoxies it was important to preserve the professional and conceptual boundaries between the disciplines of the body and the disciplines of the soul.

As to the question of what Johann Wilhelm might actually be suffering from, the theological panel carefully pointed out that he was physically melancholy by nature, and for such conditions physicians needed to give their "natural advice." It was clear, however, that Johann Wilhelm was also suffering from a "sickness of soul" (animi infirmitate), for which priests might be the source of good advice, because they were used to treating penitents suffering from despair. Here was an area of possible overlap and confusion "for experience teaches that an inner depression, anxiety and sadness, which can rightly be called a disease of the soul [animi morbus], most often afflicts those who are melancholy by nature and complexion." When the spirit of desperation blew at them, they felt assaulted in their conscience. As good Catholics, they must learn to trust the counsel and consolation of others rather than relying on their own thoughts, "which may be taught or insinuated by the Enemy." If the excessively penitent preferred to nourish their scrupulosity and thus ate out their hearts in grief, refusing to "give up their thoughts," then it was no wonder that they finally lost all their wits and understanding.[44] Aside from exorcisms for the truly possessed, there were two scriptural remedies for those afflicted by internal sadness and depression: the consolation of God's Word and especially of the Psalms, for David had known such dark and desperate conditions; and the dispensation of alms so that prayers might be said for those such as the mad duke throughout the land. In the specific case before them, though, the theologians felt that only the latter remedy might help because Johann Wilhelm was so far out of his mind that he could not absorb any spiritual consolation, at least for the moment.[45] He needed to learn to relax his overscrupulous conscience.

We should notice that, in 1590, the court theologians and the Cologne Jesuits did not think that Johann Wilhelm was demonically possessed and specifically rejected the suggestions of those who preferred to assume that he was. But the search for unorthodox cures went on all the same. Just when the physicians were drawing up their recommendations and the theologians were rejecting as superstitious the claims of Cornelius Ingenhoven, two ducal councilors, a certain licentiate Dieterich Heistermann and the well-known scholar from Berg, Dietrich Graminaeus, also undertook to examine a certain Pastor Johann from Lank (or Lenkh), near Krefeld, who had proposed to cure Johann Wilhelm with a thirty-day program that combined astrology, magic, holy water, consecrated salt, numerous Latin prayers and exorcisms, a variety of herbs soaked in beer, and amulets tied to the soles of his feet.[46] According to this pastor, Duke Johann Wilhelm was indeed a victim of poisoning, just as he feared. He had drunk it from a glass, but his troubles were also magically "blown in" (angeblasen) to him from an unspecified source. The ducal councilors put a series of skeptical questions to the pastor, probing whether his proposed therapy rested on claims of divine revelation or on the help of evil angels or on a tacit pact with the devil. The pastor was evasive here, claiming only that he traveled with God and refusing to reveal the book in which his cures could be found.[47] We can observe, then, that the ducal councilors were just as wary of strange healers at this point as the official Catholic theologians were. Writing a week later, the theologians agreed that this Pastor Johann of Lank was even more obviously superstitious and suspect than Cornelius Ingenhoven.[48]

Such efforts to squelch illicit cures were not, however, fully successful. Although the academically orthodox physicians, pastors, and councilors tried to clamp down on superstitious remedies, the court in Düsseldorf, like that in Königsberg, seemed to demand them. In 1592 Duchess Jakobe evidently ordered scraps of paper inscribed with words from the Gospel of John to be sewn into Johann Wilhelm's doublet or jerkin and unconsecrated hosts to be mixed with oysters in his food. We may be reasonably certain that these were efforts to rid Johann Wilhelm of his madness or at least to procure an heir, but commentators hostile to Duchess Jakobe saw them as magic directed against Johann Wilhelm. Unfortunately, the paranoid duke was so fearful of poisoning and of witchcraft that he reacted in panic when he discovered these measures, complaining, for example, that the devil himself was in his doublet.[49] According to his sister Sibylla, he "spoke of strange people, of witches and the like, and often says that we are all witches."[50] It may be that Johann Wilhelm's fears of the devil, of poison, and of witchcraft were only reinforced by the covert efforts of Jakobe to secure his improvement. As we have seen, he was also frightened of regular medicines, claiming in 1590, for example, "that he would rather die than use any medicine."[51] One of our reports comes from Ruprecht Silberborner, sent by the Pfalzgraf Johann of Zweibrücken to look out for his interests as the husband of Duke Wilhelm's third daughter, Magdalene. Silberborner reported explicitly that he had asked the chief ducal councilors if they suspected poison or witchcraft (*veneficium*) as a cause of Johann Wilhelm's disease. They had replied, "Absolutely not," but Silberborner himself noted that, "There are nonetheless many signs of philtres and love potions here."[52] When we consider that by this point the young duke evidently did not even want to see his wife, it becomes obvious that love potions might indeed have been part of Jakobe's or the physicians' therapeutic campaign.

The sources concerning Johann Wilhelm's mental health are so rich for the 1590s that we could continue almost ad infinitum to describe his ups and downs in remarkable detail. But the main point is already clear. The incompetent duke periodically reverted to quiet depression, although he also had weeks of lucid intervals. Some of his observers thought that his mental state coincided with the phases of the moon. Others noticed that travel helped, or pilgrimage to local shrines. But just as regularly Johann Wilhelm would manage to obtain a weapon and terrify his attendants. In November 1592, for example, he got hold of six guns and walked about shooting almost anyone he saw. At times he styled himself the "Duke of France and of Gaul."[53]

In May 1595 astrologers tried to interpret Johann Wilhelm's nativity, but with no luck, and an unspecified Countess of Hohenzollern sent a "wonderful fluid [to be used] for such kinds of madness, but there have been reservations about using it just now and the five physicians [Weyer, Wolf, Botter, Manlius, and Schlotans from Cologne] are to test it." Perhaps sensing a tricky political problem, the physicians got together but declined to express an opinion on the value of this cure.[54]

In May 1596 two women came forward with medications that they said might well help the duke. One was an "old" widow from Ertzelbach (we learn that she was about forty years old), while the other was Margaretha von Ahr, wife of the former Düsseldorf courtier, Dietrich von Enzenbroch. Both women had prepared special herbal potions that raised interest but also deep suspicion. Another of our reports on the Düsseldorf scene comes from the pen of the lawyer Dr. Alexius Moroldt, special agent and ambassador to the court of Jülich from Pfalzgraf Philipp Ludwig of Neuburg. Moroldt reported that on 6 May the corpulent widow of Ertzelbach had refused to reveal her herbs to the ducal physicians but had promised that she would administer the brew to her own children and that she would swallow it, too.[55] Under these conditions the potion was brewed, and for eight mornings the duke took it. At the end of the week the court barber-surgeon expressed his skepticism, claiming that the duke's condition showed no change. By the end of the month serious accusations were bandied about concerning the "irresponsible treatment of the prince by an immoral, medically inexperienced woman." Some councilors concluded that "only those cures recommended by experienced physicians should be undertaken."[56] In June 1596 Duke Johann Wilhelm's sister Sibylla reported to the councilors in Jülich that Margaretha von Ahr had had no luck with her remedies, either.[57] We should notice that here, as in Prussia, women healers were enlisted after professional (which is to say, male) physicians had failed to secure a return to health, but again the physicians did not silently retire from the field. They fought back as active skeptics and critics of such unauthorized folk healing.

Later in 1596 a remarkable therapy was undertaken with the help of a celebrated wonder-worker, an English doctor, residing in Holland, by the name of John Lorimer or Lumkin (or Lomkyn). He made a big splash and is thus mentioned in many sources, but our best ongoing account of his therapeutic work is probably contained in the weekly reports of the jurist Peter von Pötter to Philipp Ludwig, Pfalzgraf of Neuburg.[58] Around 10 November

1596 this "doctor" arrived full of large claims for himself, and large financial demands as well. He had required £1,000 before he would even undertake the trip to Düsseldorf—in order to equip himself and his retinue with appropriate clothing. When he arrived with sheaves of eloquent testimonials to his extraordinary abilities, he let it be known that he "had fully cured senseless and completely mad [unsinnige, gantz rasende] persons as well as those bound in iron shackles, the melancholy, and the feeble-minded" ("melancholische und mit hauptsblödigkeit und schwacheit behaffte leuth").[59] He had completely restored them, he asserted, to their former health and reason, "to which even certain Galenic physicians have testified," an important point, for Lumkin admitted openly that he was a "chemicus" (namely, a Paracelsian) and not a learned physician with a medical degree. So strong were his evidently chemical cures that the physicians of nearby Arnhem agreed that he had worked near-miracles with patients that they, the Galenists, had been unable to help.

These were strong claims, and we may guess that his invitation to Düsseldorf was a sign that the official ducal physicians no longer commanded the unqualified authority they had enjoyed seven years earlier. When asked to describe his intended therapy, Lumkin responded at great length. One of his favorite techniques at the outset was to imitate the patient and thus to infuriate him. From the patient's reaction, Pötter reported, Lumkin said he could judge whether the disease was curable or not, "for he was gifted with ability to tell whether the disease and illness were congenital [naturalis] or accidental [in Aristotle's sense of nonessential], or brought on by poison or by the influence of a disease."[60] In cases of congenital disorders ("that have been in the seed or in the complexion") he offered little or no hope, but with the effects of diseases contracted later in life he claimed amazing success, using formulas of his own devising and in tiny doses that might, he said, actually kill the healthy but could restore the sick to health.

Pötter was obviously impressed with this Paracelsian wonder-healer, pointing out that he was no papist but a Protestant, "of our religion." And despite his monetary demands, he was a "modest" man, who usually received only forty thalers a day when he treated lords and princes, although with merchants he had supposedly received fees as high as £16,000. Noting the possibility that his cures might be dangerous, Pötter observed that obviously his remedies would have to be tested before they were tried out on Duke Johann Wilhelm.[61] By 25 November Pötter had spoken personally with Lumkin and could report that he was a young man of about thirty-three years. He claimed that he was a member of the English nobility and that his father had been a physician to the king of England. Because of years spent with the English embassy in Greece, he explained to his credulous listeners, his Greek was better than his Latin. Pötter was deeply impressed by Lumkin's modesty, piety, and discretion, but also by his claim that he charged high fees to the wealthy while treating the poor at no cost. He possessed the remarkable gift of being able to determine internal problems "just from the appearance and simple contemplation of a person's nature, complexion, and properties."[62] He repeated to Pötter that he often liked to enrage a patient at first in order to tell whether he was curable. As his testimonial letters asserted, Lumkin had already cured over forty persons in the Netherlands, with no failures. His amazing abilities came in part, he said, from his experience sailing around the world with Francis Drake. No wonder he knew the virtues and uses of all the world's plants and fruits. God Himself had taught him the art of healing almost all the "species insaniae," including the frenzied, the melancholy, lunatics, and even those possessed by demons.[63] All of this rested, he said, on his simple faith in God and not on "superstitious ceremonies and charms." Here was a man whose extravagant claims and reputation obviously raised the hopes of Pötter and of others who had despaired of helping Johann Wilhelm.

Lumkin admitted that no ordinary medicine could effect such cures. He instead proposed to treat the duke with small amounts of (Paracelsian) "spirit of quintessence." When placed in the ears of deaf persons, it was so strong that it broke down blockages of hearing and generated vast outpourings of sticky, wet humors and phlegm from the nose. Of course, in Johann Wilhelm's case, the medication would have to be hidden in his food because of his well-known refusal of medicines. He warned that it was normal for the first two or three sessions of the treatment to provoke great fears and desperation. Patients often thought they were dying, but one had to be resolute in waiting for a cure.[64]

While waiting for his credentials to be checked, Lumkin showed what he could do. He took under his therapy, for example, a poor townsman's daughter who had been "out of her mind for some years now." Hopes were so high that many country people also applied to him, asking that he "experiment on them."[65] Pötter could not restrain himself from noting that Lumkin had extraordinary personal powers in dealing with the mad. He could calm the wildest lunatic merely by taking him by the hand, "and so long as he holds their hands, they remain totally calm and well-behaved, ceasing all furies and frenzied outbursts. More than that, they sometimes even answer reasonably the questions posed to them."[66] He had such an effect on the "poor daughter," who was talking and behaving strangely when Lumkin arrived at her house, "but as soon as he took her by the hand, she began behaving normally and peacefully and answered moderately to those who came before her."[67] We can wish that we knew more about this effect. Was it a form of hypnotism or of extraordinary charisma?

Another of his almost magical therapies employed an "artificial stone," with which Lumkin could painlessly operate on arms, feet, and thighs so that almost no blood flowed. Pötter had heard (was it true?) that Emperor Rudolf II had even licensed him and had invited him to come to Prague to advise the emperor personally. Lumkin intended to follow up on this offer after the projected two or three weeks that it would take to cure Duke Johann Wilhelm. Pötter also reported that some at court were fearful that Lumkin would only restore the duke to his earlier feeble condition, which was evidently not good enough.

By early December Lumkin had been to see the duke and declared that he was indeed curable but that the therapy would take perhaps four weeks (at £10, or forty thalers, a day). To begin with, he needed several days just to talk with Johann Wilhelm, a move opposed by the councilors, but Lumkin agreed to be very careful. Already the duke seemed calmer, able to take occasional walks. Pötter thought that this seemed like a very good sign: the rages had almost disappeared and his "melancholy mind" had calmed down so much that "one can hardly notice or detect his insanity, for he walks daily up and down in the castle, quietly and modestly, even though the main cures and chief medicines have not yet been employed."[68] Even so, the duke's skeptical councilors, worried that Johann Wilhelm's delicate constitution could be upset at any time, decided to call in several medical doctors from Cologne for a consultation. Indeed, the court Galenists remained unpersuaded even when Lumkin achieved dramatic effects with a poor paralyzed woman, whom he cured by giving her a pipe to smoke. We are not told what she smoked, but Pötter reported with some astonishment that smoke had come out of her mouth, nose, *and ears*, and that she claimed to be completely cured.[69]

By mid-December, however, it was not only the learned Galenists and the official councilors who were having their doubts about Lumkin's chemical cures. The lawyer Alexius Moroldt expressed his own grave doubts in a report dated 14 December 1596 to Philipp Ludwig of Neuburg. Johann Wilhelm's condition could, he thought, just as easily disintegrate as improve. And Pötter conceded about the same time that Johann Wilhelm was neither better nor worse than before. The spectacular cures that Lumkin had achieved with women had not worked with the duke. Even so, this English "chemical doctor," this Paracelsian ("medicus chymicus"), was receiving celebrity treatment, eating off silver plates and from silver bowls. Even so, despite his difficulties with the duke, Lumkin continued to score amazing successes with others, curing an official's son and a "daughter" from Jülich, both of whom had been mentally disabled but were now "restored to their God-given reason and understanding."[70]

The Galenists kept up their skeptical campaign, arguing that Lumkin's cures were highly dangerous and casting doubt on Lumkin's credentials, saying that he knew almost no Latin and had not studied or read very much. No wonder he didn't understand the duke's "weak complexion."[71] Lumkin himself seemed to be revising his advertised and overly confident expectations, claiming now that in eight or ten days (that is, by Christmas) he could free the duke "of frenzy, fury, raging, and all useless nonsense," but that it would take another three or four months to restore him "perfectly to his former understanding."[72] Slowly, too, the Paracelsian doctor was forced to reveal his therapeutic arsenal to the skeptical councilors Broel and Waldenfels on the explicit understanding that they would keep everything they learned strictly secret.

Apparently, however, this openness finally persuaded the skeptics, and a contract was signed guaranteeing Lumkin the princely sum of ten thousand imperial thalers and a substantial salary. But on 12 January 1597 the doctor betook himself to Cologne, in search of just the right medicines, he said, and also to heal the many other patients clamoring for his attention.[73] He returned to

Jülich just before Easter. By then a special imperial permit had arrived from Rudolf II sanctioning Lumkin's procedures, and so all the high nobles of Jülich-Cleves-Berg were invited to the castle at Jülich to observe the therapy. To ensure God's blessing, a public prayer for Johann Wilhelm was ordered throughout the land, and two thousand barrels of rye were distributed as alms to the poor, so that they, too, would join in heartfelt prayers for their lord. On the first day of therapy the ducal chamber was crowded; in addition to Duchess Sibylla (Johann Wilhelm's younger sister) and the princely councilors, the three ducal physicians, Galenus Weyer, Lambert Wolf, and Reiner Solenander, had been summoned, and not just as observers. In a ritual strangely reminiscent of Holy Communion but also designed to reassure the duke concerning the safety of the novel prescription, they all partook of the cup. "Then the new master himself first drank the potion intended for his princely grace, and next his servants, and thereafter the three ducal physicians, the lord chancellor and his councilors, the duchess herself and, finally, his princely grace." For three days and nights the duke could not sleep after taking this medication. He walked about restlessly under the constant guard of two noble councilors. The territorial diet was assembled on 23 April 1597 in high expectation that Duke Johann Wilhelm would appear before them, but "bad weather" kept him from attending. This novel Paracelsian therapy continued from Easter to Pentecost, and the duke improved enough that he could again take walks and enjoy public dinners. He seemed calmer, but his melancholy remained and now seemed to be shifting over into dementia or idiocy.[74]

Lumkin at least achieved an extraordinary rapport with the duke, however, and was soon deeply enmeshed in the intrigues surrounding the increasingly desperate court of Düsseldorf. Before long the ducal councilors were accusing him of the most serious crimes, including the poisoning of Johann Wilhelm. In June 1599 John Lumkin escaped to the Netherlands shortly after the council issued an order for his arrest, and thus we lose sight of one of the more remarkable therapists to try his skills on the Duke of Jülich.[75]

Meanwhile, the court intrigues to which I have referred had already produced a fatal result. On 3 September 1597 Duchess Jakobe was found dead in her bed. For years Sibylla and the ducal councilors had been deliberating over how to get rid of her, and had even contemplated poison. The conclusion is inescapable that Jakobe was murdered in order to make way for a new wife and legitimate children for Johann Wilhelm.[76]

On 20 June 1599 the duke married Antoinette, the daughter of the powerful Duke Charles II of Lorraine. At the time of their wedding she was thirty years old, and it was hoped that she would have a calming effect on her husband as well as bear him children. At first the couple traveled to well-known spas together, and Johann Wilhelm indeed seemed more peaceful. The doctors now disagreed whether the duke was suffering from a phlogosis (fever and inflammation) or from scurvy or hypochondriacal melancholy. He was treated with cooling drinks and with concoctions of alkermes (an insect), bezoar stone, and theriac (a mixture of some seventy drugs, used as an antidote to poison).[77] But this marriage too proved childless, and now the suspicion revived that Johann Wilhelm was bewitched. Around 1600 it was no easy matter to decide if witchcraft or demonic possession were at hand. Orthodox Catholic churchmen usually insisted that all physical and natural diagnoses had to be excluded (and all physical remedies exhausted) before one could conclude that supernatural forces were at work. In July 1600 the duke and his new duchess traveled with their whole court to Mönchengladbach, about fifteen miles west of Düsseldorf, to consult with a priest who claimed to be able to detect whether his grace was plagued by a "following spirit."[78] We do not know how this encounter went, but evidently after a week of observation the priest decided to withdraw from the case.

From now on most of our reports on Johann Wilhelm's condition no longer refer to his madness or raging but to his idiocy or feeblemindedness. As late as 1603 and 1604 he was trotted out before meetings of the assembled diets at Essen and at Hambach, but he was by then probably just a relic—mute but eloquent evidence, however, that he was at least still alive. At the onset of this severe mental deterioration the medical practitioners began to retreat from the therapeutic arena, for Galenic medicine had never claimed much success with retardation, "natural simplicity," and imbecility.

Since physical remedies had now been exhausted, one could turn with a good conscience to the possibility of demons. This would seem to be why the duke of Lorraine now sent two Italian priests to Düsseldorf during Lent of 1604 in a renewed effort to heal the duke spiritually. They concluded (predictably) that both the duke and Antoinette of Lorraine were bewitched. In contrast to the general attitude of skepticism with which such magical and demonic explanations had been greeted in the early 1590s, now they seemed to make more sense. About the same time, an imperial emissary also arrived with several Italian monks to perform exorcisms. From 19 March through 13 August 1604 the princely couple were under the constant care of an exorcist, and we are lucky to have a rather complete diary kept by a skeptical courtier in attendance at these exorcisms. Sometimes a monstrance holding a consecrated host was placed on the duke's head as a supplement to the prayers and exorcistic adjurations. On another occasion the duke became nauseated during the ceremony, while at other times he gaped, yawned, and rolled his eyes. But basically the duke cooperated with these procedures for a couple of months until, tired of such exercises, he declared that he couldn't bear to see the exorcist again.[79] Five priests thereupon concluded that Johann Wilhelm truly was bewitched. By October 1604 the mad duke had roused himself from his compliant torpor; he ran at his wife with a naked rapier, shouting, "Do you suppose I have a devil! Away with these rogues and exorcists!"[80]

All of this only strengthened the priests in their conviction that "the most serene duke is really and effectively infected with witchcrafts."[81] The duchess, too, was now persuaded that the rites of the church had detected a latent bewitchment of her innards. In trying to gain control of the stubborn evil spirits at work, the exorcist had commanded them that if through witchcraft they had caused the duke's madness or the infertility of his marriage, they should leave a sign of this in the left hand of the duchess. At once she had felt an unusual heat in her left arm and hand, which, under the repeated commands of the exorcist, came to be concentrated in her left hand. Antoinette was clearly an eager participant in all of these exorcisms, and she even seems to have orchestrated a campaign of princely petitions to Emperor Rudolf II, asking him to assist by sending his chaplain and confessor, Johann Pistorius, to take part in the exorcisms. In June 1605 Pistorius, the notorious convert from Protestantism and zealous Catholic propagandist, did in fact arrive in the duke's domains. Once again the physicians were consulted, but this time they gave their full blessing to the intended spiritual proceedings. In their view it was now clear that

"in this disease there is something beyond and above nature [ali-
quid praeter et supra naturam], which cannot be reduced to natural causes [cujus ratio ad naturam vel huius causas reduci non
possit]."[82]

On 20 August the second series of ducal exorcisms began. At
first Johann Wilhelm had to be tricked into accepting the prayers
and ministrations of the nine priests assembled at the castle at
Hambach, but soon enough it was clear to all, including the councilors and the Duchess Antoinette, that a rather elaborate exorcism had been prepared. The detailed report we have of these days
was composed by a noble courtier or servant of patently Protestant
sympathies, and so it is obvious that we cannot trust all the reported details. According to this account, Pater Zacharias of Milan
had printed up special adjurations, which he gravely bellowed
("thinking perhaps that the demon, lacking ears, was hard of hearing or completely deaf," as our Protestant source sarcastically put
it).[83] The Franciscan guardian of Düren, meanwhile, read specific
exorcisms intended to remove "impediments to the marital act,"
although our biased reporter claims that this ignored the possibility that Johann Wilhelm's incapacity was due to his lack of "natural affection and love" for his wife.[84] This was itself an extraordinary claim, for it seemed to presuppose that male impotence could
rest on a lack of love and might even have implied that real
affection and love were necessary for any marriage—surely an
oddly romantic notion for that age and for that class. A special ex-
orcizing cross of black wood overlaid with gilded silver was placed
on the duke's chest and head. After several days the priests looked
for some sign that the duke was in fact "afflicted by some witchcraft or possessed by the devil," and so "they finally did at the end
what they should have done at first."[85] As with the duchess the
year before, the patres tried to coax or force the devil to reveal himself in Johann Wilhelm's right hand, but this time to no avail. Unlike Antoinette, the duke was not a willing or cooperative victim
of demonic possession. Eventually he grew exasperated and, rising
up full of anger, slapped the doorkeeper, a layman, exclaiming,
"You are yourselves all demons or possessed by demons." Running
to the chapel galleries, he summoned his body guards to attack
these "treasonous tormentors," but they refused.[86]

The exorcists restored order and began to deal ever more seriously with the devil whom they thought responsible for Johann

Wilhelm's outburst. Strangely "superstitious" rituals were now attempted, using procedures that Rome might not have approved. In one, a gruesome image of the devil was engraved on a lead plate and was then beaten with rods, and four or five candles were allowed to drip on it "as if that would cause him great pain." They painted his terrifying picture ("in figura maxime horribili") on a paper that they whipped and then burned. They wrote out some fifty names of devils on separate slips of paper, which they also burned. They followed this up by throwing stones at the burning papers "so that the poor devil, in this unusual way, was first burned and then stoned."[87] None of these exercises had the desired effect, but, after some dissent among the exorcists, the rituals were evidently renewed in the renowned pilgrimage chapel at Scherpenheuvel, some twenty miles northeast of Louvain and fifty-five miles west of Jülich.[88]

Returning home, the exorcists outfitted the duke's chambers with small wax crosses and with large wooden crosses. Although Johann Wilhelm was a fervent Catholic, he may have harbored some of his father's Erasmian attitudes toward excessive rituals; the priestcraft finally became too much for him. When his would-be helpers hung a small pouch full of written blessings or conjurations and little crosses around his neck, Johann Wilhelm cut it open during the night and strewed them all about his room, "saying that these were all charms and superstitions." The exorcists also gave Johann Wilhelm a new mattress fitted out with blessings and crosses. They fumigated his chambers with incense and besprinkled clothing, bedding, and the whole chamber with holy water; on days when the duke was quiet they rubbed holy oil on his lower abdomen and on his head, which regularly annoyed him.[89] All of this proved stubbornly fruitless, and finally the priests withdrew from Hambach. When the duke learned that they had left and had no plans to return, he broke out in laughter.[90]

It is not clear from this report or from other documents when exactly the exorcists gave up their task. We do know that on 12 September 1605 Duchess Antoinette ordered a search made for the amulets and blessings that Duchess Jakobe had sewn into Johann Wilhelm's doublet ten years earlier, but they were lost. A week later Antoinette announced her intention of going on the pilgrimage to Scherpenheuvel herself, but military officers persuaded her that the situation in the Netherlands was too dangerous for such a trip at the moment.[91] In February 1606 the ducal party decided instead to go on pilgrimage to Protestant Aachen, only eighteen miles southwest of Jülich, but the burghers of Aachen closed their gates against the duchess, obviously fearing to give the Catholic party a propaganda victory. (Only eight years later Spanish troops forcibly restored Aachen to the Catholic fold.)

It is worth noticing that the professional "imperialism" we often find in contested and difficult cases, such as this one, here took a different form from what we might ordinarily expect. We frequently notice (and modern critics of the medical establishment insist) that physicians diagnosed a disease or disorder in natural terms on the assumption that it would therefore respond to a physician's care. In contrast, a priest might diagnose a demonic or sinful or supernatural origin in the same case, for which only spiritual remedies could be expected to work. We have observed that this was roughly the constellation at the beginning of Johann Wilhelm's madness in 1589–90. But over the course of the ensuing decade it appears that every kind of natural and physical therapy was exhausted. The result was that by 1605, as we have seen, the doctors were ready to concede that Johann Wilhelm's disorder was "beyond and above nature." On the spiritual side, the opposite conclusion forced itself upon Johann Pistorius, Rudolf II's confessor, who expressed his frustration that the elaborate exorcisms had failed. Writing to the papal nuncio, Giovanni Stefano Ferreri, in September 1605, Pistorius explained that Duke Johann Wilhelm would now surely die without heirs and that exorcisms could do no good, "given that the duke is really insane" ("essendo realmente pazzo").[92] When one professional expertise collided with another, pride and discretion could actually require that one yield up a contested case to the other side, rather than accept full responsibility for a therapeutic failure. This seems to be why the ducal physicians were ready to resort to supernatural explanations, while the priests a month later were just as ready to renounce heroic spiritual measures and to provide naturalistic explanations.

Even if the physicians by the early 1600s had given up hope of a cure, they did continue to encourage Johann Wilhelm to take regular exercise and to eat properly. In January 1605 we hear that the mad duke filled his day with "exercise and recreation, with painting, riding, and walking."[93] This may not be a precocious reference to painting as art therapy, but it is striking evidence that Johann Wilhelm was permitted recreation in so many areas. None of this changed his fundamental incapacity, however, and he died childless at the age of forty-seven, in 1609.[94] Antoinette followed him to the grave one year later. The chief claimants to the duchy were all Lutheran, and in the end it was split in two, with the duchies of Jülich and Berg going to Pfalzgraf Wolfgang Wilhelm of Neuburg (a Lutheran member of the Wittelsbach dynasty) and the duchy of Cleves and the county of Mark going to Elector Johann Sigismund of Brandenburg (Lutheran grandson of Duke Wilhelm V of Jülich-Cleves). Against all calculation, of course, neither one remained Lutheran for long. Wolfgang Wilhelm soon converted to Catholicism, and Johann Sigismund shortly transferred his allegiance to Calvinism, thus setting up one of the enduring tensions in Prussian, and indeed in German, history.

The putative madness of Wilhelm the Rich and the undeniable insanity of his son have permitted an unusually detailed and circumstantial view of the therapeutic options available at a Catholic court in the late sixteenth century. As in the Prussia of Albrecht Friedrich we find a persistent, even relentless, effort to cure the dukes and a willingness to try the most unorthodox remedies once the official Galenists ran out of ideas and perhaps lost some of their credibility. As in Prussia, a celebrated Paracelsian wonder-worker was called in, but his showy failure was just the sort of scandal that entrenched the orthodox Galenists in their opposition to the doctrines of Paracelsus. Chemical remedies might slowly infiltrate the pharmacopeia, but not the more ambitious religious claims about man and the cosmos.[95] Finally, after all the physical explanations had been tested and found wanting, the ducal advisers turned enthusiastically to exorcisms intended to relieve the duke and his wife of bewitchment. It is worth noticing that the exorcists did not have to claim that demonic possession was the duke's sole problem before they could go to work. Catholic demonology did not sharply distinguish demonic possession from witchcraft, and the main controversy, among Catholics, always revolved around whether a case of madness was of natural or supernatural origin. Once it was concluded that the disorder had to be supernatural, the chief worry was to exclude remedies that were patently "superstitious." But among Catholics around 1600 that border was often indistinct and thus hard to define. Madness was therefore not just political dynamite. Intellectually it was the most enigmatic disorder.

The regents and family members who looked after Duke Johann Wilhelm also demonstrated to a remarkable degree the newfound reliance of German statesmen on learned experts. The early modern German territorial state was built by men such as these, ready to depend on bureaucrats, university trained scholars, and specialized professionals in the shaping of state policy. They were, as we see here, resourceful, stoic, and pragmatic in trying to cure the state's ills and their prince's affliction.

5

A Melancholy Emperor
and His Mad Son

Emperor Rudolf II

No account of the mad princes of Renaissance Germany would be complete without the most prominent example of all, Emperor Rudolf II (1552–1612). Unfortunately, we have very few direct sources with which to assess the mental, religious, and physical condition of the emperor, for his central archive was destroyed during the Thirty Years' War. And so we are left with a buzzing and chaotic cloud of often ill-informed diplomatic rumors. Owing to the lack of direct sources that might tell us how he was actually treated, we will not be able to study his case with anything like the detail provided for Wilhelm of Braunschweig, Albrecht Friedrich of Prussia, or Johann Wilhelm of Jülich-Cleves. There are, however, a few lucid intervals in the records that do survive, and they permit us to draw a few significant conclusions.

As we have noticed, Rudolf sent imperial commissioners to Braunschweig and to the Rhineland in order to cope with repeated threats to Catholic interests in northwestern Germany, and he was often asked to intervene in cases of insanity among other princely houses. But Rudolf was himself mentally overburdened and dangerously melancholy from as early as 1577 onwards. He moved his residence and government from their traditional seat in Vienna to the Bohemian city of Prague, partly to escape the crowds and pressures of the Austrian metropolis. In the fall of 1577 an official of the Elector Palatine wrote to his master in Heidelberg that the various embassies to the imperial court had provoked such disorder that "his Imperial Majesty seems totally melancholy" ("fast melancholisch").[1] Here we find joined together two elements that came to characterize Rudolf's long reign: his loathing for crowds, confusion, and court intrigue, on the one hand, and a repeated tendency to fall into despondency and melancholy, on the other. It is true that writers (then as well as nowadays) could extend the term *melancholy* to mean little more than sad or profound, but we will see that by 1590 or 1600 those who saw Rudolf used this basically medical term in a far more pathological sense.

Physically Rudolf was frequently in ill health. In 1581, at the age of twenty-nine, he was so sick that there were fears for his life. His physicians and surgeons seemed to be having no luck in stopping an apparently rapid loss of weight.[2] His uncle, Archduke Charles of Inner Austria, began to take steps to ensure that the imperial succession would stay in Habsburg hands if the unmarried emperor died without legitimate heirs. These preparations proved unnecessary, or at least premature, because Rudolf recovered his health by the fall of 1581, but the example also reveals another characteristic of Rudolf's reign, the willingness or even eagerness of his brothers and cousins to replace him. It is also clear enough, as Winfried Schulze has shown in summarizing a large literature, that Rudolf's brothers and uncles moved as early as 1576–78 to curb Rudolf's efforts to establish primogeniture in the Austrian line. Thus the question of succession to the various parts of the Austrian inheritance was contested and uncertain well before Rudolf provoked alarm, especially after 1600, owing to his evident mental incapacity.[3] Obviously, despite earlier intentions otherwise, his obstinate refusal to marry, like the refusal of Elizabeth I of England, stimulated intrigue and speculation as well.

As the son of Emperor Maximilian II and Maria, the daughter of Emperor Charles V, Rudolf had received a double dose of the Habsburg genetic legacy (his two grandfathers were sons of Juana la Loca), and it was once common for historical eugenicists to wring their hands and to cluck knowingly about such examples of "hereditary overload." Others, more recently, have not shrunk from retrospectively diagnosing Rudolf's malady as schizophrenia.[4] Likewise, even though Rudolf kept to himself a great deal, almost everyone at court had an opinion or an anecdote to tell about the reclusive and melancholy monarch. But often these rumormongers were only repeating clichés.[5] For their part, historical popularizers have told and retold stories about the mad emperor, shut away with his smoky alchemists and mystical astrologers, frightened of marriage while dominated by lust, passive in the midst of mounting political chaos in the empire, devoutly Catholic, or bigoted, or enlightened, or fully persuaded that he was himself bewitched.

R. J. W. Evans is justified in reacting with some disdain to this mountain of sensational gossip, and his book *Rudolf II and His World* represents a serious effort to understand the emperor and to assess his reign through the distinguished entourage of poets, painters, astronomers, humanists, musicians, physicians, and hermetic magicians with whom he surrounded himself. Rudolf's glittering court included the most able astronomers of the day, Tycho Brahe and Johannes Kepler, the mannerist painters Giuseppe Arcimboldo and Bartholomaeus Spranger, the occult philosophers John Dee and (briefly) Giordano Bruno, as well as notable Paracelsians, Platonists, Cabalists, Ramists, and Jewish scholars. Together, they exemplified "an underlying atmosphere, a climate of thought in later sixteenth-century Europe, which was particularly characteristic of the Imperial court in Prague."[6] They represented, moreover, not the madness of a hopelessly insane emperor but a "universalist striving . . . an effort to preserve the mental and political unity of Christendom, to avoid religious schism, uphold peace at home, and deliver Europe from the Ottoman menace."[7] Evans argues that with lofty and logically consistent goals such as these, the intellectual world around Rudolf reflected well the goals and yearnings of the emperor himself. Evans goes far, therefore, to discount and to minimize Rudolf's evident mental problems. To be sure, he was "melancholy," Evans concedes, but that term "became a vogue word of the period," susceptible of such broad application, he implies, as to be almost meaningless.[8]

The image of Rudolf as a mad recluse survives, Evans alleges, "in sub-historical writing and belles-lettres until our own day," but a sober evaluation of Rudolf's condition teaches us otherwise. "It is doubtful," he writes, "whether Rudolf was in fact ever mad in any serious technical sense; certainly not for longer than brief intervals, as for a time during 1600 or 1606, while much hinges on the meaning which contemporaries attached to words like 'melancholy' and 'possession.'"[9] In his justified attempt to recognize Rudolf II as a man of strength, vision, and great seriousness, it seems that Evans here goes overboard. It is not clear that there even is a "serious technical sense" to the word *mad*, a word I use repeatedly in this work precisely because it is not technical. Evans seems to fear that if he concedes that Rudolf was mentally or emotionally disordered for more than a moment, we will fail to recognize the greatness and significance of Rudolf's intellectual, spiritual, and political projects. The guarantee against such a false conclusion is Evans's own book, which persuasively documents the coherence and inspiration behind the irenic, humanist, mannerist, and magical strivings of those whom Rudolf's patronage supported. That does not mean, however, that we need to doubt whether Rudolf was also for long stretches mentally ill, so disordered and irrationally frightened that he let imperial business slide for months and years, so depressed that he thought himself bewitched and even attempted suicide.

Karl Vocelka is also right to remind us that most of our sources for these episodes must be treated with exquisite care. It was papal nuncios who reported in 1600 that Rudolf had become reclusive and inaccessible and that he held no more audiences; but at the same time Protestant emissaries reported that the emperor had received them warmly. Here, Vocelka reminds us, we probably have evidence of Rudolf's growing distaste for the extreme papal curialism and for expanding papal influence throughout Europe, but the papal nuncios, in order to explain their failures, complained that Rudolf had simply gone mad.[10] We also notice that just when Rudolf and his brother Matthias began seriously to contend for control of the empire and the Habsburg hereditary lands, we begin to find references to Rudolf's alleged mental incapacity. "It is not just accidental that all of these references come from the circle around Matthias, who must have had a serious interest in portraying his ruling brother as an incompetent psychopath, thereby to improve his own position within his family and within the class of potential rulers."[11] In other words, here indeed is a case in which political rivals may have used the label of madness in an attempt to destroy an opponent.

So we need to proceed with great caution through a minefield of conflicting opinion. One way to get our bearings is to notice that Rudolf often seemed much more troubled in mind than even the depressed norm for his family would allow. As Heinz Noflatscher has recently remarked, "Depressive tendencies were a feature of most of the Habsburgs at that time." Emperor Maximilian II (1527–1576) exhibited this trait, as did King Philip II of Spain (1527–1598) and his two sisters, the Empress Maria (1528–1603, Maximilian II's wife) and the Infanta Juana (1537–1573, wife of Don Juan, Prince of Portugal), to say nothing of Philip's son Don Carlos (1545–1568). Among the Austrian Habsburgs, Archduke Ferdinand of Tirol (1529–1595, a son of Emperor Ferdinand I) and Rudolf's own brother Matthias (1557–1619, and emperor from 1612) suffered from "violent swings of emotion," to choose one sort of euphemism.[12]

Born in 1552, Rudolf spent his formative years (1563–71) with his younger brother Ernst in Spain at the court of King Philip II, where he evidently learned the newly modish Spanish manner of stiff reserve, of black and relatively simple clothing, and of exaggerated regard for one's personal grandeur and honor. He also learned to distrust and dislike the ambitions of his Spanish relatives, however, and plans that he should marry the Infanta Isabella, daughter of Philip II, dragged on for years until it became obvious that Rudolf would never commit himself to her. When she ultimately married his brother Albrecht, in 1597, Rudolf nevertheless felt deeply offended and disappointed. It seems that part of Rudolf's difficulties with various proposed marriages stemmed from his seriously inflated sense of his own imperial status. As pressure mounted on him to father a legitimate heir, he came increasingly to distrust all his brothers and other relatives, who, he felt sure, were plotting against him.[13] One might speculate about the possible political or psychological pressures on the sons of Emperor Maximilian II that conspired to prevent all five who survived infancy and childhood from fathering any legitimate heirs, but Rudolf, at least, was not impotent. Indeed, he had a reputation for libertinism and a long-standing relationship with Katharina Strada, the daughter of a favorite courtier. They had several children, one of whom we will meet soon enough, if under unfortunate circumstances. So Rudolf was clearly a sexually albeit not a maritally competent man. One might guess that it was his exaggerated and lifelong fear of entanglements and of family interference in his affairs that helped to produce the Habsburg dynastic crisis that in turn triggered off the Thirty Years' War. Evans is right to point out of Rudolf that here we may find the "crux of his dilemma: the enormous gulf between the glorious ideal and the sor-

Emperor Rudolf II, by Hans von Aachen. (Courtesy of the Kunsthistorisches Museum, Vienna)

did, niggardly reality, thwarted as he was by petty jealousies and rivalries."[14] But we should be clear on this point, too: that Rudolf thwarted *himself* through irrational fears, an unreasonable sense of his own grandeur, and at times outright emotional breakdowns. The Thirty Years' War was ultimately due in part to his madness.

The best study of Rudolf's mental, emotional, and physical problems was written over one hundred years ago by the Bavarian historian Felix Stieve. With exemplary German thoroughness, he combed through the tangled correspondence of ambassadors and legates, the web of diaries and memoirs, and the self-serving welter of proclamations, official reports, and semiofficial recommendations.[15] While new information has, of course, come to light over the years, Stieve's evenhanded evaluation of Rudolf's breakdown still commands admiration. In Stieve's estimation, Rudolf's physical ailments prompted the concern of his court as early as the late 1570s, but it was not really until the 1590s that observers began to complain of the emperor's deep sadness, his deliberate remoteness and aloofness. More and more regularly, we hear objections like that of Count Wilhelm von Zimmern in 1591: "It was hard to obtain an audience with His Majesty because he is . . . supposedly rather sad and out of sorts."[16] The growing strain of the Turkish wars took their toll during that decade, and by 1598, under the pressure of rumors of Protestant negotiations with Spain, of Spanish military excesses in northwestern Germany (in Jülich-Cleves), and of plots to depose him, Rudolf gave way to his fears of the plague and to his resentment that Archduke Albrecht had married the Infanta Isabella. "Under these influences the depression of the emperor was transmuted into an anxious and irritated agitation that made him so ill-tempered and bad-humored that virtually none of his councilors could deal with him any longer; none of his chamberlains and servants could wait on him any more."[17] In January 1599 Arnaldo van der Boye wrote to Archduke Albrecht, describing Rudolf as "very melancholy and sulky," and from now on the term *melancholy* seems almost inseparable from the emperor.[18] And the term came to imply much more than introspective gloom: increasingly the word was applied to Rudolf in the sense of severe pathology.

During this period of increased stress, Rudolf became persuaded that his two chief ministers, Wolfgang Rumpf and Paul Sixt Trautson, were dealing behind his back and against his interests. During Rudolf's retreat from public affairs, they (but especially Rumpf) had attained an almost total control over the central administration in Prague. Suddenly, in March 1599, Rudolf forced the "almost absolute" Rumpf to resign, but then took him back. Suffering a deep melancholy, Rudolf withdrew from public view, appearing only three times during the Easter holidays.[19] Erupting in rage, he fired many of his servants and banished others from court for days. News that the Protestant territories were now threatening to withhold crucial tax payments needed to fight the Turks, whom the councilors and ambassadors regularly called the "hereditary enemy," drove Rudolf wild. The Venetian ambassador reported that "every day His Majesty's mental affliction increases."[20] Rudolf was again moved to sack Rumpf and Trautson, but once again he took them back. For a couple of months Rudolf's health improved and his rages subsided, but in July he left Prague in panic-stricken flight from the plague. He shut himself up in almost perfect isolation in Pilsen for nearly a year, during which he continued both to mistreat his servants and to suffer from acute shortness of breath. His fears of being forcibly deposed prompted terrified furies, followed often enough by weeks of relative calm.[21]

In June 1600 he returned to Prague, where the plague had died down five months earlier, and for a time Rudolf seemed suffused with a new vigor. He hunted joyfully and ordered parties and recreations. But then his illness broke forth in full flower. He hallucinated, he lashed out at imagined plots against him, he raged. He announced that he had been poisoned or bewitched, and it seems he attempted suicide repeatedly.[22] In September he did finally dismiss Trautson and Rumpf for good.[23] In their place he now complained bitterly of the machinations of the Capuchins, who under Lawrence of Brindisi (later canonized as Saint Lawrence) had been especially brought to Prague in 1599 in order to spearhead the Bohemian Counter-Reformation. He ordered them to stop ringing their bells during the night and even ordered their exile from Prague. Then just as suddenly he changed his mind and allowed them to stay.[24] Rudolf showed the same tendency with his physicians, firing Guarinoni of Verona but soon offering him his position back.[25]

Spurning the advice of doctors, the increasingly Catholic monarch also had growing problems with his Catholic devotions. Stieve speculated that his courtiers, "thinking him bewitched or possessed by the devil, failed to help him to find liberation through receiving the sacrament. And, the more his sexual excesses stood in radical contrast to those religious views that he had imbibed in his youth and that still dominated him, the more any thought at all of confession and of his responsibility before God must have terrified him in his state of worried turbulence."[26] Stieve here attempts the impossible in trying to determine what Rudolf's religious emotions and reactions were, but we can at least agree with him that Rudolf obviously felt considerable conflict.

During a depressive illness in 1593 Rudolf had lashed out against the Jesuits and had refused to take the sacraments. In 1600 it was the turn of the Capuchins. He charged that the papal nuncio had bewitched him and that the Capuchins had enchanted him.[27] Far from being religiously indifferent, as some have thought, Rudolf seemed to some observers especially agitated and unsettled whenever he went to confession. At the end of 1600 he took on a new confessor, the fervent Catholic convert and propagandist Johann Pistorius (1546–1608), whom we have met already in Düsseldorf.[28] Evans makes a case for seeing Pistorius as an occult mystic, a Cabalist, and a notable scholar, as well as a tireless opponent of his former coreligionists, the Lutherans and Calvinists, but we still lack a good study of this turbulent yet productive man.[29] Crucial to his relationship with Rudolf may have been the added fact that he had also obtained a formal medical education and was thus able to care simultaneously for Rudolf's body and spirit.

From this confused crisis of 1600 we will do well to examine a couple of extraordinary documents that deal with a proposed therapy for Rudolf, for otherwise most *consilia* and opinions of this sort seem to have been destroyed along with the rest of Rudolf's personal papers. In late 1600 the suspicion became widespread throughout the Holy Roman Empire that the emperor had gone mad. Rudolf's brothers and uncles must have feared that the six other electors of the empire would send delegates to Prague to look into Rudolf's condition. If they learned the truth, they might well declare Rudolf unfit for rule and appoint the (Protestant) electors of Saxony and the Palatinate to act as "imperial vicars" (*Reichsvikariat*) in accordance with the Golden Bull of 1356. Effectively, these Protestant "vicars" would then have administered an interregnum until a proper, and perhaps non-Habsburg, claimant could be elected king of the Romans and Holy Roman emperor.[30] Naturally, Rudolf's surviving brothers, the Archdukes Matthias, Maximilian, and Ferdinand, feared that the French or Danish kings might also exploit the situation to their own advantage, and they seem to have met at Schottwien (twenty miles southwest of

Wiener Neustadt) in order to reach a brotherly understanding about how to handle the emerging crisis.[31]

Partly, though, Rudolf's brothers were concerned with the delicate matter of who exactly should be sent to speak to Emperor Rudolf. An anonymous October *Discurs* prepared for the Schottwien meeting (or for some similar meeting) survives that can give us insight into what the Catholic privy councilors in Prague thought should be done about Rudolf's health.[32] The *Discurs* starts by recognizing that Rudolf was suffering from "melancholy and serious disturbances" that endangered his heart while also provoking "great feebleness, dizziness, and flux in the head."[33] Its authors worried that Rudolf might soon die of his psychosomatic disorder. To counter this danger they recommended a "medicinische Cur," which, if Rudolf would only "follow doctor's orders a little," might drive out the melancholy within a few weeks and prevent its return. To that end, the emperor should allow himself to be bled, but not just from the veins: "An artery needs to be burst open [*gesprengt*]." Following this, he needed to take a special herbal wine and establish "order in his eating and drinking."[34] The implication of these lines would seem to be that Rudolf had been resisting venesection and had perhaps adopted wildly irregular mealtimes. In these respects he seems to have been exhibiting patterns of behavior very similar to those we have seen in Albrecht Friedrich of Prussia and Johann Wilhelm of Jülich-Cleves. These Renaissance princes all feared poisoning, resisted the recommendations of their doctors, and had difficulties with the clerics who were sent in to help as well.

The *Discurs* for Emperor Rudolf went on boldly to suggest that if he were thought to be "somewhat" possessed by demons ("von Geistern etwas angefochten"), this was no major calamity, "for if only their foundation—namely, the melancholy humor in which the spirits eagerly seek refuge and domicile—is eliminated, then with God's grace one can overpower the demons."[35] In my experience, this is the only instance in which the possibility is entertained that someone could be "somewhat" possessed, a euphemism that was probably invented to avoid the embarrassment of suggesting just how deranged the emperor was. We should also notice the cautious implication, too, that demons delighted in the melancholy humor. In fact, it was a commonplace that black bile was the devil's bath and that spirits exploited physical debilities and predispositions. Austere theologians might object to this apparent blending of body and spirit, but in the age before Descartes most scholars and ordinary people probably thought that the worlds of *soma* and *psyche* were inextricably entwined.

Rudolf's councilors also suspected witchcraft (*Zauberei*), stating at one point, "there is no doubt that it is implicated." Surprisingly, a medical cure might help here, too, but "we are not opposed to seeking to detect the witchcraft even without the medical approach. The suspected woman [*Weibesperson*] should be arrested." A proper examination would determine "whether His Majesty could be helped by exterminating the witchcraft [that is, executing the witch] or whether other means needed to be found if it should turn out that there was no witchcraft."[36] Notice the familiar assumption here that if there were witchcraft, it must be the work of a woman. The morally casual tone is also remarkable, probably a product of the vast social distance that separated these proud councilors from the sordid world of village suspicions.

In order to recover Rudolf's health and reason, the *Discurs* insisted, "evil persons who daily pour melancholy, evil thoughts into His Majesty need to be banished from His Majesty's presence"; this would do much to reduce his "perturbation." Let us observe, however, that the councilors who composed this memorandum took an open but basically medical approach to Rudolf's mental and physical health. Diet, bloodletting, and herbal cures would not only restore balance to his humors but could remove the foundation for any evil spirits that might be dwelling in the emperor's excessive black bile. The councilors did not recommend exorcism, and even if witchcraft were involved, as they thought likely, the arrest and execution of the witch would apparently suffice as the solution. It is in fact noteworthy that this document contains no suggestion that exorcism or other ecclesiastical rituals could provide any possible hope. The emperor's confessor, Pistorius, seems to have agreed with this assessment. In November 1600 he wrote to Cardinal San Giorgio: "He is not possessed, as some think, but suffers from a melancholy, which over the passage of a long time is now all too deeply rooted. To be sure I don't deny that evil spirits enjoy and abuse his disease, which they exploit by running along with it and by deceiving the emperor with all sorts of imaginings."[37] Pistorius expressed the pious hope that God would help to persuade Rudolf to subject himself to a medical cure, for if he were to do so, there was "no doubt that he would recover his health." With dark foreboding, Pistorius predicted that if Rudolf's condition worsened, "which necessarily happens through the neglect of his medications," a "German revolution both in religion and in the empire" would be unavoidable.[38] We find in Pistorius the ready willingness to find demons at work in Rudolf's mind, but surprisingly no interest in an exorcism. He perhaps foreshadowed in 1600 what he later concluded about Duke Johann Wilhelm: that spiritual remedies and exorcism would not work if a troubling disorder was basically physical.

The October *Discurs* also expressed concern that rumors of the emperor's madness (*Hauptblödigkeit*) were circulating throughout Germany. Thank God they were wrong, the authors added hopefully, but Rudolf could do much to extinguish such rumors if he showed himself often in public and if he restored good relations with the Capuchins in Prague. Such evil rumors needed to be stopped because France, Denmark, and the German Protestants were exploiting them in hopes of displacing the house of Habsburg.[39] One obvious step was becoming ever more pressing. Rudolf needed to announce a designated successor: a king of the Romans needed to be elected. Of course, these were just the sorts of recommendations that helped to persuade Rudolf that everyone was really plotting behind his back.

In trying to present these conclusions to the moody and suspicious Rudolf, another October memorandum, probably from the imperial councilors in Prague, suggested gently that His Majesty needed "a little therapy" ("ein kleine Cur"), not because he was really ill, he was to be told, but so that he might avoid the future difficulties that the doctors and astrologers thought likely to flow "from the stars and from your nature."[40] The dizziness of which Rudolf had evidently already complained was just a foretaste of much worse trouble to come unless Rudolf would resolve to follow doctor's orders a bit more often. To be sure, the memorandum went on soothingly, Rudolf was right to suspect that he was the victim of witches: "Evil women are indeed guilty of causing Your Majesty's weakness." If they were just arrested "a little" and examined, the full truth would soon come out.[41] Here we find the same mood of nervous euphemism—the councilors suggested having "a little" witchcraft trial, for indeed he might be "somewhat" possessed and need "a little" therapy. The tone of this brief is evidence enough of just how jittery Rudolf's madness had made all his closest advisers.

The so-called Schottwien Treaty that emerged in late October 1600 from the consultation of Archdukes Matthias, Maximilian, and Ferdinand took up all these points again and urged Rudolf to "follow the advice of his learned doctors according to God's order." They worried that his wrath and fury might produce such a "paroxysm" (a seizure or stroke) that he could die. He should not cut himself off from the means ordained by God by which he could become strong again. But the "Treaty" went on, as the prior memoranda had not, to note that Rudolf should also deal with the "deep *Anfechtungen* of his mind" and with that despondency that made him tire of life itself. He needed help with his religious scruples and with his resistance to prayer, divine services, and specific clerics. "You yourself think that you are bewitched, which could be so," but his complaints could just as well come from the heavy burdens of office. And so it was important to provide Rudolf "along with [physical] medicine, the spiritual medicine of prayer, confession, communion, and the consolation of eminent theologians."[42] In shorthand fashion the archdukes referred to their remedy as a "spiritual and physical therapy" ("geist- und leibliche Cur") that corresponded well to the emerging consensus of doctors and theologians of the late sixteenth century.[43] During the Renaissance, very few doctors or priests were so fully persuaded of their own exclusive omnicompetence that they rejected other professional help. We remember that Duke Albrecht Friedrich's physicians had listed his spiritual problems and their spiritual, Lutheran remedies as well.

Even if Rudolf did not need exorcism, then, he required the comforts and spiritual aids of the church, and this all the more so since Rudolf was sometimes tempted to make common cause with the Protestants, "who are also reasonable people," as he had said in 1605. Pistorius in fact became so discouraged at Rudolf's rejection of papal policy and of certain Catholic priests that he concluded the emperor "thought no more of God." Perhaps he came to agree with Rudolf's own repeated conviction that he was doomed. Shortly before Easter of 1605 Rudolf stated, "I know for certain that I belong to the devil."[44] By 1606 Pistorius had given up hope of having any useful influence over Rudolf. Excluded from the emperor's presence, he too now joined the ranks of those who Rudolf thought had betrayed him.[45]

I have spent so much time on Rudolf's condition in 1600 because the surviving documents allow us to glimpse the ways that his physical and spiritual concerns could overlap and supplement each other. For a few months we do not seem completely captive to the normal diplomatic rumor mill. And by early 1601 Rudolf seemed to be better again. His fears, rages, and hallucinations quieted down (except when he had to confess, as in Holy Week); he took pleasure again in holy communion and stopped abusing his servants. He even reestablished harmonious relations with the Capuchins.[46]

But now we are again looking in through a haze of rumor and distanced report, and Rudolf took steps to make it ever harder to observe him. He appeared hardly at all in public and ordered his galleries and walkways covered over so that he could move about and go to church completely unobserved.[47] Delegates and ambassadors in Prague now had to wait months to see him, and those who did meet with him reported that Rudolf (at age fifty) seemed old and pale, depressed, introverted, and still afraid that he might be assassinated. (Tycho Brahe had persuasively predicted that the emperor would suffer the same fate as Henry III of France—that a monk would kill him). Once again the administration and court fell under the absolute control of servants such as Hieronymus Makovski and, gradually, Philipp Lang.[48] Rudolf was not uninformed about events, however, and continued to show a keen political intelligence, but outsiders continued to wonder if he was mad. He evidently took his meals alone in exactly the same room and at the same times, resisting any changes. Despite this desirable (or perhaps eccentric) regularity, he continued to refuse all medications, and suspicious observers could not determine even which religion he favored.[49] Given the buzzing rumors, it is not surprising to learn that speculation raged concerning just what the emperor's problem was.

Writing to the elector of the Palatinate in June 1601, Margrave Georg Friedrich of Brandenburg-Ansbach painted a picture of imperial catastrophe, of weakness at the center, and of the desperate condition of Protestants in Bohemia and in the empire generally. He attached two anonymous reports aimed at providing much more detail on Rudolf's mental and physical condition. From these reports it is evident that some observers blamed the "devilish" Makovski for bewitching Rudolf, for it was "well known" that he practiced the "devil's art."[50] Another informant held that the papal and Spanish party now regarded Rudolf as "crazy, possessed, and incompetent to rule" ("unsinnich, besessen und unduchtich zum regiment"). The reference to demonic possession was evidently meant in earnest, but the councilors could not follow up on this diagnosis, apparently because Rudolf himself remained so thoroughly uncooperative. Complaining again of the Capuchins he said, "How they torture me, these rogues." He couldn't stand priests or prayers now of any sort. The councilors generally concluded that "because His Majesty has for eight years tried to use the black arts to make a 'philosophic mirror' and because they [the councilors] were now trying to intervene too late, he was being driven by the Evil One as if by the furies."[51]

Not everyone accepted this demonic interpretation, of course. Others, including Margrave Georg Friedrich's Protestant informant in Prague, thought that Rudolf was suffering instead from a "most profound melancholy." He had seen the emperor in good moments able to discuss politics "without any disturbance of mind." The informant reminded Georg Friedrich that Rudolf was in his climacteric fiftieth year, the same year in which his father Maximilian had died, and argued that natural causes were at the root of the emperor's madness.[52] What with all the intrigues going on behind his back, aimed at securing a Catholic and Habsburg successor, and what with Rudolf's love of "Wissenschaft," it was no wonder that he had fallen into melancholy of a deep and dangerous sort.

One could go on and on retailing such rumors of the recluse in the Hradčany Castle, but for our purposes the psychiatric portrait would not change much. Rudolf oscillated between times of animated engagement with the problems of his day and a mannerist, philosophically and emotionally alienated retreat into what Evans has aptly described as a magic universe. This retreat was not in itself a mad seclusion, a senseless or irrational denial of worldly realities, and Evans has gone far toward retrieving the high moral and irenic intellectual ideals that inspired Kepler and Brahe, Arcimboldo and Spranger, and the alchemists, Platonists, Ramists, Cabalists, pansophists, neostoics, utopians, and occult mystics who flocked to Prague.[53] Retreat also served Rudolf well when he was cast down into despondent, morbid, or suicidal melancholy.

From at least 1600 onwards, though, the emperor was so often subject to attacks of uncontrollable rage, to paranoid introversion, and to fears that he had been bewitched that it is understandable his brothers tried to replace him as emperor. In the end he was kaiser in title only, for his roles as king of Hungary, Bohemia, and the other Habsburg hereditary lands had all shifted to his brother Matthias.[54] I do not think it helps our understanding of Rudolf to attach to him the label of schizophrenia, as some scholars have done. As we have seen, the sources are often so indirect, biased, and problematic as to render such a modern diagnosis suspect, if not impossible. But it seemed clear enough to his contemporaries that he was suffering from serious mental troubles, as well as cardiac problems, and that any therapy would have to be both physical and religious. Without any effective treatment for the periodically mad emperor, the Holy Roman Empire lurched toward the war of the Bohemian succession and the beginnings of the Thirty Years' War (1618–1648), Europe's first world war.

DON JULIUS CAESAR OF AUSTRIA

The emperor seems to have passed some of his troubles on to an illegitimate son, Don Julius Caesar, or Giulio Cesare (ca. 1585–1609), who was for a time the apple of his father's eye. Unfortunately, we know little about him or about his brothers and sisters. The papal nuncio Ferreri reported in September 1605 that Julius came to Prague, supposedly to see his father and to obtain the lordship of Krumau (or Kromau, Cromnau, Krumlov), but at first Rudolf merely spied on him walking about the castle garden.[55] Three weeks later Julius left Prague without ever speaking to his father.[56] Evidently by then relations between father and son were strained. In July of the next year Julius, whom Ferreri described as undisciplined and wild, seized a weapon and so seriously wounded one of his servants that Rudolf ordered him disarmed and interned in a castle for a time.[57] Up to this point Don Julius had displayed many of the character traits of his father, such as a grandiose illusion of himself as the imperial Caesar and, as Evans says, a "passion for the mechanical." He ran up numerous unpaid bills for clocks.[58] He merits mention in this study, however, because he also displayed, in exaggerated form, Rudolf's own madness.

As lord of the district of Krumau (fifteen miles southwest of Budweis and near the border of Lower Austria), Julius soon established himself as a lecherous tyrant. By December 1606 we find official protests over his wild advances against the maidens of the town.[59] Frightened servants began to flee his service.[60] His excessive expenditures also rapidly outran the allowance his father had granted him, but, by employing brutal threats, he continued to live a high life. During 1607 he took the daughter of a local barber-surgeon and bathhouse operator as his concubine, with whom he lived for some time. For reasons we can no longer reconstruct, he grew angry with her in early 1608—so enraged, in fact, that he attacked her with a sword or knife and threw her, bleeding, from his window. As with other Czech defenestrations, however, this fall was not fatal. She landed in the castle pond and managed to make her way back to her father's house, where she recovered her health. No sooner did Julius hear of this recovery than he ordered her returned to his castle, an order her father quite reasonably refused. For this offense Don Julius now threw the poor man in prison and commanded the town councilors to condemn him to death. After five weeks of this desperate situation, the wife and daughter of the barber-surgeon caved in to Julius's threats and presented themselves at the castle. The mother extracted an oath from Julius that he would do the daughter no harm, and on the Monday before Shrovetide the girl's father was released from his dungeon.

But that evening, as a servant was bringing candles to Julius's chambers, the tyrant received him in a towering rage, stabbing him twice in the hand and once in the chest, so that he barely escaped with his life.[61] Then Julius ordered the barber's daughter to don a fur-lined nightgown and lie down on the bed, whereupon he went berserk with mortal fury, stabbing her countless times and cutting off her ears, gouging out one eye, smashing out her teeth, and splitting her skull so violently that her brain was found hanging out. He flung pieces of her flesh all around the room. For three hours this butchery proceeded without interruption. Evidently the castle servants were too terrified to intervene. Recovering from his frenzy, he ordered her wrapped in linen and carried away.

By the next day he appeared somewhat repentant, visiting her corpse and fingering her wounds.[62] Now he had his victim laid out in a double coffin and personally nailed down the lid, and she was buried in a local cloister with great pomp. But Julius himself did not improve his own appearance for some time. For four days he wandered about, covered with gore, terrifying and nauseating his servants. One hostile witness claimed that not even the dogs would come near him.[63] Finally, after a month of unaccountable delay on Emperor Rudolf's part, a group of imperial commissioners arrived to arrest Don Julius and take him to prison. Appalled at his bestiality, the captain and the town council of Krumau refrained from calling Rudolf's wastrel son a madman and preferred legal and moral terms with which to condemn his wicked and corrupt will. But Julius showed clear signs of full-fledged madness in the prison to which he was confined for the remaining year of his life. He refused to change his clothes; he smashed his crockery, threw his silverware around the room, tore up his clothing, and continued to terrify his servants. With the warmer weather of the summer of 1608, Don Julius threw off all his clothes and went about naked in his room, speaking in turn nonsensically and then reasonably enough.

In the late fall of 1608 efforts began to be made to effect a cure of the crazy Don Julius. The former Hofmeister Georg Zagel (or Cagl, Czakhl) visited Julius, together with a doctor by the name of Mingonius and an apothecary. After six examinations this expert team recommended that Julius might obtain more help if he would confess his sins to a priest, a suggestion to which the emperor's son merely reacted with embittered rage.[64] During the first half of 1609 they tried the various cures that we have seen tried in other cases: they cut his hair and bathed him frequently in special herbal baths, trimmed his fingernails, and tried to make him look more presentable. Meanwhile, Julius insisted throughout that he was perfectly healthy and in no need of a doctor. When they tried to bleed him and give him medications, though, he resisted far more strenuously than he had with the baths, shouting out, "You sacrament-fools, leave me in peace!"[65] One day they found him collapsed on the floor with his eyes staring weirdly, but under care he recovered his former insolence. He especially hated the ministrations of the priests and confessors sent to console him. At one point his thighs and genitals became severely swollen, but this condition spontaneously improved before his doctors could decide what to do. Ethically, they felt torn between the options of forcing him to take the prescribed medications and of simply waiting for God to act "to bring him back to his former health and reason."[66] We can easily imagine which was the easier policy.

Among the lists of expenditures on Julius for lemons and Seville oranges, for sleeping caps, nightgowns, and stockings, there is one distinctly odd reference. One thaler and thirty-five kreuzers (the equivalent of a week's wages for a servant) were spent on a two-volume edition of the "Malleus Maleficionis." Surely this was the well-known *Malleus Maleficarum*, which we may surmise was purchased not to amuse Don Julius but on the suspicion that he, like his father, was bewitched and that perhaps some further steps toward locating the responsible witch needed to be taken.[67] Unfortunately, we have no evidence of exorcisms or witchcraft trials that might bear out this interpretation. On 25 June 1609 the unfortunate Don Julius died. He had obviously been very ill in body and mind and soul for well over a year.

CONCLUSION

Don Julius of Austria is the last example of a mad German Renaissance prince that I propose to treat at length. That is not at all to say, however, that the seventeenth century does not have a full supply of its own. In the Ernestine Saxon line, for example, Duke Johann (1573–1605) was melancholy in his last years, prompting at least one observer to worry about his "agitated, melancholy depression," which had grown so extreme in 1603 that he once invaded the women's bathhouse and, after staying there for some time, asked the peasant occupants which woman they thought was the prettiest. "His [mental] feebleness and heavy thoughts grow more dangerous with each passing hour . . . and they show no sign of improvement because he is getting no sleep, he talks endlessly, screams horribly, curses fiercely, and then rejoices but then falls into great fear, trembling, and horrors, imagining that he sees a 'black man' standing before him or fearing that he will fall into the water or elsewhere."[1] His son, Johann Friedrich VI of Saxony-Weimar (1600–1628), the brother of the great military leader Bernhard of Saxony-Weimar, was regarded as weak, undisciplined, and mad for almost all of his short life.[2] The Saxon court at Altenburg was also the home of Duchess Anna Maria, sister of Pfalzgraf Wolfgang Wilhelm of Neuburg and wife of Friedrich Wilhelm I (1573–1602). Widowed in 1602, she felt isolated and forlorn in her separate residence at Dornburg, especially because her sons were being reared at the court of Leipzig, and wrote frequently in 1613 to her brother complaining of her deep depressions and expressing the conviction that she had been bewitched by her steward's wife.[3] In November 1613 she felt physically attacked by Satan but was assured that her deep piety would protect her.[4]

The early seventeenth century also took its psychic toll on the princely house of Hesse, where Moritz the Learned (1572–1632) attempted to moderate between the orthodox Lutherans of Saxony and the Calvinists of the Palatinate. His peaceful efforts met the steadfast resistance of the Hessian territorial estates, and his relations with his sons were deeply troubled. His son Otto shot himself dead during a delirium induced by a feverish illness. His son Philipp died a hero's death at the Battle of Lutter in 1626, fighting on the side of Denmark. And Moritz found himself entangled in a bitter struggle with his son Wilhelm over who should govern Hesse. In 1627 Moritz gave up his landgraviate and devoted himself full time to "alchemy, metaphysical distillations, and to the unworldly poetry of Dante."[5] Broken by bad luck and by ingratitude, he lived out his remaining years in a state of bitterness that struck some observers as madness.

In the case of Duke Friedrich Ulrich of Braunschweig-Wolfenbüttel (1591–1634) we have the pathetic example of a prince whose every scheme, plan, and policy ended in failure. Childless, he watched helplessly as his wife engaged in a scandalous affair with Duke Julius Ernst of Saxony-Lauenburg. Contemporaries joked that even his divorce from her was a failure. By the end of his inadequate reign he was hopelessly dependent upon his four chief councilors and upon Anton von Streithorst. "One of the weakest and least assertive rulers of all times," he ruined the little territory he had been given to govern.[6] Although such massive incompetence does not necessarily imply outright insanity, to his poor subjects Duke Friedrich may well have seemed a mad prince. And the list of such stories could be almost indefinitely extended.

Obviously, the crises prompted by princely madness were far more threatening politically and dynastically when they concerned the "weakness" of a ruling prince or of his heir, which is why it is not too surprising that we have so much more information about men than women. It is striking, however, to notice how much more attention, both medical and spiritual, was devoted to the mentally disordered princes of the mid- to late sixteenth century in contrast to their cousins and ancestors from the earlier part of the century. As we have seen, the princes of Baden, Württemberg, Braunschweig, Brandenburg, and Hesse were summarily deposed and replaced in the years from 1490 to 1520, with little or no concern for their health or possible recovery. Brothers, sons, and

cousins often united to displace a ruling lunatic without waiting
for expert testimony or doctors' opinions. As we have seen, it is
questionable whether these princes were regarded as sick at all, for
the relevant documents do not use a medical vocabulary. If we did
not have independent testimony concerning the willful and im-
prudent actions of the prince, in fact, we might be led to suspect
that power-hungry relatives were merely using the excuse of madness to lock up an inconvenient father or cousin. Actually, I think
that in almost every case we can be sure that the supposedly mad
prince was indeed mentally or emotionally disabled. Moreover, by
the middle of the century the voice of doctors was becoming ever
more audible, and by the last decades of that century we often
enjoy access to extremely detailed dossiers of medical opinion.
Here we find little confirmation of our modern, cynical suspicions
that inconvenient monarchs were being shunted aside under the
politically convenient label of melancholia.

Indeed, the very willingness with which a prince's relatives
embraced all sorts of potential cures tends to argue against such an
interpretation. As we have seen, by the late decades of the sixteenth century and on into the seventeenth, an extremely varied
arsenal of therapies was deployed in efforts to secure the recovery
or at least to halt the decline of a failing prince or princess. First
and most prominent were the scholastic physicians, trained in the
thought of Aristotle, Hippocrates, and Galen. While we naturally
look for signs of Renaissance rebellion against medieval traditions, our records are rather full of the Renaissance revival of the
ancients that clearly included and even emphasized Aristotle. But
once the academically orthodox Galenic physicians had had their
opportunity to effect a cure, it became customary to turn to the
truly novel healers of the sixteenth century: Paracelsian physicians, alchemists, and folk healers. In desperation the court sometimes even had recourse to those women practitioners whom the
Galenic ducal physicians usually held in the deepest contempt as
ignorant and superstitious frauds. Usually, however, the Galenists
did not withdraw gracefully from the ideological field. From the
1570s onwards, the court records often allow us to reconstruct
bitter confrontations between rival therapies.

It is sometimes thought that the sixteenth-century Paracelsians prompted a massive paradigm shift away from Galenic medicine toward a more observational or more "scientific" medicine,

but it seems clear that at the German courts most court physicians remained staunchly Galenist in their assumptions and procedures. There were exceptions, notably at the court of Hesse-Kassel, but generally these doctors ridiculed Paracelsian therapists and warned of the fatal consequences that one might expect from the harsh and experimental chemical remedies favored by Paracelsian "adventurers." Such warnings did not deter princesses and princely councilors from employing Paracelsians; then as now, patients and their families wanted effective cures and were less concerned with doctrinal purity than were their learned court physicians. But the sixteenth century saw no real, theoretical shift of medical paradigms. What we can see rather more clearly is the way that Galenists themselves exploited the experimental and observational resources of the Aristotelian and Galenic traditions. The Galenic physician of 1600 was not only usually a better philologist than his counterpart in 1500, in fuller command of the nuances in the ancient Greek medical texts, but he was also likely to be more committed to a research program that sought causal interconnections between observed events and experimental verification (sometimes even falsification) of theories. But princes were understandably reluctant to become part of anyone's research project.

Among both Protestant and Catholic ruling houses it also became customary by the late sixteenth century to suspect that the devil was somehow implicated in any prince's stubborn insanity and to conclude that clerical intervention might be necessary. For Lutherans this usually meant that the court chaplains would undertake to preach daily or even more often to the afflicted prince, offering him God's consolation but also trying to provoke his repentance for a supposedly willful resistance to God's Word and obstruction of orthodox doctrine. They might also organize days of prayer in which the congregations of a whole territory might beseech God for a merciful act of healing. Since Lutherans rejected exorcism (except, among some, at baptism),[7] they generally held that Satan's direct assault could only be countered by massive communal bouts of prayer, hymn singing, and fasting. It is, however, noteworthy that Protestant princes often resented these clerical admonitions, especially the incessant preaching, just as much as they resisted any medical orders to follow a regular routine of eating, drinking, and sleeping. Catholic courts were generally quicker to suspect that the devil was involved in a prince's incapacity, perhaps because Catholics were taught that they had effective countermeasures at hand, and by the late sixteenth century we know of several Catholic princes who thought that they had been bewitched. Even so, a vehemently Catholic prince such as Duke Johann Wilhelm of Jülich-Cleves could deeply resent the exorcistic rituals and blessed objects employed in efforts to relieve his madness.

Not only insanity but especially marital infertility came to seem the special province of the devil, a point made forcefully by witchcraft theorists in the fifteenth century and frequently adopted among princely families by the 1580s and 1590s. In fact, the famous contention of the *Malleus Maleficarum*—that witches were often mainly concerned with interrupting the sex lives of married people—seems to have been more widely believed among the princes of late Renaissance Germany than among any other social stratum. For most people, harmful magic was thought to ruin the weather through frost or hail and thus to threaten the food supply or the local economy.[8] Occasionally, *maleficium* (harmful magic) was thought to cause diseases in cattle, the death of children, or nonfatal human ailments. Rarely did the average German witchcraft trial register complaints of impotence or infertility induced by the *maleficium* of the Evil One, but the world of princes was different. We have here a good litmus test of just how politically important hereditary succession in the male line was: late Renaissance German princes and their advisers, unlike ordinary people, had come to think of witchcraft or possession as the likely causes of marital failure.

The general of the Barnabite Order, Michael Murazanus (or Marrano), seems to have specialized in the disenchantment of noblemen and particularly of noble ladies, claiming, with what accuracy we cannot say, that he had successfully exorcised the cardinal of Lorraine, the bishop of Verdun (these two, we hope, not for impotence), as well as the duchess of Mantua along with Don Amadeo of Savoy.[9] We can surmise, however, that he was exaggerating when he claimed a similar success with Duchess Antoinette of Jülich during her visit to Nancy, for we know that her union with Duke Johann Wilhelm remained childless.[10] Murazanus was called in early in the second decade of the seventeenth century to exorcize Duchess Elisabeth Renate of Bavaria (1574–

1635, daughter of Duke Charles II of Lorraine), the childless and melancholy wife of Duke Maximilian I. Although Murazanus combined his spiritual remedies with a recommended series of therapeutic baths, his efforts again failed.[11] Here, as in the other cases we have considered, exorcism was indeed an option, but it was usually employed, if at all, only after physical and medical therapies had been exhausted and after expert medical opinion had come to agree that the prince's madness was due to more than natural causes.

Experts such as the imperial confessor Johann Pistorius, however, remained cautious about the claims made for exorcism, reserving in his mind the possible conclusion that any psychic disorder might be of natural origins after all: the result of bad breeding, bad environment, and bad habits. The highest church officials and theologians we have considered were not quick to claim omnicompetence for clerical remedies. Turf battles between physicians and theologians did break out in the late sixteenth century, as extremists on both sides claimed exclusive jurisdiction over illnesses of various sorts, but most medical and religious specialists recognized that they had much to gain from cooperation and much to lose if they staked out unrealistic claims to therapeutic supremacy.

Surely this system of cautious compromise and cooperation provides some of the necessary background for understanding the publication in 1614 of the Catholic *Rituale Romanum*, the Roman rituals for exorcism that were to be employed not when demonic influence was merely suspected or possible but only when all natural explanations for a strange disorder had failed.[12] Thus the *Rituale Romanum* claimed that exorcism for demonic possession could be used only if: (1) the supposed demonic spoke a foreign language he or she had never heard or learned; or (2) the suffering person displayed instant (supernatural) knowledge of what was going on far away; or (3) he or she exhibited superhuman (and therefore supernatural) strength in some way. Obviously, these criteria were and were intended to be hard to meet and did not depend in any way upon the conscious or subjective conviction of the disordered or apparently possessed person that he or she was bewitched or possessed by an alien force. Orthodox theologians came to recognize that such feelings of alienation and of loss of personal control and integrity could all have natural and humoral

explanations. Just as clearly the ducal physicians we have observed generally admitted that the princes under their care needed
a well-regulated spiritual life just as much as they needed bugloss,
borage, and a good night's sleep. Physicians and clerics generally
cooperated, too, in opposing the efforts of "ignorant" and "superstitious" village empirics as well as the offers by local faith healers. Thus, academically trained theologians and physicians could
use their Aristotelian categories not only to keep from getting
entangled in each other's hair but also to keep out the riffraff.

What explains the apparent rise of therapy as a response to
princely madness in the sixteenth century? Once upon a time,
historians would have claimed that physicians were more knowl-
edgeable or more humane in 1600 than a century earlier, but such
a claim would be almost impossible to substantiate. There was
no victory of empirical science over hidebound, dogmatic, doc-
trinaire, and hopelessly scholastic (Aristotelian) reactionaries.
The court physicians we have looked at managed to be a remarkably flexible, pragmatic, and humane group, even though they
remained devoted to Aristotle, Hippocrates, and Galen. Instead, it
may make more sense to suggest that the sixteenth century saw a
general rise in the status of ducal or princely physicians. If such a
rise in status could be demonstrated, as I think it could, it might
help to explain why their point of view was more prominent by the
mid- to late sixteenth century than before. Generally speaking,
the early modern German state was coming to rely on academic
learning as a guarantor of proper procedures and of legitimacy, and
doctors shared in this development.

It may also be that with the rise and proliferation of academic
Galenism not only among academically trained doctors but also
among the educated laity, such as those addressed by Timothy
Bright and Robert Burton in England or by André du Laurens and
Jacques Ferrand in France, the popular preconditions were established for a greater sense of therapeutic optimism about madness
and melancholy. Perhaps princes became the objects of a more
intensive therapy partly because their relatives came to conclude
that their lamentable conditions were no longer irremediable. We
could also speculate that the mad princes of the late sixteenth
century received more care from their doctors and priests simply
because their councilors and relatives were more desperate to
avoid a dynastic crisis or collapse than had been the case fifty or a
hundred years earlier.

I have suggested, too, that certain princes, such as Wilhelm the Younger of Braunschweig-Lüneburg or Albrecht Friedrich of Prussia, came to be treated with so much respect that we can perhaps feel the effect of a doctrine like that of the "king's two bodies," in which an increasing reverence for the state led to an increased awe for the prince's person. If the body politic was incorruptible and immortal, there were jurists who held that the prince, as head of the body politic, must participate in that perfection. This could help us to understand why the mentally disordered prince came to be handled so gingerly. It is also true that the prince of the late sixteenth century was more of a bureaucrat and state symbol than a warrior. It was no longer so crucial that the prince be able to lead his troops in the field, and so, in one sense, the court could better afford an inept ruler even as the early modern state increasingly needed a pompous symbol of its authority and might.

One thing that apparently remained constant, however, was the desperation felt by those close to a prince if he could no longer behave responsibly. No matter what one did, and no matter that the addled monarch was no longer needed in the army camps, his mental incompetence posed a threat to the legitimacy of the state and its apparatus. But instead of taking charge with the kind of brutal coups d'état and depositions that punctuated the early decades, councilors came to vacillate in the face of obvious lunacy, unable to decide, for example, how to disarm and confine a dangerous prince, lost as they were in a maze of novel claims to princely sovereignty and entangled in a web of court intrigue, in which the prince's wife often formed a political focal point of opposition to the official councilors. Under these conditions it could take cautious relatives decades to decide what to do about a ruler such as Emperor Rudolf II, who was not acting in the perceived interests of his dynasty. Perhaps some combination of these factors led to the increase in therapy for mad monarchs by 1550 or 1600, but the observed fact itself seems inescapable: by the end of the century, princes were more often complaining of too much medical and spiritual attention than of too little.

We can also hazard a few generalizations about the madnesses regarded as incapacitating in the sixteenth century. We have seen that simple retardation, as was likely in the case of Duke Albrecht Friedrich of Prussia, was not considered unmanageable unless it was combined with emotional and mental disorder. It was his delusions and rages that brought on the crises of his reign, both shortly before his marriage to Marie Eleanore of Jülich and for years thereafter. In fact, and somewhat surprisingly, raging and furious outbursts constitute the most common feature of melancholic disorders during the late sixteenth century. Not fiscal irresponsibility, as in the early sixteenth century, but abuse, wounding, and towering furies against servants and noble advisers now became standard features of the medical dossier. We need to recognize that a large part of the spectrum of the term *melancholy* referred not to depression (or to wisdom, genius, or whimsy) but to raging insanity. The rise of melancholy, however, did mean that we now find far more frequent references to the sad, morose, despairing, and especially tearful prince than we have detected in the earlier part of our period. It is, of course, hard to say whether princes really were more desperate and lachrymose than before, or if their observers were now simply more able to see their depressions and their breakdowns into uncontrollable weeping as understandable components of melancholy madness. The rising discourse of melancholy may have made certain kinds of madness more comprehensible, more expectable, and therefore more prominent than earlier.

It could also be that princes really did feel under more pressure to conform to manly standards of self-control and religious orthodoxy and really did fear more for the salvation of their souls after about 1550, both because of the rise of a stricter Spanish-style courtly austerity and because of the new demands for spiritual orthodoxy made by clerics and councilors of the Reformation and Counter-Reformation state. This is a topic that would reward further study.

Thus the pressures on young princes may have actually intensified after about 1550. Perhaps there were good reasons for more princes to break down in the second half of the sixteenth century than earlier, but let us remember that these are essentially statistical judgments for which we have no appropriate statistical data. We do not know that there really were more mad princes by 1580 or 1600; we only know that the cases we have studied were more prominent, more talked about, and better documented than the instances of mental illness or insanity from fifty to a hundred years earlier. The question of reality is a tangled one, as any reader knows, and it might just as well be the case that the rise of therapy for the deranged and incompetent princes of the Holy Roman

Empire was more the product of therapeutic relabeling and the general rise in awareness that led to an increased attention to court diseases, *morbi aulici,* in general.

Indeed, as Werner Friedrich Kümmel has shown, a whole genre of medical and semimedical literature arose in the sixteenth and seventeenth centuries to cope with the perceived threats of a demoralizing atmosphere at court.[13] Certainly court doctors and preachers became convinced that they needed to take firm measures to curb the excessive eating, drinking, and general libertinism at court, those marks of courtly and aristocratic license (and licentiousness) that collided head-on with other advice, given especially to young princes, to the effect that they must strictly control themselves and maintain an emotional reserve. It could even be, therefore, that what Norbert Elias called the "civilizing" demands of the early modern court, the rise of a stricter code of manners that repressed the body and the dissemination of a new set of courtly embarrassments, helped create the psychologically immobilizing conditions of a princely melancholia that found expression in pathological indecision, weeping, and self-contempt but also in excessive pride, and in the double bind of desire for public display together with yearnings for retreat from courtly spectacle.[14] Shakespeare's somber, agonized, and melancholy Prince of Denmark was a recognizable figure by 1600 at many a German Renaissance court.

We have also encountered a world of madness that seems rather different from the sorts of discourse outlined and examined by Michel Foucault in his *Madness and Civilization.* The German princes who lost their wits suffered a confinement as bitter and at times as dehumanizing as the mad of eighteenth-century England or France—except, of course, that they were not put on vulgar display and were not lumped together with derelicts, vagabonds, and the poor. And by 1540, or by 1560 at the latest, court physicians were making strenuous efforts to cure them of their insanity or at least to alleviate their symptoms. As we have noted, when orthodox Galenic methods failed, it became common to turn to unorthodox healers, Paracelsians, barber-surgeons, cunning women, folk healers, and (at least in Catholic parts of the empire) exorcists. We could say that each of these presupposes its own underlying perception, its own discourse, but, considering the state of our sources, it is difficult to reconstruct the discourse of the illiterate. When these differing perceptions clashed at court, the records do sometimes contain the exasperated remonstrances of the court physicians, challenged but far from defeated. At other times, though, physicians concluded that their patients must actually be bewitched or possessed by demons, for that was one way to explain their own therapeutic failures. As we have seen, the exorcists, too, were often equally ready to concede that a prince was not enchanted or possessed but was suffering from a purely natural condition or ailment.

Our records are too sparse to provide answers to the important question of gender, but it is probably significant that Princess Anna of Saxony was not given the benefit of a medical diagnosis. Her behavior was regarded (at least by the men who wrote and controlled the records) as unpardonably outrageous, unfaithful, and immoral, and her confinement was intended as punitive rather than therapeutic. To the very end, her doctors were arguing about whether she was basically sinful or sick. It was not a debate that erupted, at least not so explicitly and tenaciously, in the case of any prince we have examined. The question can thus properly be posed whether women were more often subjected to the gaze of moral judgment whereas men were more likely to come under the medical gaze, the *perception medicale.* Unfortunately, with so few mad princesses and so many mad princes, it would be hazardous to speak with certainty here of the gendering of madness or of melancholy.

In one regard, however, this study confirms Foucault's observation of the sheer complexity of social responses to madness. Without sharing Foucault's particular taste for allegory, I too have tried to call attention to certain situations, especially in the early sixteenth century, in which the madman was not spoken of or treated as sick. Should we regard this as an adumbration of the perspective of the eighteenth-century asylum? Or would it be better to recognize that certain institutional settings are more conducive to medical discourse while others encourage moral discourse? However we choose to answer such questions, we can conclude that the rise of melancholy was one of the fundamental transformations of discourse as well as of practice in the Renaissance. With the new medical and philosophical theories about black bile and about the way in which improper habits could cause the burning or roasting of the normal humors and thus the production of an unnatural melancholy, Renaissance men and women had a powerful new set of metaphors with which to experience and describe what was wrong with their world.[15]

In the end, of course, this book has dealt with the world of princes, with the curiously privileged and precarious society in which they lived. Let us by no means forget that their lives were not the same as those of their subjects, even if they did pull on their baggy brocade trunk hose one leg at a time. Like the wealthy in all times, they were permitted to act out more of their whims and obsessions than were ordinary folk; but if they turned dangerously irresponsible, their relatives and counselors may have been even quicker to confine them than were the village relatives of Mad Tom O'Bedlam. As mad princes, moreover, they could repeatedly threaten the peace and stability of whole kingdoms. It is striking how often princely madness triggered a constitutional or successional crisis within the Holy Roman Empire, but perhaps just as striking that not one of these territorial incidents led to war. Few territories managed their succession crises as serenely as the principality of Mecklenburg in the mid-sixteenth century, and the continued intervention and regulation by the emperors, even by unhappy Rudolf II, went far to temper the turbulent humors of the imperial body politic. When the emperor himself went mad, however, there was no easy solution. The succession crisis brought on by Rudolf II's refusal to marry, and by his melancholy retreat from so many of the major problems of the empire, finally pushed the Bohemians and indeed the whole empire over the edge and into catastrophe.

APPENDIX
NOTES
INDEX

Appendix:
The Seductions of Genealogy

When examining a genealogical table representing the distribution of mental disorder among the ruling houses of the Holy Roman Empire (such as table 1 above), the casual observer can be sorely tempted to conclude that madness was inherited from a few original progenitors. Such genealogies seem to compel the eye and the mind to see linkages, which are in fact only apparent. By this means, a historian might explain the misfortunes of later generations by pointing to the archetypal disorders of earlier generations. In his popular Tübingen lecture course, for example, Professor Hans-Martin Decker-Hauff was fond of pointing to the troubles that beset the ruling house of Württemberg during the nineteenth century; he used to explain them by referring to what he saw as the defective genetic load they had all inherited from Count Heinrich of Württemberg (d. 1519), who, as we have seen, was imprisoned because of his madness. Living under arrest with his wife, he fathered the future Duke Ulrich and thus became the ancestor of the whole surviving house of Württemberg. Unfortunately, the case is not so easily proved. By a judicious choice of selected examples, genealogical tables can seem to prove almost anything the historian might want to claim.

A careless reading of the table that follows could draw the inference that the house of Braunschweig was unusually subject to madness *because of* the lines of inheritance that the genealogical table highlights. The flaw in this sort of reasoning is easy to see once one recognizes the fundamental fact that the German nobles were all interrelated. Any noble feature or characteristic, therefore, whether madness or genius, honesty or tyranny, could be

APPENDIX TABLE. Madness in and around the House of Braunschweig

Princes and Princesses Known as Mad Are in Italics

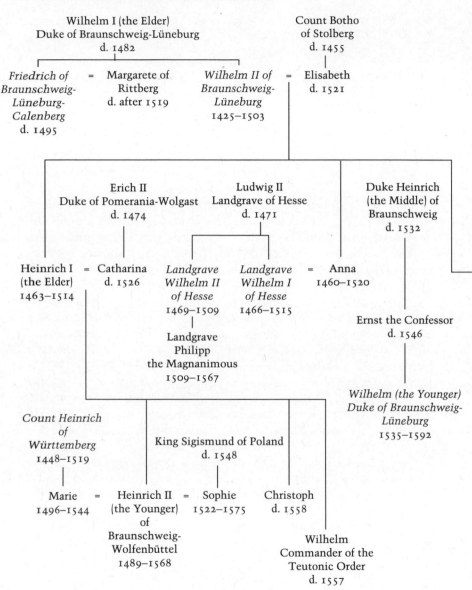

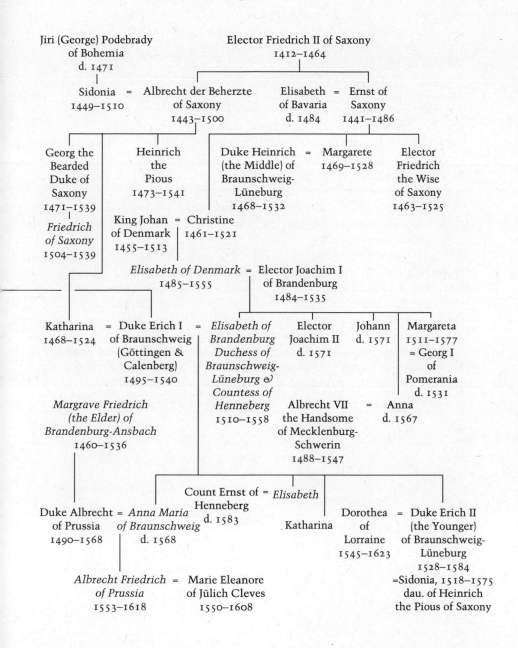

Jiri (George) Podebrady
of Bohemia
d. 1471

Sidonia = Albrecht der Beherzte
1449–1510   of Saxony
1443–1500

Elector Friedrich II of Saxony
1412–1464

Elisabeth = Ernst of
of Bavaria   Saxony
d. 1484   1441–1486

Georg the   Heinrich   Duke Heinrich = Margarete   Elector
Bearded   the   (the Middle) of 1469–1528   Friedrich
Duke of   Pious   Braunschweig-   the Wise
Saxony   1473–1541   Lüneburg   of Saxony
1471–1539   1468–1532   1463–1525
Friedrich   King Johan = Christine
of Saxony   of Denmark   1461–1521
1504–1539   1455–1513

Elisabeth of Denmark = Elector Joachim I
1485–1555   of Brandenburg
                       1484–1535

Katharina = Duke Erich I = Elisabeth of   Elector   Johann   Margareta
1468–1524   of Braunschweig   Brandenburg   Joachim II   d. 1571   1511–1577
            (Göttingen &   Duchess of   d. 1571   = Georg I
            Calenberg)   Braunschweig-   of
            1495–1540   Lüneburg &   Pomerania
                              Countess of   d. 1531
Margrave Friedrich   Henneberg   Albrecht VII = Anna
(the Elder) of   1510–1558   the Handsome   d. 1567
Brandenburg-Ansbach   of Mecklenburg-
1460–1536   Schwerin
                                              1488–1547

                     Count Ernst of = Elisabeth
                     Henneberg
Duke Albrecht = Anna Maria d. 1583   Dorothea = Duke Erich II
of Prussia   of Braunschweig   Katharina   of   (the Younger)
1490–1568   d. 1568   Lorraine   of Braunschweig-
                                             1545–1623 Lüneburg
                                                        1528–1584
        Albrecht Friedrich = Marie Eleanore   =Sidonia, 1518–1575
        of Prussia   of Jülich Cleves   dau. of Heinrich
        1553–1618   1550–1608   the Pious of Saxony

displayed on a genealogical table that might give the thoroughly misleading impression that they shared these qualities because of their fortunate or unfortunate inheritance.

Of course, if we could compare large numbers of complete family trees from ordinary families with those of presumably inbred princely families, we might be able to draw some inferences about the predominance of madness in one group or another. But as I have explained earlier, we do not have anything like adequate information about the incidence of mental disorder among the common people, and so such comparisons are as impossible for the sixteenth century as they would be problematic even in our own day. Many deviant mental qualities may in fact have had a genetic component, of course, but my only point is that we cannot prove such connections simply from the reconstruction of family trees. And proving these hereditary links is so difficult that we will rarely have the necessary data from an age as far removed as the sixteenth century.

These tables, however, do have their appropriate uses. From them we can observe the sets of family relationships that tied nobles and princes together and that structured their experiences. We can also see why it was that particular princes became so deeply involved in the care and custody of specific relatives and why a given illness or reproductive failure could be so threatening to a whole princely house. With these cautions in mind, I hope that readers can use this table and table 1 to situate many of my protagonists without leaping to unjustified conclusions.

NOTES

ABBREVIATIONS OF ARCHIVES

BHStAM	Bayerisches Hauptstaatsarchiv München
GLAK	Generallandesarchiv Karlsruhe
GStAPK	Geheimes Staatsarchiv Preußischer Kulturbesitz, Berlin-Dahlem
HStAD	Hauptstaatsarchiv Düsseldorf
HStAH	Hauptstaatsarchiv Hannover
HStAM	Hauptstaatsarchiv Marburg
HStAS	Hauptstaatsarchiv Stuttgart
StAB	Staatsarchiv Bamberg

INTRODUCTION

1. Lawrence Stone, "The Revival of Narrative: Reflections on a New Old History," in his *The Past and the Present* (Boston, 1981), 74–96. Because even the strictest proponents of quantitative history and of structural social analysis tell a kind of story (a "narrative"), Stone is perhaps really describing the revival of confidence in exemplary detail and anecdote rather than in stories as such.

2. For a brief history of the genre and its problems, see Edward Muir, "Introduction: Observing Trifles," in Edward Muir and Guido Ruggiero, eds., *Microhistory and the Lost Peoples of Europe* (Baltimore, 1991), vii–xxviii.

3. See, for example, Roy Porter, *A Social History of Madness: The World through the Eyes of the Insane* (London, 1987); Lilian Feder, *Madness in Literature* (Princeton, 1980); Andrew Scull, *Museums of Madness* (London, 1979); Thomas S. Szasz, *The Manufacture of Madness* (New York, 1970); and D. A. Peterson, ed., *A Mad People's History of Madness* (Pittsburgh, 1982).

4. For an introduction, see Erwin Ackerknecht, *A Short History of*

Psychiatry, 2d ed., trans. Sula Wolff (New York, 1968); George Rosen, *Madness in Society: Chapters in the Historical Sociology of Mental Illness* (New York, 1969); George Mora, "The History of Psychiatry: A Cultural and Bibliographic Survey," *International Journal of Psychiatry* 2 (1966): 335–55 (with 188 bibliographical footnotes); Raymond Klibansky, Erwin Panofsky, and Fritz Saxl, *Saturn and Melancholy: Studies in the History of Natural Philosophy, Religion and Art* (London, 1964); H. H. Beek, *Waanzin in de Middeleuwen: Beeld van de gestoorde en bemoeienis met de zieke* (Nijkerk, 1969); Werner Leibbrand and Annemarie Wettley, *Der Wahnsinn: Geschichte der abendländischen Psychopathologie* (Freiburg i. Br., 1961); and Esther Fischer-Homberger, *Hypochondrie: Melancholie bis Neurose: Krankheiten und Zustandsbilder* (Bern, 1970).

5. On madness and religion, see Penelope B. R. Doob, *Nebuchadnezzar's Children: Conventions of Madness in Middle English Literature* (New Haven, 1974); Judith Neaman, *Suggestion of the Devil: The Origins of Madness* (Garden City, N.Y., 1975); Michael MacDonald, *Mystical Bedlam: Madness, Anxiety and Healing in Seventeenth-Century England* (Cambridge, Eng., 1981); Michael MacDonald and Terence R. Murphy, *Sleepless Souls: Suicide in Early Modern England* (Oxford, 1990); D. P. Walker, *Unclean Spirits: Possession and Exorcism in France and England in the Late Sixteenth and Early Seventeenth Centuries* (Philadelphia, 1981); and H. C. Erik Midelfort, "The Devil and the German People: Reflections on the Popularity of Demon Possession in Sixteenth-Century Germany," in Steven Ozment, ed., *Religion and Culture in the Renaissance and Reformation* (Kirksville, Mo., 1989), 99–119.

6. Unfortunately, the full version has never appeared in English, and as a result the scholarly reception of Foucault in English-speaking countries has sometimes degenerated into a question of whether readers, no matter how careful, have really understood Foucault's larger intentions, a task that seems already difficult enough for those who are at least commenting on the full French text of 1961. See, for example, H. C. Erik Midelfort, "Madness and Civilization in Early Modern Europe: A Reappraisal of Michel Foucault," in Barbara C. Malament, ed., *After the Reformation: Essays in Honor of J. H. Hexter* (Philadelphia, 1980), 247–65; and Lawrence Stone, "Madness," *New York Review of Books,* 16 Dec. 1982, as well as his exchange of letters with Foucault, *New York Review of Books,* 31 March 1983.

7. The discussion of "experience" has become uncommonly tangled. See Jacques Derrida, "Cogito and History of Madness," in his *Writing and Difference,* trans. Alan Bass (Chicago, 1978), 31–63, 307–10; Allan Megill, *Prophets of Extremity: Nietzsche, Heidegger, Foucault, Derrida* (Berkeley, 1985), 191, 200–205, 221–25; Colin Gordon, "*Histoire de la folie:* An Unknown Book by Michel Foucault," in Arthur Still and Irving Velody, eds., *Rewriting the History of Madness: Studies in Foucault's Histoire de la folie* (London, 1992), 19–42, esp. 35–38.

8. Michel Foucault, *Histoire de la folie à l'âge classique* (Paris, 1972), chap. 2 ("Le grand renfermement") and chap. 3 ("Le monde correctionnaire"); for "cités d'exil," see p. 95.

9. For a clear discussion of discourse, see Hayden V. White, *Tropics of Discourse: Essays in Cultural Criticism* (Baltimore, 1978), 1–25, 235–38; for a discussion specifically of Foucault's discourse, see Hayden V. White, *The Content of the Form* (Baltimore, 1987), 104–41.

10. See, for example, Robert Castel, *L'ordre psychiatrique: L'âge d'or d'aliénisme* (Paris, 1976), published in English as *The Regulation of Madness: The Origins of Incarceration in France*, trans. W. D. Halls (Berkeley, 1988); and Françoise Castel, Robert Castel, and Anne Lovell, *The Psychiatric Society*, trans. Arthur Goldhammer (New York, 1982).

11. Roy Porter, *Mind Forg'd Manacles: A History of Madness from the Restoration to the Regency* (London, 1987). See also Roy Porter, "Foucault's Great Confinement," in Still and Velody, eds., *Rewriting the History of Madness*, 119–25.

12. MacDonald, *Mystical Bedlam*, xi–xii.

13. See Martin Schrenk, *Über den Umgang mit Geisteskranken: Die Entwicklung der psychiatrischen. Therapie vom "moralischen Regime" in England und Frankreich zu den "psychischen Curmethoden" in Deutschland* (Berlin, 1973); Klaus Dörner, *Madmen and the Bourgeoisie: A Social History of Insanity and Psychiatry* (London, 1981); and Wolf Lepenies, *Melancholy and Society*, trans. Jeremy Gaines and Doris Jones (Cambridge, Mass., 1992).

14. Thus, for example, Allan Megill, "Foucault, Structuralism, and the Ends of History," *Journal of Modern History* 51 (1979): 451–502; and "The Reception of Foucault by Historians," *Journal of the History of Ideas* 48 (1987): 117–41.

15. For further discussion, see Feder, *Madness in Literature*; Porter, *A Social History of Madness*; and Peterson, ed., *A Mad People's History of Madness*. Two excellent accounts that have illuminated the medical and mental histories of monarchs from the late eighteenth century are Richard Hunter and Ida Macalpine, *King George and the Mad Business* (London, 1969); and Hugh Ragsdale, *Tsar Paul and the Question of Madness: An Essay in History and Psychology* (New York, 1988). It would be useful to have studies of their mad contemporaries, Queen Maria I of Portugal, King Christian VII of Denmark, and King Fernando VI of Spain.

16. Doob, *Nebuchadnezzar's Children*; Neaman, *Suggestion of the Devil*; Mark Hansen, *The Royal Facts of Life: Biology and Politics in Sixteenth-Century Europe* (Metuchen, N.J., 1980); and Basil Clarke, *Mental Disorder in Earlier Britain: Exploratory Studies* (Cardiff, Wales, 1975) all go some way toward providing a few case studies from the fourteenth and fifteenth centuries, especially of kings Henry VI of England and Charles VI of France, or, in the case of Hansen's book, for the royal houses of sixteenth-century England, France, Spain, and Austria.

17. For a brief introduction to the constitution of the German nations in the early modern period, see John Gagliardo, *Germany under the Old Regime: 1600–1790* (London, 1991). See also Bernard Guenée, *States and Rulers in Later Medieval Europe* (Oxford, 1985); and Bernd Moeller, *Deutschland im Zeitalter der Reformation* (Göttingen, 1977).

18. Gerhard Oestreich, *Verfassungsgeschichte vom Ende des Mittelalters bis zum Ende des Alten Reiches,* vol. 11 of the paperback ed. of Bruno Gebhard's *Handbuch der deutschen Geschichte,* 9th ed., ed. Herbert Grundmann (Stuttgart, 1970), 137–51; cf. the impressive list of signatories to the 1555 diet of Augsburg in Arno Buschmann, ed., *Kaiser und Reich: Klassische Texte und Dokumente zur Verfassungsgeschichte des Hl. Römischen Reiches Deutscher Nation* (Munich, 1984), 275–82.

19. On classical medicine, see Owsei Temkin, *Galenism: The Rise and Decline of a Medical Philosophy* (Ithaca, N.Y., 1973); Per-Gunnar Ottosson, *Scholastic Medicine and Philosophy: A Study of Commentaries on Galen's* Tegni *(ca. 1300–1450)* (Naples, 1984); Nancy Siraisi, *Medieval and Early Renaissance Medicine: An Introduction to Knowledge and Practice* (Chicago, 1990); Lawrence Babb, *The Elizabethan Malady* (East Lansing, Mich., 1951); Ruth Harvey, *The Inward Wits: Psychological Theory in the Middle Ages and the Renaissance* (London, 1975); Klibansky, Panofsky, and Saxl, *Saturn and Melancholy;* and E. Patricia Vicari, *The View from Minerva's Tower: Learning and Imagination in* The Anatomy of Melancholy (Toronto, 1989).

20. See Andrew Cunningham, "Fabricius and the 'Aristotle Project' in Anatomical Teaching and Research at Padua," in A. Wear, R. K. French, and I. M. Lonie, eds., *The Medical Renaissance of the Sixteenth Century* (Cambridge, Eng., 1985), 195–222; Charles B. Schmitt, *Aristotle and the Renaissance* (Cambridge, Mass., 1983); and Allen G. Debus, *Man and Nature in the Renaissance* (Cambridge, Eng., 1978), 2–8.

21. See J. B. deC. M. Saunders and Charles D. O'Malley, eds., *The Anatomical Drawings of Andreas Vesalius: With Annotations and Translations, a Discussion of the Plates and Their Background, Authorship, and Influence, and a Biographical Sketch of Vesalius* (New York, 1982), 17–19. Most Galenists saw Vesalius as being "on their side": M. F. Ashley Montague, "Vesalius and the Galenists," in E. Ashworth Underwood, ed., *Science, Medicine, and History: Essays . . . in Honour of Charles Singer,* 2 vols. (London, 1953), 1:374–85.

22. This was the celebrated starting point of the pseudo-Aristotelian *Problem* XXX.1, which generated a huge literature. See Klibansky, Panofsky, and Saxl, *Saturn and Melancholy,* 15–42.

23. See Oskar Diethelm, *Medical Dissertations of Psychiatric Interest Printed before 1750* (Basel, 1971); see more generally Ewald Horn, *Die Disputationen und Promotionen an den Deutschen Universitäten vornehmlich seit dem 16. Jahrhundert* (Leipzig, 1893).

24. On Paracelsian theory, see Walter Pagel, *Paracelsus: An Introduction to Philosophical Medicine in the Era of the Renaissance* (Basel, 1958); Allen G. Debus, *The Chemical Philosophy: Paracelsian Science and Medicine in the Sixteenth and Seventeenth Centuries*, 2 vols. (New York, 1977); Ernst Wilhelm Kämmerer, *Das Leib-Seele-Geist Problem bei Paracelsus und einigen Autoren des 17. Jahrhunderts* (Wiesbaden, 1971); and H. C. Erik Midelfort, "The Anthropological Roots of Paracelsus' Psychiatry," *Medizinhistorisches Journal* 16 (1981): 67–77.

25. See Walter Pagel, *Jan Baptista van Helmont: Reformer of Science and Medicine* (Cambridge, Eng., 1982).

26. Johannes Albertus Wimpenaeus, *De concordia Hippocraticorum et Paracelsistarum* (Munich, 1569).

27. See Allen G. Debus, *The French Paracelsians: The Chemical Challenge to Medical and Scientific Tradition in Early Modern France* (Cambridge, Eng., 1991).

28. See especially Bruce T. Moran, *The Alchemical World of the German Court: Occult Philosophy and Chemical Medicine in the Circle of Moritz of Hessen (1572–1632)* (Suttgart, 1991).

29. This allegation is an example of Foucault's penchant for confident oversimplifications that scarcely accord with his own evidence. Foucault seems to have meant that the peculiar creation of the classical age was the *perception asilaire*, in which the mad were regarded not as sick but as dangerous and therefore confinable. He viewed the continued existence of medical models of madness among physicians and medical care for the mad in hospitals as survivals from the Middle Ages and not, therefore, representative of the classical age itself (*Histoire de la folie*, 124–39). Given this radically symbolic interpretation of classicism, Foucault could go on to assert: "Madness in its ultimate forms is, for classicism, man in immediate relation to his animality. . . . There would come a day when this presence of animality in madness would be considered, from an evolutionary perspective, as the sign (or even as the very essence) of sickness. By way of contrast, in the classical age the fact is remarkably clear that *the madman is not sick*. His animality, in effect, protects the madman from all that could render man fragile, precarious, sick" (ibid., 166; Foucault's emphasis; my translation; cf. *Madness and Civilization*, 68–69). For a fascinating study of an early exploitation of the idea of the "animality of madness," see Joseph Scalzo, "Campanella, Foucault, and Madness in Late-Sixteenth-Century Italy," *Sixteenth Century Journal* 21 (1990): 359–71.

30. See Rainer Christoph Schwinges, *Deutsche Universitätsbesucher im 14. und 15. Jahrhundert: Studien zur Sozialgeschichte des alten Reiches* (Stuttgart, 1986), 467–68. At Cologne and Louvain between 1445 and 1495 only ten students in all matriculated in medicine out of a total of 3619 students. See also E. T. Nauck, "Die Zahl der Medizinstu-

denten deutscher Hochschulen im 14.–18. Jahrhundert," *Sudhoffs Archiv für Geschichte der Medizin* 38 (1954): 175–86.

31. This general topic is now best approached through Vivian Nutton, ed., *Medicine at the Courts of Europe, 1500–1837* (London, 1990). For the health care of German villagers, see Sabine Sander, *Handwerkschirurgen: Sozialgeschichte einer verdrängten Berufsgruppe* (Göttingen, 1989).

32. See Ernst Kantorowicz, *The King's Two Bodies: A Study in Mediaeval Political Theology* (Princeton, 1957), 9, and, more generally, 7–41. Thomas Brady and Edward Ayers have stimulated my thinking along these lines.

33. See the similar conclusion (based on French evidence) of Natalie Z. Davis, *Fiction in the Archives: Pardon Tales and Their Tellers in Sixteenth-Century France* (Stanford, 1987). This tentative conclusion, however, stands in contrast to the careful work of Magdelena Sanchez on the early-seventeenth-century court of Spain, in which she finds a strongly gendered discourse on melancholy: "Melancholy, Illness, and Age: Female Images and Politics in Philip III's Spain" (unpublished paper). See also Juliana Schiesari, "The Gendering of Melancholia: Torquato Tasso and Isabella di Morra," in Marilyn Migiel and Juliana Schiesari, eds., *Refiguring Woman: Perspectives on Gender and the Italian Renaissance* (Ithaca, N.Y., 1991), 233–62; and *The Gendering of Melancholia: Feminism, Psychoanalysis, and the Symbolics of Loss in Renaissance Literature* (Ithaca, N.Y., 1992). Schiesari is mainly concerned with the patriarchally dictated absence of melancholy genius as a topos applied to women and not with melancholia as a debilitating madness. Sander Gilman has noted that in the Middle Ages and Renaissance visual representations of melancholy and madness used both female and male images: *Seeing the Insane* (New York, 1982), 8–15.

34. MacDonald, *Mystical Bedlam*, 152, 153.

35. See, for example, Angelo S. Rapport, *Mad Majesties: Or, Raving Rulers and Submissive Subjects* (New York, 1910); P. J. Kowalewskij, *Wahnsinnige als Herrscher und Führer der Völker: Psychiatrische Studien aus der Geschichte*, trans. from the 6th Russian ed. by Wilhelm Henckel, pt. 1 (Munich, 1910); Auguste Brachet, *Pathologie mentale des rois de France: Louis XI et ses ascendants . . . 852–1483* (Paris, 1903); Victor Galippe, *L'heredité des stigmates de dégénérescence et les familles souveraines* (Paris, 1905); and Georg Buschau, "Entartungserscheinungen an regierenden Häusern," in *Die Umschau*, vol. 10, no. 13 (24 March 1906).

36. Walter Grube, *Der Stuttgarter Landtag, 1457–1957: Von den Landständen zum demokratischen Parlament* (Stuttgart, 1957), 43–66.

37. See the article on Fortunatus in *Allgemeine Deutsche Biographie* 5:648–49.

38. Sigmund von Riezler, *Geschichte Baierns* (Gotha, 1899), 4:672–80; *Allgemeine Deutsche Biographie* 42:717–23.

39. In fact, Duke Wilhelm himself was so concerned about his pious and "melancholy" son, Maximilian, that he urged Maximilian to change his diet and follow his doctor's orders: Kurt Pfister, *Kurfürst Maximilian von Bayern und sein Jahrhundert* (Munich, 1948), 87–88.

40. See Benno Hubensteiner, *Vom Geist des Barock: Kultur and Frömmigkeit im alten Bayern*, 2d ed. (Munich, 1978), 110–12; Helmut Dotterweich, *Der junge Maximilian: Jugend und Erziehung des bayerischen Herzogs und späteren Kurfürsten Maximilian I. von 1573 bis 1593* (Munich, 1980); and Sigmund Riezler, *Geschichte Baierns*, 9 vols. (Gotha, 1899), 4:673–80.

41. Walter Goetz, "Ladislaus von Fraunberg, der letzte Graf von Haag," *Oberbayerisches Archiv für vaterländische Geschichte* 46 (1889–90): 108–65, esp. 159. I owe this reference to the kindness of Niklas Schrenck von Notzing.

42. See the discussion of Landgrave Wilhelm in chap. 1.

43. Wolfgang Sedelius, *Wie sich ain Christenlicher Herr, so Landt unnd Leüt zuo Regieren under jm hat, vor schedlicher Phantasey verhueten, unnd in allen noeten troesten soll* (Munich, 1547).

44. Ibid., fol. B2r.

45. Sigmund Riezler evaluated the work briefly in *Allgemeine Deutsche Biographie* 54:308–10; but the most thorough discussion is in Bruno Singer, *Die Fürstenspiegel in Deutschland im Zeitalter des Humanismus und der Reformation* (Munich, 1981), 90–93, 250–70.

46. *Wie sich ain Christenlicher Herr*, fol. A2r.

47. Werner Friedrich Kümmel, "*De Morbis Aulicis:* On Diseases Found at Court," in Nutton, ed., *Medicine at the Courts of Europe*, 15–48. I am grateful to Professor Kümmel for allowing me to consult his manuscript before it was published.

48. Norbert Elias, *The Civilizing Process*, vol. 1, *The History of Manners*, trans. Edmund Jephcott (New York, 1978); vol. 2, *Power and Civility*, trans. Edmund Jephcott (New York, 1982); and *The Court Society*, trans. Edmund Jephcott (New York, 1983).

49. For a later period, see Werner Troßbach, "Fürstenabsetzungen im 18. Jahrhundert," *Zeitschrift für historische Forschung* 13 (1986): 425–54.

50. Michael Roberts, *The Early Vasas: A History of Sweden, 1523–1611* (Cambridge, 1968), 207, 233–41.

51. David P. Daniel, "Piety, Politics, and Perversion: Noblewomen in Reformation Hungary," in Sherrin Marshall, ed., *Women in Reformation and Counter-Reformation Europe: Private and Public Worlds* (Bloomington, Ind., 1989), 68–88. See also Raymond T. McNally, *Dracula Was a Woman: In Search of the Blood Countess of Transylvania* (New York, 1983).

1: THE EARLY SIXTEENTH CENTURY

1. See Christian Friedrich Sattler, *Geschichte des Herzogthums Würtenberg unter der Regierung der Graven*, 4 vols. (Tübingen, 1767–68),
3:113–14, 134; Christoph Friedrich von Stälin, *Wirtembergische Geschichte*, 4 vols. (Stuttgart, 1841–73), 3:575–76; Albert Moll, "Die
Krankheits- und Todesfälle im württembergischen Regentenhause," *Medizinisches Correspondenz-Blatt* 30 (1860): 281–87, esp. 286; and Christian Friedrich Sattler, *Geschichte des Herzogthums Würtenberg unter der
Regierung der Herzogen* (Ulm, 1769), Beylagen nos. 103, 266.

2. Thus, for example, Ingrid Karin Sommer, ed., *Die Chronik des
Stuttgarter Ratsherrn Sebastian Küng*, Veröffentlichungen des Archivs
der Stadt Stuttgart, vol. 24 (Stuttgart, 1971), 116; Stälin, *Wirtembergische
Geschichte* 3:576–77; Moll, "Krankheits- und Todesfälle," 286; J. C. Pfis-
ter, *Herzog Christoph zu Wirtemberg aus größentheils ungedruckten
Quellen*, 2 vols. (Tübingen, 1819–20), 1:15; and *Allgemeine Deutsche
Biographie* 11:627–28.

3. The Rathsamhausen were a leading family of the Lower Alsatian
free nobility.

4. Sattler, *Geschichte des Herzogthums Würtenberg . . . Graven*, 2d
ed., part 4 (Tübingen, 1777), 8.

5. Moll, "Krankheits- und Todesfälle," 287.

6. HStAS, A602/519c, no. 2.

7. It appears that Cicero invented the word *furor* in order to push the
medically loaded terms *mania* and *melancholia* to the side: see his *Tus-
culan Disputations* 3.5. But we have no adequate history of the word or
the concept.

8. See Sattler, *Geschichte des Herzogthums Würtenberg . . . Graven*
4:339; Stälin, *Wirtembergische Geschichte* 3:601 (in which Stälin cites, at
n. 4, the *Anshelm Berner Chronicle* 1:246); and Sommer, ed., *Chronik des
Stuttgarter Ratsherrn Sebastian Küng*, 116.

9. Sommer, ed., *Chronik des Stuttgarter Ratsherrn Sebastian Küng*,
116, using the terms *feel und mangel* and *blodickhait*.

10. HStAS, A602/519c, nos. 6 and 7. In his reply Eberhard allowed the
venesection with the following words: "With respect to the barber we are
pleased to allow him the old Hussler whenever he needs him, but no one
else."

11. Ibid., nos. 7 and 10. In addition to fathering children during his
long captivity, Heinrich also annotated some of the books that he was
allowed to use. See Klaus Graf, *Exemplarische Geschichten: Thomas
Lirer's "Schwäbische Chronik" und die "Gmünder Kaiserchronik"* (Munich, 1987), 36.

12. Christoph quickly agreed to obey his father and was pensioned off
with a few hundred gulden a year and a house in Durlach. See Friedrich
Wieland, "Markgraf Christoph I. von Baden, 1475–1515, und das Badische

Territorium," *Zeitschrift für die Geschichte des Oberrheins* 85 (1932–33): 527–611, esp. 552–57.

13. GLAK, D 1165: "Urkunde Maximilians I. vom 15.1.1516." I found this document with the help of Archivdirektor Weber, to whom I am most grateful.

14. Friedrich Wieland, private communication 25 April 1988; see also Wieland, "Markgraf Christoph I. von Baden, 1475–1515," and especially Wieland's essay, "Porträtstudien zum Stundenbuch Markgraf Christofs I. von Baden," *Zeitschrift für die Geschichte des Oberrheins* 128 (1980): 464–75.

15. *Allgemeine Deutsche Biographie* 4:227–32, at 232.

16. For a quick summary, see "Die Gefangenhaltung Markgraf Friedrichs des Aeltern von Brandenburg auf der Plassenburg," *Hohenzollerische Forschungen: Jahrbuch für die Geschichte der Hohenzollern* (Munich) 2 (1893): 435–46.

17. See Robert Scribner, "Reformation, Carnival and the World Turned Upside Down," in his *Popular Culture and Popular Movements in Reformation Germany* (London and Ronceverte, 1987), 71–101; Emmanuel Le Roy Ladurie, *Carnival in Romans*, trans. Mary Feeney (New York, 1979); Yves-Marie Bercé, *Fête et revolte: Des mentalités populaires du XVIe au XVIIIe siècle* (Paris, 1976); and Natalie Z. Davis, *Fiction in the Archives: Pardon Tales and Their Tellers in Sixteenth-Century France* (Stanford, 1987), 30, 33–34.

18. *Allgemeine Deutsche Biographie* 7:480; and 4:43–53.

19. "Vidimus der Urkunde des Markgrafen Friedrich des Aelteren zu Brandenburg vom Jahr 1515, durch welche derselbe die Regierung an seinen Sohn Casimir abtritt, mitgetheilt von demselben," *Archiv für Geschichte und Alterthumskunde von Oberfranken*, ed. E. C. von Hagen, 3 (1845): 101–4, at 102.

20. Ibid., 102.

21. "Gebrechlichait halben seiner gnaden gemuts": Reinhard Seyboth, *Die Markgrafthümer Ansbach und Kulmbach unter der Regierung Markgraf Friedrichs des Älteren (1486–1515)* (Göttingen, 1985), 424–25.

22. "Aydt deren die uff meinen alten gn. Herrn wartten sollen," *Archiv für Bayreuthische Geschichte und Alterthumskunde* (Bayreuth) 1 (1828): 95–98.

23. StAB, C3/247, no. 9, fol. 45r–v.

24. Seyboth, *Markgraftümer Ansbach und Kulmbach*, 415–21. Seyboth is, however, not the first to make these claims in defense of the old margrave: two hundred years ago this political view of Friedrich's deposition was expressed by the historian who probably knew the Brandenburg archives better than anyone at that time (or perhaps since). See Karl Heinrich von Lang, *Neuere Geschichte des Fürstenthums Baiereuth*, pt. 1: 1486–1527 (Göttingen, 1798), 118–32.

25. StAB, C3/247, no. 10, fol. 47v.

26. Ibid., fol. 48r.

27. "Aydt deren die uff meinen alten gn. Herrn wartten sollen," 95–98.

28. Karl August Barack, ed., *Zimmerische Chronik*, 4 vols. (Stuttgart, 1869), 4:252–54; Seyboth, *Markgraftümer Ansbach und Kulmbach*, 420.

29. Seyboth, *Markgraftümer Ansbach und Kulmbach*, 421.

30. "Atrum bile maligno induravetur ut lenitiur amplius mederi non posset": StAB, C3/247, no. 14: "Excerptum ex Rationario Sebaldi Abbatis Heilsbronnensis ad A. MDXV," p. 225, fols. 67–68.

31. StAB, C3/246, no. 5: "Extract aus dem Landtags- Abschied d.d. Önolzbach am Dienstag nach dem Suntag Invocavit ao. 1528."

32. Ibid.

33. *Allgemeine Deutsche Biographie* 42:738–41.

34. Both the cases of Wilhelm I and Wilhelm II of Hesse are treated in the short but competent article by Hermann Stutte, "Beitrag zur Geschichte der Irrenfürsorge im ausgehenden Mittelalter," *Die medizinische Welt* 20 (1951): 1000–1002. See also *Allgemeine Deutsche Biographie* 43:27–28.

35. Hans Glagau, *Hessische Landtagsakten*, vol. 1: 1508–1521 (Marburg, 1901), 120–22, 126, 141–43.

36. Ibid., 143.

37. Ibid., 93.

38. Ibid., 98.

39. Ibid., 147.

40. Ibid.

41. Ibid., 159–61.

42. Ibid., 159, n. 1.

43. See Hermann Stutte, "Zur Geschichte der luetischen Geistesstörungen," *Deutsche medizinische Wochenschrift* 75 (1950): 794–97; and Oswald Feis, "Die Krankheit Wilhelms des Mittleren (Ein Beitrag zur Frühgeschichte der Lues)," *Janus: Archives internationales pour l'histoire de la médicine et la géographie médicale* 4 (1937): 75–87.

44. Glagau, *Hessische Landtagsakten*, 14.

45. Ibid., 15.

46. Ibid., 16.

47. Ibid., 16.

48. HStAM, Bestand 2: I A 7, nos. 1, 2, and 3. These fragments have been effectively interpreted by Feis, "Die Krankheit Wilhelms des Mittleren," 80–87.

49. In the case of Count Philipp of Ysenburg (1467–1526), the records are evidently so fragmentary that we can say little more than that he went mad after his return from a pilgrimage to Jerusalem (like Wilhelm the Elder of Hesse) and had to be assigned a guardian in 1517. His story rings with echoes of vehement family conflicts. See G. Simon, *Die Geschichte des reichsständischen Hauses Ysenburg und Büdingen*, 3 vols. (Frankfurt, 1865), 2:251–54.

50. For the general problem of the mad monarch in the Middle Ages, see Edward Peters, *The Shadow King: Rex Inutilis in Medieval Law and Literature, 751–1327* (New Haven, 1970). For an excellent review of the problem, focusing on the eighteenth century and on supposedly "absolute" princes, see Werner Troßbach, "Fürstenabsetzungen im 18. Jahrhundert," *Zeitschrift für historische Forschung* 13 (1986): 425–54. German investigations of this sort all depend, in part at least, on Johann Jacob Moser, *Persönliches Staatsrecht derer Teutschen Reichs-Stände,* pt. 1 (Frankfurt and Leipzig, 1775); this became pt. 11 of Moser's twenty-part *Neues Teutsches Staatsrecht.*

51. Actually, Foucault seems to emphasize that the classical age (the eighteenth century) was divided among various institutional discourses or perspectives and that eighteenth-century doctors and medical hospitals most certainly did treat the mad according to the categories of illness and with whatever therapies they deemed appropriate. In his accounting, it was only the *perception asilaire* that rigorously excluded the category of mental illness (*Histoire de la folie,* 125–43).

52. See Norman Dain, *Concepts of Insanity in the United States, 1789–1865* (New Brunswick, N.J., 1964), 35–52.

2: MID-CENTURY: THE TURN TO THERAPY

1. I have managed to find out very little about Count Sighard V of Schwarzburg (?–1560), the son of Count Johann Heinrich (1496–1555), who governed his county from 1525 to his death in 1555. Sighard apparently became visibly disturbed in February 1554 and died in 1560 after falling from a window. Did he jump? See Johann Christian August Junghans, *Geschichte der Schwarzburgischen Regenten* (Leipzig, 1821), 68.

2. J. C. Pfister, *Herzog Christoph von Wirtemberg,* 2 vols. (Tübingen, 1819–20), 2:154–55.

3. Ibid., 155.

4. Ibid., 152–53.

5. Ibid., 155. See also Christoph Friedrich von Stälin, *Wirtembergische Geschichte,* 4 vols. (Stuttgart, 1856), 4:779; *Allgemeine Deutsche Biographie* 4:244.

6. HStAS, Württembergisches Hausarchiv G48, Büschel 12.

7. Ludwig Spengler, *Die Geisteskrankheit des Herzogs Philipp von Mecklenburg: Ein Beitrag zur Geschichte der Psychiatrie im 16. Jahrhundert,* 2d ed. (Neuwied, 1863), 4–7.

8. Ibid., 7.

9. Ibid., 8; on Willich, see *Allgemeine Deutsche Biographie* 43:278–82.

10. Spengler, *Geisteskrankheit des Herzogs Philipp,* 8.

11. Ibid., 8–9.

12. Ibid., 15.

13. Ibid., 16.

14. Ibid., 17.

15. Ibid., 20.

16. See Axel Wilhelmi, *Die mecklenburgischen Ärzte von den ältesten Zeiten bis zur Gegenwart: Eine Neuausgabe*, ed. A. Blanck (Schwerin, 1901), no. 48; and Hans Schröder, *Lexikon der hamburgischen Schriftsteller bis zur Gegenwart*, 8 vols. (Hamburg, 1851–53), 1: no. 396.

17. Spengler, *Geisteskrankheit des Herzogs Philipp*, 23.

18. See Heinrich Schnell, *Mecklenburg im Zeitalter der Reformation, 1503–1603* (Berlin 1900), 133–34; and Otto Vitense, *Geschichte von Mecklenburg* (Gotha, 1920), 160–66.

19. *Neue Deutsche Biographie* 6:227. The biography by Heinrich Freiherr von Welck, *Georg der Bärtige, Herzog von Sachsen: Sein Leben und Wirken* (Braunschweig, 1900), is marred by Protestant bias.

20. Erich Brandenburg, "Herzog Heinrich der Fromme von Sachsen und die Religionsparteien im Reich (1537–1591)," *Neues Archiv für sächsische Geschichte und Altertumskunde* 17 (1896): 121–200, 241–303, at 125–26.

21. See Woldemar Goerlitz, *Staat und Stände unter den Herzögen Albrecht und Georg, 1485–1539*, Sächsische Landtagsakten, vol. 1 (Leipzig, 1928), 548, 550–51; Brandenburg, "Herzog Heinrich," 132–33; and Oswald Artur Hecker, *Religion und Politik in den letzten Lebensjahren Herzog Georgs des Bärtigen von Sachsen* (Leipzig, 1912), 55.

22. See the discussion in Hecker, *Religion und Politik*, 7–72.

23. Ibid., 72. See also C. A. H. Burckhardt, "Hofnachrichten über Herzog Georg und seinen Sohn Friedrich (1539)," *Neues Archiv für sächsische Geschichte und Altertumskunde* 9 (1888): 137–39.

24. Otto Richter, "Prinz Friedrichs Hochzeit und Tod, 1539," *Dresdner Geschichtsblätter* 13 (1904): 273–79, at 276.

25. Veit Ludwig von Seckendorf reported in his history of Lutheranism that Friedrich died from a combination of sex and strong medications. See J. S. Ersch and J. G. Gruber, *Allgemeine Encyklopädie der Wissenschaften und Künste* (Leipzig, 1855), sec. 1, vol. 60: 86. But the autopsy performed on Friedrich found that his lungs, liver, and heart were all "corrupt and disabled" (Richter, "Prinz Friedrichs Hochzeit," 274, 277).

26. See Ludwig Pfandl, *Johanna die Wahnsinnige: Ihr Leben, Ihre Zeit, Ihre Schuld* (Freiburg i. Br., 1930); Johan Brouwer, *Johanna die Wahnsinnige: Ein tragisches Leben in einer bewegten Zeit* (Munich, 1978; trans. from the 4th Dutch ed., Amsterdam, 1949); Isabel Altayo and Paloma Nogues, *Juana I: La reina cautiva* (n.p. [Spain]: Silex, ca. 1985); Barberá Carmen, *Juana la loca* (Barcelona, 1992), a fictionalized biography; and Townsend Miller, *The Castles and the Crown: Spain, 1451–1555* (London, 1963). See also Ghislaine de Boom, *Don Carlos, l'héritier de Jeanne la Folle* (Brussels, 1955).

27. Hans Kruse, "Wilhelm von Oranien und Anna von Sachsen: Eine fürstliche Ehetragödie des 16. Jahrhunderts," *Nassauische Annalen* 54 (1934): 1–184, at 10–13, a valuable reference I owe to Georg Schmidt. See also C. V. Wedgwood, *William the Silent: William of Nassau, Prince of Orange, 1533–1584* (New York, 1968 [1944]), 44.

28. A. J. van der Aa, ed., *Biographisch Woordenboeck der Nederlanden* (Haarlem, 1852–78), 1:94.

29. Kruse, "Wilhelm von Oranien," 30–32; Wedgwood, *William the Silent*, 64–65.

30. Kruse, "Wilhelm von Oranien," 38; Wedgwood, *William the Silent*, 66.

31. Kruse, "Wilhelm von Oranien," 39; Wedgwood, *William the Silent*, 65.

32. Kruse, "Wilhelm von Oranien," 39.

33. Wedgwood, *William the Silent*, 112.

34. Kruse, "Wilhelm von Oranien," 56, 152.

35. Ibid., 78–80.

36. Ibid., 137, 139.

37. Ibid., 136–37.

38. Ibid., 137.

39. Ibid., 137, 90–92.

40. Ibid., 114, 116–17, 119, 129, 132.

41. Ibid., 135.

42. See above, p. 41, and chap. 1, n. 33.

43. A pious biography of Wilhelm exists: H. C. Heimbürger, *Wilhelm der Jüngere, Herzog von Braunschweig-Lüneburg und Stammvater des Hauses Hannover* (Celle, 1857).

44. *Allgemeine Deutsche Biographie* 43:2.

45. Hans Joachim von der Ohe, *Die Zentral- und Hofverwaltung des Fürstentums Lüneburg (Celle) und ihre Beamten: 1520–1648* (Celle, 1955), 3–5, 14–16. On the general question of dynastic calculation, division of territories, and family feeling, see Paula Sutter Fichtner, *Protestantism and Primogeniture in Early Modern Germany* (New Haven, 1989).

46. H. Hoogeweg, "Fürst und Hof zu Celle während der Krankheit Wilhelms des Jüngeren (1573–1592)," *Zeitschrift des Historischen Vereins für Niedersachsen* 67 (1902): 348–442, at 350–51.

47. Ibid., 349.

48. Ibid., 353–55.

49. Ibid., 356.

50. Ibid., 359–60. See also Ohe, *Zentral- und Hofverwaltung*, 11.

51. Hoogeweg, "Fürst und Hof zu Celle," 362–63.

52. Ibid., 364.

53. Ibid., 370–72.

54. Ibid., 372.

55. Ibid., 380–81.

56. *Allgemeine Deutsche Biographie* 32:568–69.

57. HStAH, Celle Briefe 44, no. 992: letter of 21 Dec. 1588 from Dr. Schroeter to Duchess Dorothea; and no. 1004, I: "Protocolle betr. die Verhandlungen der Gesandten, Besserungsvorschläge für Herzog Wilhelm den Jüngeren, 12–19 June 1589"; and Anlage J: "Bericht der Mediziner Mellinger, Schröter, und Mithobius (25 February 1589)," fols. 63–68.

58. HStAH, Celle Briefe 44, no. 992: "Briefwechsel mit Herzogin Dorothea." On Mellinger, see O. von Boehm, "Dr. Johann Mellinger, ein Kartograph des 16. Jahrhunderts und seine Landtafel des Fürstentums Lüneburg," *Hannoversche Geschichtsblätter* n.s. 2 (1933): 308–317.

59. HStAH, Celle Briefe 44, no. 992, 16–17 Oct. 1588.

60. Ibid., fols. 29–32.

61. Ibid., 3 Dec. 1588, fols. 50–52.

62. Ibid., 24 Dec. 1588.

63. Ibid., Celle Briefe 44, nos. 960–1016, all deal with Wilhelm's illness.

64. Ibid., Celle Briefe 44, no. 1004, I: "Protocolle betr. die Verhandlungen der Gesandten," puncto 8, fols. 40v, 43v.

65. Hoogeweg, "Fürst and Hof zu Celle," 432.

3: DUKE ALBRECHT FRIEDRICH OF PRUSSIA

1. Johann Voigt, however, made out a case for the basic health and normalcy of Albrecht Friedrich's childhood so that he could blame his later madness on the mistreatment and contempt shown him by his councilors and regents: "Über die Erziehung und die Krankheit des Herzogs Albrecht Friedrich," *Neue preußische Provinzialblätter*, 3d ser., 8 (1861): 1–43, 93–105.

2. Rita Scheller, *Die Frau am preussischen Herzogshof, 1550–1625* (Cologne, 1966), 66–71.

3. See F. L. Carsten, *A History of the Prussian Junkers* (Aldershot, Eng., 1989), 23–25; Klaus-Dietrich Staemmler, *Preußen und Livland in ihrem Verhältnis zur Krone Polen, 1561 bis 1586* (Marburg, 1953), 25–26; Otto Hintze, *Regierung und Verwaltung: Gesammelte Abhandlungen zur Staats-, Rechts- und Sozialgeschichte Preussens*, ed. Gerhard Oestreich, 2d ed. (Göttingen, 1967), 37; Fritz Gause, *Die Geschichte der Stadt Königsberg in Preussen*, 3 vols. (Cologne, 1972), 1:305, 322–24; and Walther Hubatsch, *Albrecht von Brandenburg-Ansbach: Deutschordens-Hochmeister und Herzog in Preußen, 1490–1568* (Heidelberg, 1960), 203–9.

4. See Jürgen Petersohn, *Fürstenmacht und Ständetum in Preußen während der Regierung Herzog Georg Friedrichs, 1578–1603* (Würzburg,

1963), 3–6, 9–20, 44–47; Walther Franz, *Geschichte der Stadt Königsberg* (Munich, 1934; repr. Frankfurt a. M., 1979), 116–17, 121; Gause, *Geschichte der Stadt Königsberg* 1:323–29.

5. Iwan Bloch, "Der rheinische Arzt Solenander und die Geisteskrankheit des Herzogs Albrecht Friedrich von Preußen," *Klinisch-Therapeutische Wochenschrift* 19 (1922): 147–62. On the marriage negotiations and the wedding party, see Bernhard Vollmer, "Die Reise Herzog Wilhelms des Reichen von Jülich-Kleve-Berg mit seiner Tochter Maria Leonora zu ihrer Hochzeit nach Preußen," *Düsseldorfer Jahrbuch* 42 (1940): 276–90; Erich Scholtis, "Aus einer alten Chronik," *Westpreußen Jahrbuch* 1959: 138–42; Rita Scheller, "Die enttäuschenden Brautbriefe des Herzogs Albrecht Friedrich an Prinzessin Marie Leonore," *Das Ost Preußenblatt* 24 (1973): F-12, p. 11; Harry Scholz, "Die Leibärzte Herzog Albrechts von Preußen," *Deutsches medizinisches Journal* 13 (1962): 625–28.

6. Harry Scholz, "Die Geisteskrankheit des Herzogs Albrecht Friedrich von Preußen," *Sudhoffs Archiv für Geschichte der Medizin und der Naturwissenschaften* 46 (1962): 211–28, at 219.

7. Karl Faber, "Tagebuch über Albrecht Friedrichs Gemüths-Krankheit: Nach einem im geheimen Archiv befindlichen Manuscript des Lukas David," *Prussisches Archiv* 2 (1810): 127–78.

8. Ibid., 131–32.

9. In 1572 his mother's brother, Duke Erich II of Braunschweig, had brought charges of magic and poisoning against his wife, Sidonie, in an unsuccessful effort to obtain a divorce from her. Such charges may also have inflamed Albrecht Friedrich's fears for his own life. See Johannes Merkel, "Die Irrungen zwischen Herzog Erich II. und seiner Gemahlin Sidonie (1545–1575)," *Zeitschrift des Historischen Vereins für Niedersachsen* 64 (1899): 11–101.

10. Faber, "Tagebuch," 134. On Albrecht Friedrich's continuing fear of poison, see 138–39, 142.

11. This may well have been the so-called Trithemius powder recommended to Duke Albrecht by the imposter Paul Skalich. See Harry Scholz, "Über Ärzte und Heilkundige zur Zeit des Herzogs Albrecht von Preussen," *Jahrbuch der Albertus Universität zu Königsberg* 12 (1962): 45–106, at 82.

12. Faber, "Tagebuch," 137.

13. Ibid., 141–42.

14. Ibid., 150.

15. Walther Hubatsch, *Geschichte der evangelischen Kirche Ostpreussens*, 3 vols. (Göttingen, 1968), 1:110–13. The best portrait of one of Heshusius's main targets, the Calvinist nobleman and extreme spokesman for the rights of the territorial estates Friedrich von Aulack, is in Petersohn, *Fürstenmacht und Ständetum*, 148–53.

16. Hubatsch, *Geschichte der evangelischen Kirche* 1:114.

17. On Osiander in general, see Gottfried Seebaß, *Das reformatorische Werk des Andreas Osiander* (Nuremberg, 1967). On his influence in Prussia, see Martin Stupperich, *Osiander in Preussen, 1549–1552* (Berlin, 1973); and Jörg Fligge, "Zur Interpretation der osiandrischen Theologie Herzog Albrechts v. Preußen," *Archiv für Reformationsgeschichte* 64 (1973): 245–80. On the survival of the Osiandrians, see Gause, *Geschichte der Stadt Königsberg* 1:329.

18. Hubatsch, *Geschichte der evangelischen Kirche* 1:120; Gause, *Geschichte der Stadt Königsberg* 1:338–39.

19. On, for example, 14 June 1573: Faber, "Tagebuch," 157 and 158–62.

20. Ibid., 157, 160.

21. Ibid., 169–70; Scholz, "Geisteskrankheit des Herzogs Albrecht Friedrich," 218–19.

22. Faber, "Tagebuch," 261–62.

23. Ibid., 176–77.

24. Kaspar von Nostitz, *Haushaltungsbuch des Fürstenthums Preussen, 1578: Ein Quellenbeitrag zur politischen und Wirthschaftsgeschichte*, ed. Karl Lohmeyer (Leipzig, 1893), Anhang 20, 300–319.

25. Report of Dr. Adrian to the Elector, 26 Nov. 1573, in ibid., Anhang 19, 299.

26. Ibid., 300.

27. Ibid., 301; cf. the Obermarschall's opinion on 312.

28. Ibid., 302–4.

29. Ibid., 306.

30. Ibid.

31. Ibid., 307.

32. Ibid., 308; cf. 315.

33. Ibid., 309.

34. Ibid., 310.

35. Ibid., 311. Melchior Creutz expressed the view that even now Albrecht Friedrich could not count past thirty (315).

36. Ibid., 312.

37. On Thurneisser, see J. C. W. Moehsen, "Leben Leonhard Thurneisser zum Thurn," in his *Beiträge zur Geschichte der Wissenschaften in der Mark Brandenburg* (Berlin and Leipzig, 1783), 1–198; on this episode in his life, 98–99. See also *Allgemeine Deutsche Biographie* 38:226–29; and the extensive entries in Christian Gottlieb Jöcher, *Allgemeines Gelehrten-Lexikon: Fortsetzungen und Ergänzungen*, ed. H. W. Rotermund, vol. 4 (1751); and in Leonard Meister, *Helvetiens berühmte Männer* (Zurich, 1799). On his thought, see Peter Morys, *Medizin and Pharmazie in der Kosmologie Leonhard Thurneissers zum Thurn (1531–1596)* (Husum, 1982); and Rudolf Schmitz, "Medizin und Pharmazie in der

Kosmologie Leonhard Thurneissers zum Thurn," in Jean François Bergier, ed., *Zwischen Wahn, Glaube und Wissenschaft: Magie, Astrologie, Alchemie und Wissenschaftsgeschichte* (Zurich, 1988), 141–66.

38. H. R. Trevor-Roper, "The Court Physician and Paracelsianism," in Vivian Nutton, ed., *Medicine at the Courts of Europe, 1500–1837* (London, 1990), 79–94. For the example of Hesse-Kassel, see Bruce T. Moran, "Prince Practitioning and the Direction of Medical Roles at the German Court: Maurice of Hesse-Kassel and His Physicians," in the same volume, 95–116; and especially his *The Alchemical World of the German Court: Occult Philosophy and Chemical Medicine in the Circle of Moritz of Hessen (1572–1632)* (Stuttgart, 1991).

39. GStAPK, XX.HA, HBA. A4: report of 20 April 1574.

40. Ibid.

41. GStAPK, XX.HA, Etats-Ministerium 85c, no. 3, fols. 5–6. Let me here record my deep thanks to Dr. Klaus Neitmann for his guidance in these archival materials.

42. Ibid., fols. 9–32. See also Scholz, "Geisteskrankheit des Herzogs Albrecht Friedrich," 214.

43. GStAPK, XX.HA, Etats-Ministerium 85c, no. 3, fol. 30v.

44. Ibid., fol. 11r. Christian Krollmann followed out these suggestions using modern terminology in "Die Krankheit des Herzogs Albrecht Friedrich von Preußen und die hereditäre Belastung," *Sitzungsberichte des Vereins für die Geschichte von Ost- und Westpreußen* 8 (1912): 286–88.

45. "Discursus in melancholia," GStAPK, XX.HA, Etats-Ministerium 85c, no. 3, fols. 11v, 13r.

46. Ibid., fol. 17v.

47. Ibid., fols. 20v–22v.

48. Ibid., fols. 23r, 28v–29r.

49. Ibid., fols. 30v, 32r.

50. Ibid., fol. 32r.

51. GStAPK, XX.HA, HBA. K5, Kasten 1064: Valerius Fidler, "De impedimento curae," 14 Oct. 1575.

52. GStAPK, XX.HA, HBA. A1 (Konzepte 1568–1579), Kasten 1106: draft of a letter from Albrecht Friedrich to Maximilian II, 10 Dec. 1575.

53. Ibid., HBA. K5, Kasten 1064: *consilium* of Paulus de Lapide.

54. Ibid., HBA. K5, Kasten 1064: *consilium* of Severinus Göbel (1575).

55. Duke Albrecht had often trusted experts and advisers who had no academic credentials, Andreas Osiander and Paul Skalich being the two best examples.

56. GStAPK, XX.HA, Etats-Ministerium 85c, no. 3, fols. 8, 33–43, at fol. 41r.

57. GStAPK, XX.HA, HBA. K5, Kasten 1064: letters of Albrecht Friedrich to Naevius (Nefe) dated 29 March 1576, 21 July 1576, and 30 Sept. 1576, and of Naevius, 19 Feb. 1577. According to Christian Gottlieb

Jöcher's *Allgemeines Gelehrten-Lexikon*, vol. 5 (1816), Caspar Naevius of Leipzig died on 7 July 1574, but this must be an error.

58. *Medicorum rationes cur dux Prussiae curari non possit*, GStAPK, XX.HA, HBA. K5, Kasten 1064. See also Scholz, "Geisteskrankheit des Herzogs Albrecht Friedrich," 214–15; and Scheller, *Die Frau am preussischen Herzogshof*, 83–85, 195–97.

59. Actually, Wilhelm V never was fully Protestant, but he had sponsored an Erasmian reform-Catholicism; by the 1570s he was moving toward a stricter Tridentine observance.

60. It is not clear what vice this may be, but the tone leaves little doubt they were sexual abuses. Masturbation?

61. Flacians were hyperorthodox Lutheran partisans of Matthias Flacius Illyricus.

62. *Medicorum rationes*; and Scheller, *Die Frau am preussichen Herzogshof*, 196, n. 61.

63. GStAPK, XX.HA, HBA. K5, Kasten 1064: "Vorschlag des Wundarztes Hans Markhauser, 19.12.1577."

64. Ibid., "Gutachten über obige Schrift, 30.12.1577."

65. GStAPK, XX.HA, Etats-Ministerium 85c, no. 3, fols. 45–47, at fol. 45r–v.

66. Ibid., fol. 46r.

67. Ibid., fol. 45r. On mummy, see Karl Dannenfeldt, "Egyptian Mumia: The Sixteenth-Century Experience and Debate," *Sixteenth Century Journal* 16 (1985): 163–80; and Robert W. Carrubba, "The First Detailed Report on Persian Mummy," *Physis* [Italy] 23 (1981): 459–71, on the researches of Dr. Engelbert Kämpfer, 1651–1716.

68. GStAPK, XX.HA, HBA. K5, Kasten 1064: a folder labeled "Die Krankheit des Herzogs Albrecht Friedrich" contains Frese's report, dated 16 Nov. 1581.

69. Voigt, "Über die Erziehung und die Krankheit," 94–95.

70. The word *bezoar* comes from the Persian *pad* and *zahr* meaning "protecting against poison." For a stunning display of the continued importance of bezoar as late as the mid-eighteenth century, see the entries in Johann Heinrich Zedler, ed., *Grosses vollständiges Universal-Lexicon aller Wissenschaften und Künste*, 64 vols. (Leipzig and Halle, 1732–50), vol. 3, cols. 1656–83.

71. GStAPK, XX.HA, HBA. K 5, Kasten 1064. The legal case ran from 13 July to 10 Oct. 1590.

72. Heinz Immekeppel, *Das Herzogtum Preussen von 1603 bis 1618* (Cologne, 1975), 20.

73. On the importance of the title, "Dux Prussiae," and the term of address, "Fürstliche Durchlaucht," that went with it, see Petersohn, *Fürstenmacht und Ständetum*, 29–33.

74. Ibid., 35–38.

75. Ibid., 75–87.

76. Ibid., 104, 120–27.

77. Helmut Quaritsch, *Souveränität: Entstehung und Entwicklung des Begriffs in Frankreich und Deutschland vom 13. Jh. bis 1806* (Berlin, 1986). I owe this reference to Thomas Brady.

78. Gause, *Geschichte der Stadt Königsberg*, 344.

79. Rita Scheller, "Die Entwicklung des Königsberger Hofes unter Herzog Albrechts Nachfolgern (1568–1654)," *Jahrbuch der Albertus-Universität zu Königsberg* 20 (1970): 12–39, at 25.

80. Scheller, *Die Frau am preussischen Herzogshof*, 140–66.

81. See the excellent set of colloquium papers edited by Johannes Kunisch and Helmut Neuhaus, *Der dynastische Fürstenstaat: Zur Bedeutung von Sukzessionsordnungen für die Entstehung des frühmodernen Staates* (Berlin, 1982).

4: THE LAST DUKES OF JÜLICH-CLEVES

1. Regarding these principalities, the best brief orientation in English is Francis L. Carsten, *Princes and Parliaments in Germany: From the Fifteenth to the Eighteenth Century* (Oxford, 1959), 258–69; a much denser picture is presented in the massive exhibition volume *Land im Mittelpunkt der Mächte: Die Herzogtümer Jülich-Kleve-Berg*, ed. by the Städtisches Museum Haus Koekkoek Kleve and the Stadtmuseum Düsseldorf (Kleve, 1984).

2. See Otto R. Redlich, *Jülich-Bergische Kirchenpolitik am Ausgange des Mittelalters und in der Reformationszeit*, 3 vols. (Bonn, 1907–15), 1:120*–121*; 3:49*–52*; Dorothea Coenen, *Die katholische Kirche am Niederrhein von der Reformation bis zum Beginn des 18. Jahrhunderts: Untersuchungen zur Geschichte der Konfessionsbildung im Bereich des Archidiakonates Xanten unter der klevischen und brandenburgischen Herrschaft* (Münster, 1967), 10–22, 281–85; Erwin Mülhaupt, *Rheinische Kirchengeschichte von den Aufängen bis 1945* (Düsseldorf, 1970), 115–84, esp. 167; J. P. Dolan, *The Influence of Erasmus, Witzel and Cassander in the Church Ordinances and Reform Proposals of Cleve during the Middle Decades of the Sixteenth Century* (Münster, 1957); and A. Walters, *Konrad von Heresbach und der clevische Hof zu seiner Zeit* (Elberfeld, 1867).

3. See Redlich, *Jülich-Bergische Kirchenpolitik* 3:49*; Stephan Ehses, ed., *Nuntiaturberichte aus Deutschland: Die Kölner Nuntiatur*, vol. 2, pt. 1, *Nuntius Ottavio Mirto Frangipani (1587 Juni–1590 September)* (Paderborn, 1899; repr. Paderborn 1969), liv, 228; and P. B. Bergrath, "Zur Geschichte der Geistesstörung des Herzogs Wilhelm des Reichen und seines Sohnes Johann Wilhelm von Jülich-Cleve-Berg," *Allgemeine Zeitschrift für Psychiatrie* 10 (1853): 249–80, 396–419, at 262–65.

4. Emil Pauls, "Zauberwesen und Hexenwahn am Niederrhein," *Beiträge zur Geschichte des Niederrheins: Jahrbuch des Düsseldorfer Geschichts-Vereins* 13 (1898): 134–242, at 214. See also A. Franzen, *Die Kelchbewegung am Niederrhein im 16. Jahrhundert: Ein Beitrag zum Problem der Konfessionsbildung im Reformationszeitalter* (Münster, 1955).

5. *Allgemeine Deutsche Biographie* 43:106–13; "Gulielmi Ducis . . . vitae obitusque succincta enarratio," HStAD, JB II/2018, fols. 24–31 at fol. 28r.

6. Max Lossen, "Zur Geschichte des Laienkelches am Hofe des Herzogs Wilhelm von Jülich-Cleve-Berg, 1570–79," *Zeitschrift des Bergischen Geschichtsvereins* 19 (1883): 1–30; 20 (1884): 234–38.

7. Moriz Ritter, *Deutsche Geschichte im Zeitalter der Gegenreformation und des dreissigjährigen Krieges (1555–1648)*, 3 vols. (Stuttgart, 1889), 1:552–54, 562–64; Ehses, ed., *Nuntiaturberichte, II/1: Frangipani (1587–1590)*, xxvi, 2, 25–26. The fullest picture of Duke Wilhelm's efforts to navigate between the fervent certainties of both confessions may be extracted from the remarkable work of Ludwig Keller, *Die Gegenreformation in Westfalen und am Niederrhein: Actenstücke und Erläuterungen*, 3 vols. (Leipzig, 1881–95). See also Alois Schröer, *Die Kirche in Westfalen im Zeichen der Erneuerung: 1585–1648*, vol. 2, *Gegenreformation in den geistlichen Landesherrschaften* (Münster, 1987).

8. See Carsten, *Princes and Parliaments*, 273–82. See also Karl Heckmann, "Der Siegeburger Vergleich des Herzogs Jülich-Berg mit dem gräflichen Hause Wittgenstein über die Teilung der Herrschaft Homburg vom Jahre 1604 und ihre Vorgeschichte," *Zeitschrift des Bergischen Geschichtsvereins* 61 (1932/33): 55–119.

9. Wilhelm Muschka, *Opfergang einer Frau: Lebensbild der Herzogin Jakobe von Jülich-Kleve-Berg, geborene Markgräfin von Baden* (Baden-Baden, 1987), 240–41; Heinz Schweitzer, "Zur Identifizierung der in der Fürstengruft der St. Lambertuskirche zu Düsseldorf aufgefundenen Gebeine," *Düsseldorfer Jahrbuch: Beiträge zur Geschichte des Niederrheins* 50 (1960): 1–27.

10. For the portraits, see the reproductions in Muschka, *Opfergang einer Frau*, esp. 292; and in *Land im Mittelpunkt der Mächte*, 404–6, 411–19. Wilhelm's illness has been much studied. In addition to Bergrath's essay of 1853 (above, n. 3), see Wilhelm Crecelius, "Urkundliche Beiträge zur Krankheitsgeschichte der Herzoge Wilhelm und Johan Wilhelm von Jülich, Cleve und Berg," *Zeitschrift des Bergischen Geschichtsvereins* 23 (1887): 1–29, 186–94; K. W. Bouterwek, ed., "Bericht von der letzten Krankheit und selig Absterben unsers weyland Edlen Landts Fursten, H. Wilhelmen, hertzogen zu Gulich, Cleve und Berg etc., uff befehlch der h.h. Rähte etc., uffgesetzt durch Reinerum Solenandrum, M.

Dr. . . . 1592, i. Januarii," *Zeitschrift des Bergischen Geschichtsvereins* 2 (1865): 172–76; more completely available as "Bericht des Leibmedicus Dr. Solenander über Krankheit und Tod des Herzogs Wilhelm III. von Jülich-Cleve-Berg (1592)," *Archiv für die Geschichte des Niederrheins* 6 (1868): 168–79; Anton Wackerbauer, "Dr. Reiner Solenander (Reinhard Gathmann), ein niederrheinischer Arzt, Leibarzt am Düsseldorfer Hofe (1524–1601)," *Düsseldorfer Jahrbuch* 37 (1932/33): 95–140.

11. See Ehses, ed., *Nuntiaturberichte*, 19, 23–24, 31–32, 56–60, 65–67, 211–13, 339–40, 348–55, 414–17, 516–19; Stieve, *Zur Geschichte der Herzogin Jakobe von Jülich* (Bonn, 1877), 146–48; and Muschka, *Opfergang einer Frau*, 241.

12. "Bericht des Leibmedicus Dr. Solenander," 175.

13. Ibid., 176; Muschka, *Opfergang einer Frau*, 294–95, gets the tone right.

14. "Bericht des Leibmedicus Dr. Solenander," 179.

15. His case has been discussed often. See Emil Pauls, "Zur Geschichte der Krankheit des Herzogs Johann Wilhelm von Jülich-Kleve-Berg," *Zeitschrift des Bergischen Geschichtsvereins* 33 (1897): 7–38; "Gutachten und Erklärungen abergläubischer Art des Pfarrers zu Lank bei Krefeld über die Art der Krankheit und die ärztliche Behandlung des geisteskranken Jülicher Jungherzogs Johann Wilhelm," in ibid. 33 (1897): 39–48; "Geisteskrankheit, Ableben und Beerdigung Johann Wilhelms, des letzten Herzogs von Jülich-Kleve-Berg," in Alfred Herrmann, ed., *Beiträge zur Geschichte des Herzogthums Kleve*, Veröffentlichungen des historischen Vereins für den Niederrhein, vol. 2 (Cologne, 1909), 257–75; and "Zur Geschichte Jakobes von Baden und der Geisteskrankheit ihres Gemahls (Johann Wilhelm)," *Monatsschrift des Bergischen Geschichtsvereins* 21 (1914): 141–52, 162–70. See also Friedrich Schubert, "Die Geisteskrankheit Johann Wilhelms, des letzten Herzogs von Jülich-Kleve-Berg," *Jan Wellem: Monatsschrift für Düsseldorf* 3 (1928): 297–304 (I have not yet obtained a copy of this article); Crecelius, "Urkundliche Beiträge zur Krankheitsgeschichte," 1–29; Muschka, *Opfergang einer Frau*, 236–47, 432–35; Bergrath, "Zur Geschichte der Geistesstörung"; K. W. Bouterwek, "Drei Huldigungstage der Stadt Wesel" [with documentary appendices], *Zeitschrift des Bergischen Geschichtsvereins* 2 (1865): 151–96; Wackerbauer, "Dr. Reiner Solenander," esp. 113–15, 135–38.

16. "Videbatur splendidus in vestibus, prae se ferens parum cerebri": Bergrath, "Zur Geschichte der Geistesstörung," 256.

17. Ibid., 254–55; see also *Land im Mittelpunkt der Mächte*, 31, 123, 343, 375.

18. Bergrath, "Zur Geschichte der Geistesstörung," 267–71; Muschka, *Opfergang einer Frau*, 241–42; excellent discussion of the problem in Pauls, "Zur Geschichte Jakobes von Baden," 146–47.

19. Pauls, "Zur Geschichte der Krankheit des Herzogs Johann Wilhelm," 23; HStAD, JB II/2232, fols. 43–47: Ärztliches Gutachten of 18 October 1589.

20. Pauls, "Zur Geschichte der Krankheit des Herzogs Johann Wilhelm," 23–24.

21. *Land im Mittelpunkt der Mächte*, 158–66, 431–32.

22. Max Lossen, "Die Verheiratung der Markgräfin Jakobe von Baden mit Herzog Johann Wilhelm von Jülich-Cleve-Berg (1581–1585)," *Zeitschrift des Bergischen Geschichtsvereins* 31 (1895): 1–77; Else Rümmler, "Die Düsseldorfer Hochzeit im Jahre 1585: Die Beschreibung des Festes von Dietrich Graminaeus," in *Land im Mittelpunkt der Mächte*, 169–80, 432–43.

23. Pauls, "Zur Geschichte Jakobes von Baden," 144; and "Geisteskrankheit, Ableben und Beerdigung Johann Wilhelms," 262; Stieve, *Zur Geschichte der Herzogin Jakobe*, 13.

24. Pauls, "Zur Geschichte Jakobes von Baden," 149. In February 1590 the ducal councilors blamed this fear on the insinuations of "the Jesuit Brillenmacher." See Crecelius, "Urkundliche Beiträge zur Krankheitsgeschichte," 4, 20; Stieve, *Zur Geschichte der Herzogin Jakobe*, 19.

25. HStAD, JB II/2232, fols. 43–47 and 56–61; a copy of this *consilium* is found in BHStAM, JB h 273/1, fols. 47–52. The report is printed in Pauls, "Zur Geschichte der Krankheit des Herzogs Johann Wilhelm," 22–27; the quotation is on 23. On Solenander, see *Allgemeine Deutsche Biographie* 34:563–65; and Wackerbauer, "Dr. Reiner Solenander."

26. In the copy prepared for Johann Wilhelm's father and for his wife, Jakobe, these references to his hereditary or congenital weaknesses were discreetly omitted. Pauls, ed., "Zur Geschichte der Krankheit des Herzogs Johann Wilhelm," 26–27.

27. In the copy of this medical report sent to Jakobe the medical reasons for limiting sexual intercourse were slightly expanded. The doctors noted that the young duke's seed was crucial to his fertility, "and because so much rests on this point for those in his estate, one must pay strict attention to this matter" (ibid., 27, 25).

28. Ibid., 25, 30. Actually, the trip was also arranged so that Johann Wilhelm would not learn of the death of his favorite councilor, Dietrich von Horst. While on their travels, the accompanying councilors complained regularly that Johann Wilhelm was still not in any condition to be told of this death (ibid., 31–38). For the letters from father to son, see ibid., 32–34; HStAD, JB II/2232, fols. 22–23, 70–71.

29. Pauls, "Zur Geschichte der Krankheit des Herzogs Johann Wilhelm," 27–28.

30. Ibid., 29.

31. See Crecelius, "Urkundliche Beiträge zur Krankheitsgeschichte," 10, 27, 29; Stieve, *Zur Geschichte der Herzogin Jakobe*, 21–23; Bouter-

wek, "Drei Huldigungstage der Stadt Wesel," 155, n. 27; Pauls, "Geistes-krankheit, Ableben und Beerdigung Johann Wilhelms," 268–69; Max Spindler, gen. ed., *Handbuch der Bayerischen Geschichte*, 2d ed., vol. 2, *Das alte Bayern*, ed. Andreas Kraus (Munich, 1988), 396–406.

32. HStAD, JB II/2233, fols. 10–121, esp. fols. 10–29. The Hessian Hauptstaatsarchiv in Marburg is another repository of information on Johann Wilhelm's condition: HStAM, Bestand 4f, Jülich-Berg, Herzöge, nos. 30–35, 38–42.

33. HStAD, JB II/2233, fols. 12–13, 79–82.

34. *Prima pars consilii medici quae vitae et victus rationem tractat*: HStAD, JB II/2232, fols. 56–61; I have also used the copy sent to Munich under the same title: BHStAM, JB h, 273/1, fols. 53–60.

35. HStAD, JB II/2232, fol. 59v.

36. "Nam venus moderata melancholicis salubris": ibid., fol. 58v.

37. Crecelius, "Urkundliche Beiträge zur Krankheitsgeschichte," 18, 21.

38. HStAD, JB II/2232: "Anacephaleosis seu recapitulatio," fols. 121–22; BHStAM, JB h 273/1, fols. 62–65.

39. BHStAM, JB h 273/1, fols. 67–69; HStAD, JB II/2232, fols. 79–82, 96–97. Actually, Wilhelm V lived on in steadily deteriorating health until January 1592.

40. Bergrath, "Zur Geschichte der Geistesstörung," 408, citing the 1593 investigation into Jakobe's role in Johann Wilhelm's illness.

41. Muschka, *Opfergang einer Frau*; Stieve, *Zur Geschichte der Herzogin Jakobe*, 86–99.

42. Ingenhoven's recommendations are preserved in HStAD, JB II/2232, fols. 125–39.

43. HStAD, JB II/2232, fols. 89, 111v, and 139–43 at fol. 140v.

44. Ibid., fol. 142r-v.

45. Ibid., fol. 143v.

46. The proposed exorcisms are preserved in the beautiful copy of HStAD, JB II/2232, fols. 107–12.

47. Pauls, "Zur Geschichte der Krankheit des Herzogs Johann Wilhelm," 39–48; HStAD, JB II/2232, fols. 85–88.

48. HStAD, JB II/2232, fol. 141v.

49. Bergrath, "Zur Geschichte der Geistesstörung," 402–4 and note on 404; Emil Pauls, "Der Exorcismus an Herzog Johann Wilhelm von Jülich in den Jahren 1604 und 1605," *Annalen des Historischen Vereins für den Niederrhein* 63 (1896): 33, 45–46.

50. Stieve, *Zur Geschichte der Herzogin Jakobe*, 147.

51. Crecelius, "Urkundliche Beiträge zur Krankheitsgeschichte," 18.

52. "Sed philtri seu poculi amatorii exhibiti multa sunt inditia": ibid., 20–22, quoting Silberborner's report of his interview with the councilors on 10 February 1590.

53. HStAD, JB II/2236, report dated 13 Nov. 1592. See also the similar outbursts reported in BHStAM, JB h 252/1, fols. 249–55 (21 May 1595); JB h 252/2, fols. 312–15 (28 Aug. 1595) and fol. 343 (3 Sept. 1595). My deepest thanks go to Dr. Heike Preuß of the Nordrhein-Westfälisches Hauptstaatsarchiv in Düsseldorf for introducing me to the complexities of these sources and for lending me her notes.

54. BHStAM, JB h 252/1, fol. 251r.

55. Philipp Ludwig (d. 1614) had married Johann Wilhelm's sister Anna in 1574 and was therefore one of the "Interessenten." His son Wolfgang Wilhelm inherited the duchies of Jülich and Berg.

56. BHStAM, JB h 252/4, fols. 85r–v, 143v–145r, and 239v–240v.

57. There is some confusion in the records concerning which woman, the widow from Ertzelbach or the wife of von Enzenbroch, is under discussion. Bergrath compounds the confusion ("Zur Geschichte der Geistesstörung," 409–10).

58. See the brief echoes of his activities in Bouterwek, "Drei Huldigungstage der Stadt Wesel," 176–77; and Bergrath, "Zur Geschichte der Geistesstörung," 410–12.

59. BHStAM, JB h 278/1, fol. 243r.

60. Ibid., fol. 243v.

61. Ibid., fol. 244r–v.

62. Ibid., fol. 263v.

63. Ibid., fol. 264v. These claims in particular are reminiscent of Paracelsus, for whom demonic possession might be an illness listed along with others. See also Bouterwek, "Drei Huldigungstage der Stadt Wesel," 176–77, for further evidence of this English doctor's reputation.

64. BHStAM, JB h 278/1, fol. 265r.

65. "Alsolche mit ihre fürstliche gnaden furhapende Cur an sich zu probiren unnd experimentiren zulassen": ibid., fol. 268v. This is a noteworthy early example of the use of "experiment" as a verb. See Charles B. Schmitt, "Experience and Experiment: A Comparison of Zabarella's View and Galileo's in *de Motu*," *Studies in the Renaissance* 16 (1969): 80–138.

66. BHStAM, JB h 278/1, fol. 268v.

67. Ibid., fol. 269r.

68. Ibid., fols. 269r–v and 287v.

69. Ibid., fol. 289r.

70. Ibid., fols. 302r–v, 311r–v, 318v, and 319r.

71. Ibid., fols. 319v and 339–44.

72. Ibid., fol. 339v.

73. Bergrath, "Zur Geschichte der Geistesstörung," 410–11.

74. Ibid., 411–12.

75. Bouterwek, "Exorcizatio an Herzog Johann Wilhelm geübt," *Zeitschrift des Bergischen Geschichtsvereins* 2 (1865): 201–11 at 201.

76. Muschka, *Opfergang einer Frau,* 324–26, 357–69. Until Jakobe

was dead, no remarriage for Johann Wilhelm would have been legitimate in the eyes of Rome and therefore able to produce legitimate Catholic heirs. Thus divorce, even for proven adultery on Jakobe's part, did not offer a Catholic solution to the succession crisis in Jülich-Cleves.

77. Bouterwek, "Drei Huldigungstage der Stadt Wesel," 176–77.

78. Bergrath, "Zur Geschichte der Geistesstörung," 413–14; Pauls, "Der Exorcismus an Herzog Johann Wilhelm," 35–53, at 37.

79. Pauls, "Der Exorcismus an Herzog Johann Wilhelm," 33, 37–38.

80. BHStAM, JB h 282/1, report dated Cologne, 12 Oct. 1604.

81. E. Pauls, "Der Exorcismus an Herzog Johann Wilhelm," 38, n. 4; 39, n. 2.

82. Report by doctors Botter, Weyer, and Dominicus Berthemius of Lorraine, 16 August 1605, reprinted in ibid., 49, n. 3.

83. Ibid., 41–42; the report was published by M. Goebel as "Exorcisation des Herzogs Johann Wilhelm von Cleve in August 1605," *Monatsschrift für die evangelische Kirche der Rheinprovinz und Westfalen* (1853), no. 1: 20–34; and in an improved transcription by Bouterwek, "Exorcizatio an Herzog Johann Wilhelm geübt" (the quoted passage is at 205).

84. Bouterwek, "Exorcizatio an Herzog Johann Wilhelm geübt," 206.

85. Ibid., 206.

86. Ibid., 207.

87. Ibid., 209.

88. It seems unlikely to me that Duke Johann Wilhelm and his entire entourage went on this pilgrimage.

89. Writing in the wake of their failure, the Barnabite general Michael Murazanus (Marrano) claimed that he had taken part in these efforts and that they had all been carried out in accord with the doctrines of "Mangi" and of the *Malleus Maleficarum*. This was evidently a reference to Girolamo Menghi, the prolific Italian compiler of exorcisms. See Felix Stieve, ed., "Wittelsbacher Briefe aus den Jahren 1590 bis 1610: Abteilung VI," *Abhandlungen der Historischen Classe der Königlich Bayerischen Akademie der Wissenschaften*, vol. 20, pt. 2 (1892): 363–514, at 481. Stieve mistakenly takes Mangi to be a reference to Albertus Magnus.

90. Bouterwek, "Exorcizatio an Herzog Johann Wilhelm geübt," 211.

91. Pauls, "Der Exorcismus an Herzog Johann Wilhelm," 43.

92. Arnold Oskar Meyer, ed., *Nuntiaturberichte aus Deutschland, Siebzehntes Jahrhundert: Nebst ergänzenden Aktenstücken. Die Prager Nuntiatur des Giovanni Stefano Ferreri und die Wiener Nuntiatur des Giacomo Serra (1603–1606)* (Berlin, 1913), no. 559e (19 Sept. 1605), p. 508.

93. BHStAM, JB h 281, letter of 23 Jan. 1605 from Melchior Erasmus and Ludwig Veit Fuchs to Pfalzgraf Philipp Ludwig.

94. A detailed autopsy report was filed, as in his father's case. See

Pauls, "Geisteskrankheit, Ableben und Beerdigung Johann Wilhelms," 257–75, at 271–72.

95. Allen G. Debus shows how resilient the Paracelsian theories were in France, surviving down to the eighteenth century, but few mainline physicians were converted. See *The French Paracelsians: The Chemical Challenge to Medical and Scientific Tradition in Early Modern France* (Cambridge, Eng., 1991).

5: A MELANCHOLY EMPEROR AND HIS MAD SON

1. Felix Stieve, *Die Verhandlungen über die Nachfolge Kaiser Rudolfs II. in den Jahren 1581–1602* (Munich, 1879), 33 and n. 92. In the sixteenth century, *fast* was an intensifier meaning "totally" or "extremely."

2. Ibid., 4–5.

3. Winfried Schulze, "Hausgesetzgebung und Verstaatlichung im Hause Österreich vom Tode Maximilians I. bis zur Pragmatischen Sanktion," in Johannes Kunisch and Helmut Neuhaus, eds., *Der dynastische Fürstenstaat: Zur Bedeutung von Sukzessionsordnungen für die Entstehung des frühmodernen Staates* (Berlin, 1982), 252–71, esp. 260–62.

4. See Hans Luxenburger, "Psychiatrisch-erbbiologisches Gutachten über Don Julio (Cesare) de Austria," *Mitteilungen des Vereins für Geschichte der Deutschen in Böhmen* 70 (1932): 41–54; Karl Vocelka, *Rudolf II. und seine Zeit* (Vienna, 1985), 9–10; and *Die politische Propaganda Kaiser Rudolfs II. (1576–1612)* (Vienna, 1981), 95–105.

5. See the sharp critique in R. J. W. Evans, *Rudolf II and His World* (Oxford, 1973), 43–49.

6. Ibid., 2.

7. Ibid., 2–3.

8. Ibid., 44, n. 2.

9. Ibid., 45, 47.

10. Vocelka exaggerates this basically good point. It was not only papal ambassadors who reported on Rudolf's madness. The Venetians did also, and in 1600 they were hardly tools of papal ambition.

11. Vocelka, *Rudolf II. und seine Zeit*, 10; cf. his *Die politische Propaganda*, 104. This argument, too, contains a useful element of cautious source criticism, but the implicit conclusion (that Rudolf was really competent to rule all the time) goes well beyond the evidence.

12. Heinz Noflatscher, *Glauben, Reich und Dynastie: Maximilian der Deutschmeister (1558–1618)* (Marburg, 1987), 240.

13. Evans, *Rudolf II*, 55–60; Felix Stieve, *Verhandlungen*, 34–35; Johannes Janssen, *History of the German People at the Close of the Middle Ages*, 17 vols. (London, 1896–1910), 9:273–75.

14. Evans, *Rudolf II,* 58.

15. Stieve, *Verhandlungen;* see also Stieve's excellent, balanced sketch in *Allgemeine Deutsche Biographie* 19:493–515.

16. Stieve, *Verhandlungen,* 33–34 and n. 93.

17. Ibid., 34–35.

18. Ibid., 35, n. 95.

19. Ibid., 40–41 and n. 117.

20. "Si accresce in tanto ogni giorno evidemente la afflitione dell'animo di S. C. M.": ibid., 41, n. 122, a report dated 8 May 1599.

21. Ibid., 42–46.

22. Evans, *Rudolf II,* 71–72, 89–90; Stieve, *Verhandlungen,* 47–48. See also Franz Dvorský, ed., *Die böhmischen Landtagsverhandlungen und Landtagsbeschlüsse vom Jahre 1526 an bis auf die Neuzeit,* vol. 10: 1600–1604 (Prague, 1900), 104–5, 113.

23. Anton Gindely, *Rudolf II. und seine Zeit, 1600–1612,* 2 vols. (Prague, 1863–65), 1:46–47.

24. Dvorský, ed., *Die böhmischen Landtagsverhandlungen* 10:245; Evans, *Rudolf II,* 90.

25. Stieve, *Verhandlungen,* 57–58.

26. Stieve, *Verhandlungen,* 48; for similar speculations see Arnold Oskar Meyer, ed., *Nuntiaturberichte aus Deutschland, Siebzehntes Jahrhundert. Nebst ergänzenden Aktenstücken. Die Prager Nuntiatur des Giovanni Stefano Ferreri und die Wiener Nuntiatur des Giacomo Serra (1603–1606)* (Berlin, 1913), lxv.

27. Stieve, *Verhandlungen,* 58 n. 181, 141.

28. Ibid., 48, n. 141.

29. The inadequate article by Gaß in the *Allgemeine Deutsche Biographie* 26:199–201 concentrates mainly on Pistorius's connections with the history of Baden.

30. Stieve, *Verhandlungen,* 61 and n. 194; Hellmuth Rössler and Günther Franz, eds., *Sachwörterbuch zur deutschen Geschichte* (Munich, 1958), 1042–43.

31. Stieve, *Verhandlungen,* 63; Johannes Janssen, *History of the German People* 9:276, n. 1, claims that research by J. Fischer, *Der sogenannte Schottwiener Vertrag vom Jahre 1600* (Fribourg, Switzerland, 1898), has debunked the legend of this meeting and "treaty" at Schottwien. I have not yet consulted this apparently important work of Fischer's.

32. Stieve, *Verhandlungen,* 137–40, prints a detailed abstract of the memorandum as appendix 10 and argues that its authors were the privy councilors; a fuller edition is available in Dvorský, *Die böhmischen Landtagsverhandlungen* 10:92–96: "Kurzer Discurs, wie der Röm. Kais. Mt. in ihrem itzigen Anliegen vor ihr Person und sonsten zu helfen sein möcht."

33. "Die melancolische, schwere Perturbationes Ihrer M[ajestä]t

Herz allgemach ausnagen und im Haupt grosse Blödigkeit, Schwindel und Fluss . . . erwecken": Dvorský, *Die böhmischen Landtagsverhandlungen* 10:92–93.

34. Ibid., 93.

35. Ibid.

36. Ibid.

37. Meyer, ed., *Nuntiaturberichte* (Ferreri), lxiii, n. 3. For guidance into the thickets of the reports of the papal nuncios I have found helpful Felicitas Rottstock, *Studien zu den Nuntiaturberichten aus dem Reich in der zweiten Hälfte des sechzehnten Jahrhunderts: Nuntien und Legaten in ihrem Verhältnis zu Kurie, Kaiser und Reichsfürsten* (Munich, 1980), esp. 11–41.

38. Meyer, ed., *Nuntiaturberichte* (Ferreri), lxiii–iv, n. 3.

39. Dvorský, *Die böhmischen Landtagsverhandlungen* 10:93–94; cf. 97.

40. Ibid., 96.

41. Ibid., 97.

42. Ibid., 98–99.

43. Ibid., 99; cf. Archduke Matthias to Archduke Albrecht, 16 and 21 Oct. 1600: Stieve, *Verhandlungen*, Beilage viii, 133–34.

44. Meyer, ed., *Nuntiaturberichte* (Ferreri), xvii, and no. 372i, p. 300; no. 403, p. 333.

45. Ibid., no. 755, p. 722.

46. Stieve, *Verhandlungen*, 102–3, nn. 344–47.

47. Ibid., 108.

48. Ibid., 109; Friedrich Hurter, *Philipp Lang: Kammerdiener Kaiser Rudolphs II.* (Schaffhausen, 1851).

49. Leopold von Ranke, *Zur deutschen Geschichte: Vom Religionsfrieden bis zum dreißigjährigen Krieg* (Leipzig, 1868), 188.

50. Ibid., 282.

51. Ibid., 284.

52. Ibid., 285.

53. See also Hugh Trevor-Roper, *Princes and Artists: Patronage and Ideology at Four Habsburg Courts, 1517–1633* (London, 1976), 95–125; R. J. W. Evans, "The Austrian Habsburgs," in A. G. Dickens, ed., *The Courts of Europe: Politics, Patronage and Royalty, 1400–1800* (New York, 1977), 121–45; and T. D. Kaufmann, *The School of Prague* (Chicago, 1988).

54. Vocelka, *Die politische Propaganda*, 104–5.

55. On the brothers and sisters, see Gindely, *Rudolf II. und seine Zeit* 2:337–38; Meyer, ed., *Nuntiaturberichte* (Ferreri), no. 551f, p. 503, no. 559c, p. 508.

56. Meyer, ed., *Nuntiaturberichte* (Ferreri), no. 572d, p. 521.

57. Ibid., no. 796a, p. 784.

58. Evans, *Rudolf II*, 49.

59. Gindely, *Rudolf II. und seine Zeit* 2:338.

60. Anton Blaschka, "Das Schicksal Don Julios de Austria: Akten und Regesten aus seine letzten Lebensjahren," *Mitteilungen des Vereins für Geschichte der Deutschen in Böhmen* 70 (1932): 220–55, at 227, 229–30.

61. Gindely, *Rudolf II. und seine Zeit* 2:339.

62. Luxenburger, "Psychiatrisch-erbbiologisches Gutachten über Don Julio," 47.

63. Václav Březan, *Posledni Rožmberkové,* ed. J. Dostal (Prague, 1941), 239, with warmest thanks to Dr. Dana Koutná for her help with translation.

64. Blaschka, "Das Schicksal Don Julios," 245.

65. Ibid., 246–48.

66. Ibid., 248–52.

67. Ibid., 252.

Conclusion

1. Wolfgang Lemble to Pfalzgraf Philipp Ludwig of Neuburg, 29 July 1603, reporting from Weimar: BHStAM, JB h 350.

2. See *Allgemeine Deutsche Biographie* 14:352; Ottokar Lorenz, *Lehrbuch der gesammten wissenschaftlichen Genealogie* (Berlin, 1898), 434–39.

3. BHStAM, JB h 345/2: Sachsen-Altenburg, fols. 37, 92–97.

4. Ibid., fol. 99v; see also BHStAM, JB h 345/1, for letters on her condition by ducal physicians Johann Walter Eben and Gregor Silbermann. I must again express my thanks to Dr. Heike Preuß for introducing me so generously to these materials.

5. *Allgemeine Deutsche Biographie* 22:268–83 at 282–83. He had long cultivated Paracelsian alchemy: Bruce T. Moran, *The Alchemical World of the German Court: Occult Philosophy and Chemical Medicine in the Circle of Moritz of Hessen (1572–1632)* (Stuttgart, 1991).

6. *Allgemeine Deutsche Biographie* 7:501–5.

7. Exorcism at baptism was retained, for example, by Lutherans in Brandenburg but rejected by Lutherans in some other territories.

8. Brian P. Levack, *The Witch-Hunt in Early Modern Europe* (London, 1987), 152–56; Wolfgang Behringer, *Hexenverfolgung in Bayern: Volksmagie, Glaubenseifer und Staatsräson in der frühen Neuzeit* (Munich, 1987), 96–112, 169–71.

9. Sigmund von Riezler, *Geschichte Baierns,* 9 vols. (Gotha, 1903; repr. Aalen, 1964), 5:102.

10. As he flatly claimed in November 1604, "fuit a similibus maleficiis liberata." See Felix Stieve, ed., "Wittelsbacher Briefe aus den Jahren

1590 bis 1610: Abteilung VI," *Abhandlungen der Historischen Classe der Königlich Bayerischen Akademie der Wissenschaften,* vol. 20, pt. 2 (1892): 363–514, at 480–81.

11. Ibid., 371. Murazanus regarded Duchess Elizabeth's bewitchment as "notorious," but Duke Maximilian actually rejected the notion that his wife was bewitched, pointing out that if she were indeed subject to demonic attack, her natural parts would be corrupted and weak, which they were not: ibid., 497, 502. See also Kurt Pfister, *Kurfürst Maximilian von Bayern und sein Jahrhundert* (Munich, 1948), 348.

12. The Roman Church had been trying for centuries to sharpen the rules for "testing the spirits" (*probatio spirituum*). In the late sixteenth century it was not only demonic possession but also harmful magic (*maleficium*) that frequently needed to be distinguished from natural symptoms. Girolamo Menghi was one of many who devoted himself to making the distinction clearer: *Fuga Daemonum* (Venice, 1596), cap. xii, fol. 59r, as cited by Mary R. O'Neil, "*Sacerdote ovvero strione:* Ecclesiastical and Superstitious Remedies in 16th-Century Italy," in Steven L. Kaplan, ed., *Understanding Popular Culture: Europe from the Middle Ages to the Nineteenth Century* (Berlin, 1984), 53–83, at 80, n. 31. The whole topic needs detailed study.

13. Werner Friedrich Kümmel, "*De Morbis Aulicis:* On Diseases Found at Court," in Vivian Nutton, ed., *Medicine at the Courts of Europe, 1500–1837* (London, 1990), 15–48.

14. Norbert Elias, *The History of Manners* and *Power and Civility,* vols. 1 and 2 of *The Civilizing Process,* trans. Edmund Jephcott (New York, 1978, 1982). Hans-Peter Duerr is engaged in a massive effort to debunk this theory of Elias, and while I agree with large parts of Duerr's critique, I think that Elias may still describe an important shift in the civilizing pressures at princely courts. See Hans-Peter Duerr, *Der Mythos vom Zivilisationsprozess,* 3 vols. to date (Frankfurt, 1988–92): vol. 1, *Naktheit und Scham;* vol. 2, *Intimität;* vol. 3, *Obszönität und Gewalt.*

15. For the seventeenth- and eighteenth-century development of these metaphors, see Wolf Lepenies, *Melancholy and Society,* trans. Jeremy Gaines and Doris Jones (Cambridge, Mass., 1992); Ludwig Völker, "*Komm, Heilige Melancholie*": Eine Anthologie deutscher Melancholie-Gedichte, mit Ausblicken auf die europäische Melancholie-Tradition in Literatur- und Kunstgeschichte (Stuttgart, 1983); Ute Mohr, *Melancholie und Melancholiekritik im England des 18. Jahrhunderts* (Frankfurt, 1990); and Günter Bader, *Melancholie und Metapher: Eine Skizze* (Tübingen, 1990).

INDEX